GE

Mud
Lake

Victor

Darby

Trail Creek

Warm Creek

Fox Creek

Chapin

gs

Darby Creek

Little Pine Creek

Teton River

Cedron

Bates

Mahogany Cr.

M O U N T A I N S

Horseshoe Cr.

Sam

Richvale

B I G   H O L E

oasis

SPINDRIFT
STORIES OF TETON BASIN

SPINDRIFT

STORIES OF TETON BASIN

Edited by Jeanne Anderson,
Marilyn Elliott Meyer and
Michael B. Whitfield

Bonnie Krafchuk,
Project Coordinator

TETON ARTS COUNCIL

Spindrift: Stories of Teton Basin is published by Teton Arts Council
with funding provided by the Spirit of the Northwest Project
through the Idaho Commission on the Arts and the
National Endowment for the Arts, in partnership with
Teton Regional Land Trust and Teton County Historical Society.

Some pieces in this anthology appeared previously in other publications.
Permission to use provided by authors. See full list in Appendix.

Library of Congress Cataloging-in-Publication Data is available.

Dust-jacket art and map of Teton Basin on endpapers
by Alan McKnight.

Book design by Alan McKnight with production assistance
by Mary Lou Hansen, Sage Services, Driggs, Idaho.

ISBN 0-9706235-1-8
First edition

"The sensitive shall inherit the Earth."
—Dr. LeRoy Shelton

Nourished by our landscape,
in the adventurous spirit of Richard "Beaver Dick" Leigh,
with the perseverance of the early pioneers
and the sensitivity gained from facing mutual challenges,
we dedicate this anthology
to the people of Teton Valley.

Coyote

STANDING IN THE PARKING LOT, laden with groceries and waiting for my husband, I spied Coyote behind the dumpsters. He was rummaging around amongst the boxes and debris, discreet, but not overly so. He has never been too modest or careful and has, in fact, seemed to enjoy his blunders and indiscretions as much as his occasional good judgment. Still, annoying and bad-smelling as he can be, every now and then I learn something—always unexpected—from him. Knowing I had a bit of a wait, I moved into the shadow and gave a low whistle. He lifted his head, cocked his ear and sniffed the air. Then he turned toward me, gave a leering grin of recognition and sauntered over.

"You don't generally hang in such a busy place," I wondered at Coyote.

"No worries here," he replied. "Look around. Everyone's self-absorbed, running around, harried, doin' their thing. No worries for me," he repeated.

I scanned the scene before us, and he appeared to be correct, though I was still somewhat anxious for his safety. We watched as mothers loaded their vans with children and groceries, as tourists pulled in their rigs loaded with kayaks and mountain bikes. Various folks I knew to be teachers, realtors and construction workers parked and went into the store for provisions. Mexican families often went in all together as a family unit, and because, for now at least, there's only one show in town, the fashionable and wealthy were also shopping here.

José saw me and came over. "What are you doing talking to this riffraff?" he scolded seeing Coyote.

"We're observing diversity here in downtown Driggs," Coyote replied disdainfully. "Your demeanor towards me is surprising considering it was I who brought you here."

"For a price," José scowled, "a high price."

"But with your hide and a new life besides," Coyote retorted looking over José's fine leather cowboy boots and jacket.

"Diversity, yes," I interrupted to distract them from their argument. "Things have sure changed a lot since Beaver Dick Leigh's time."

Coyote got a faraway look in his eyes. "Incredible change," he agreed, "and in little more than a hundred years."

"You're not waxing nostalgic on us, are you?" I teased him.

"Of course not!" he snorted. "This valley couldn't support many Beaver Dicks. Do you know how many thousands of animals he killed?"

"It must have been incredible living here in the late 1800s. But I don't envy the existence; between the harsh elements and epidemics, survival back then was a daily occupation."

"Much like surviving in Mexico," José commented. "Folks are kept in check when they're wondering where their next meal is coming from."

"But now, we got prosperity!" Coyote raucously declared. He was absurdly drooling over some rotten meat he'd found in the dumpster.

"The valley is changed and hard in a different way," I mused mostly to myself. "We've got modems, faxes, scanners and e-mail. We've got all the conveniences of modern communication, and city people can come to the country and do their city thing right here."

"And have a view!" José added.

"And expresso, too!" said Coyote.

"Well, that's what worries me. What is our view? What is important to us? Who is seeing what? Who are all these people here shopping for jello, pork chops, French roast and tofu?" I asked.

Coyote stopped chewing and regarded me coolly through narrowed, yellow eyes. "They're the people who blew in. Just as you blew in. Just as the soil was blown in. Just as the spindrift off the peaks is blown who knows where."

"The spindrift nourishes the high mountain forget-me-nots. Perhaps it even feeds the small tributaries that eventually make it to the Teton or Badger or Bitch Creeks. But what does each of us do? Are we here only to take? How much can we use this landscape and its gifts before it has nothing more to give?" I was now so involved in my out-loud thinking I hadn't noticed my husband was back, loading up the groceries and visiting with José. Coyote, of course, had made himself scarce.

"A better question," I announced as I climbed into the pickup, "might be how we can know ourselves. Who are all these folks who have drifted in? What are the themes of this valley that spin hither and yon?"

"Huh?!" was my husband's response as he climbed in beside me.

"We'll write our stories," I answered. "In our sharing of stories, we'll discover our common culture—maybe even deepen our connection to this beloved place and to each other."

I leaned out the window to say good-bye to José. "I love your boots. You have excellent taste!" I winked at him.

—*Bonnie Krafchuk*

Table of Contents

AFTER OUR BONES ARE ASHES

APPENDIX

List of Illustrations

Endpapers: Map of Teton Valley *drawn by Alan McKnight with production assistance by Mary Lou Hansen*
Frontispiece: *Alan McKnight*

About this Project

WRITING AN ANTHOLOGY ABOUT TETON BASIN was a serendipitous and unpremeditated endeavor. In 1997, our community was chosen to participate in the Spirit of the Northwest Project funded by the National Endowment for the Arts and administered by the Idaho Commission on the Arts. Along with another Idaho community and two each from Oregon and Washington, we were selected because our valley is undergoing such rapid change and development that our identity and values are under siege. The Spirit Project was unusual in that each community was awarded funds before knowing how they were to use them. The project chosen was not to be imposed upon the community but rather to come from the community's essence and need.

The process of deciding on a project was long and uncomfortable. The ICA folks and state coordinators advised us that discomfort was a necessary part of the process. We had community forums. We sent representatives to Yamhill, Oregon, for inspiration and to meet with the other communities. The TAC board canvassed local groups and individuals for ideas for possible projects. A Spirit committee was formed, meeting outside of regular TAC board meetings. Our mission was to discover a suitable project. We compiled a list, which grew.

We knew we wanted to express our common culture, our deep connection to place and our desire to listen and learn from each other. When we finally stumbled upon the anthology project, it felt so right that we dropped all other ideas. We decided our genius is here, in each of us. We felt certain that the actual process of gathering stories and writing them would inform us as to who we are. Members of the community—young and old, native and newcomer—were invited to contribute their stories on what it means to inhabit this high mountain valley. The Teton Regional Land Trust and the Historical Society have been invaluable partners throughout. With great delight, we invite you to read *Spindrift: Stories of Teton Basin*, the work of nearly 60 authors and artists.

—*Bonnie Krafchuk*

Editors' Notes

THE GOAL OF THIS SPIRIT OF THE NORTHWEST PROJECT was not to produce a book. The Arts Council and partners decided to embark on this journey called an anthology as a way of bringing people together. This goal arose as a conscious recognition that we have some social work to do in Teton Valley. We sincerely hope that what you read here takes us toward that target—a more understanding society. The editorial effort has certainly achieved that aim for us.

We came together with little experience of editing as a group. Our challenge was particularly difficult: our friends and neighbors produced the works you read here, not unknown people from another place.

We have tried to assure a variety of perspectives. We have attempted to make the material read more smoothly, to correct factual, grammatical and spelling errors, and to fit it all into one small volume. Overall we have tried not to get in the way of each author's voice, each writer's manner of speaking and thinking. We have tried to better understand one another.

We recently heard an analysis of Teton Valley's social scene in the vernacular of a marriage counselor. Consider the marriage of newcomers and oldtimers in our evolving society.

Many newcomers feel left out, frustrated that things don't work here as they do in other places. Teton Valley institutions don't seem to use logical procedures to make decisions. Many oldtimers wonder why the new people are complaining.

In Teton Valley, decisions, even the administration of local government, are made on the basis of relationship. Genuine communication is personal, one on one. This has worked in the past—people knew one another, personally. Today it doesn't work as well because our community is changing rapidly. We are overwhelmed by the change.

In the pages of *Spindrift*, you will hopefully hear some of the diverse voices that make Teton Valley a great place, and could make it a better society. If these voices help us to better understand one another, to get to know one another, the efforts of the past year have been worthwhile.

—*The Editors*

WALKING THE LAND

LAURIE KUTCHINS

Weather Diary

SUMMER AFTERNOON STORMS—the sky a puzzle of clouds and light and darkness. Vertical shafts of rain, horizontal sweeps of wind. A crossword puzzle of wind and rain, shadows and clearings, all afternoon, all day. Looking west from this ridge northeast of Tetonia, who needs a weather map? You can see with your own eyes how the weather rolls into Teton Valley from the coast. Pacific lows lugged inland, eastward, like an enormous, soaked, feather pillow. Far off, west across the valley, there's a crosshatch of light and rain where three creeks fold together into the Teton River canyon country. On a cloudless day you don't see this fierce chasm in the gentle undulations of earth and grain. It takes a day of storms, a complexity of ever-shifting shadows and light, to see the valley's wild, secret marking where the land otherwise appears plainly groomed and unwild. Looking east, the Tetons are harbored in layers of grey-black clouds. The valley's western sky will probably clear by nightfall, stars will shine above the canyon, but the Tetons might be locked under weather for days. Looking southwest, occasional breaks in the clouds make blue promises over the Big Holes. Looking north, the sky is an ominous purple bruise over Yellowstone country. Keep turning around. In all directions, this is a sky to watch. The storms keep changing, the clouds keep brushing light or shadow, rain or lightning against the land.

Now that I am under the tutelage of the clouds, I begin to see that everything is a subject of weather. This hand-hewn pine table, for example, is the subject of weather by virtue of its placement beside windows that take in the long summer afternoons, the haze of dusk as the sun slides north and west of the Big Holes and drops somewhere far beyond the Lemhis. At summer solstice, it's light here until well after ten o'clock. The table fades from blonde to whitish against such generous sun. And in winter, it seems to shrink and crack from contrast, from deep, stark cold, darkness by five in the afternoon. The table withers from long nights that bring no one home to stoke up the wood stove or place a steaming supper on its surface. This, an inside weathering.

To Teton Valley, I am a summer person. My migrations to and from my family's place in the north end of the valley follow the school year and the instinctual calendar of the sandhill cranes. Like the sandhills, I return each spring to settle in for what I know best of Teton Valley—

the season of growing crops, hot-air balloons and local rodeo, coyote pups, wildflowers, mountain bluebirds, thimbleberries, streams of RVs along Routes 32 and 33, and the drama of summer storms that level off into the brief dry lull of August. Our days can be simple up here without phones, without electricity, without schedules, looking out at so much of the valley. Summer nights are a dome of starlight and three full moons bright enough to read by. I live here only three to four months out of the year, but I know it as family, home.

I've been making this migration for 20 years. I remember when, after nightfall, Driggs and Victor were a modest sprinkle of lights off in the southern end of the valley—two distinct, separate and unconnected sprinkles surrounded by the vast dark expanse of the valley. I remember each year coming back and night-counting the lights north of Tetonia—for almost a decade there were seven lights that I could see from our cabin. Seven lights, mostly the bright machine shed lights of the big crop ranches strewn across the northern end of the valley. Almost ten years ago, it became apparent that the nightscape of Teton Valley had changed and was going to continue changing. I knew this hadn't happened over night, but being away for eight months at a time made it seem as if the incremental increases had been an overnight explosion. In the southern half of the valley, the lights of Victor and Driggs had grown together. They were no longer separate sprinkles but an extended blur of lights north to south, west to east. It was as if the darkness itself was under siege. Now, when I look down into the southern half of the valley, I cannot tell where one town ends and the other begins. It's a rural sprawl. Several years ago, when the first seven tripled, I stopped counting the north-of-Tetonia lights altogether.

Reluctantly, I leave for milder winters as the school calendar beckons, around the time when the barley is two weeks from harvest and the first yellow flecks among the aspens announce another summer's gone. That dawn I'm not awakened by the crane's thin-throated cry, that certain dusk I no longer see them flapping low across the fields to bed down along the nearby creek, I know it's time.

In winter I miss the Teton Valley storms and clearings. I miss the winter habits of the moose that forage and make snowbeds all up and down the creek drainage. I miss the skiing in and out of the cabin, the wind like an encouraging palm at my back, or a constant slap across my shoulders and cheeks. I miss the winter night skies, either moonless and black as water dreams, or pure lavender, reflecting snow. I miss the cabin, its smell of old sunlight in the logs, its masculine arms, its soft shadows by kerosene light, its large windows black against the night, its clutter of knicknacks strewn on shelves and walls—the family tracks of three generations—its pine table pocked, sun-faded, and weathered. I admire our neighbors—how intimately they live with winter, quietly going about their business inside its cold skull for so many months at a time. I admire and sometimes envy their tenacity and choice. To live that closely and succinctly with your partner. To live that alertly within this landscape, beneath this sky, and in humble accordance with seasonal earth-sky rhythms. In winter I live with the ache of distance. How many times have I awakened elsewhere with the blood language of this place on my tongue: *aspen, sagebrush, elk, wind, outcrop, blizzard, spit-snow?*

This is a place, a landscape, that has taught me weather as a verb. To weather a storm, a change, a loss. To remember how it looked before a road gouged out the field and the ridge slope, how it looked before the cabin, the house, the settlement was built, how it flowed before the subdivision came of age. To notice and to remember in the sensory immediacy of the present the silence of nightfall before there are so many more lights. To speak the names of the animals that are of this place before and as they vanish: grouse, great-horned, whooper, eagle, elk, cougar, moose, coyote, porcupine, badger, beaver, bear. To hope for their weathering, their homes. To survive the storms, and to weather the natural and human evolutions of the place.

SUSAN AUSTIN

Little's Peak
for K and D

rusting coffee can
in a rock cairn—family names
snow, wind, clouds *horsetails*

MARY MAJ

Cranes Signal Spring

I WAS SITTING BY THE TETON RIVER RECENTLY, listening and watching the clangorous arrival of sandhill cranes. The cranes were vigorously feeding along melted-out river bank and coursing the water edge looking for bugs and roots. Their long, slender, probing beaks are used to penetrate deep into soft soil, dissect an occasional cow-pie and forage through the remnants of last year's plant growth. Cranes seem to be able to nicely mix feeding with dancing and singing to their could-be mates and co-travelers.

The cranes that stage in Teton Valley in the spring and fall are greater sandhill cranes, the largest subspecies of crane found in central and western North America. The Teton Valley birds are part of the "Rocky Mountain" population.

The cranes I was watching began arriving in the valley in mid-March. Only a few of these birds will remain as pairs and nest in the valley, the surrounding foothills and meadows. Cranes disperse widely in the summer and are thus quite difficult to survey. However, one count performed in 1969 located 50 pairs summering in the valley.

Most of our spring cranes will disperse as pairs to wetlands and high mountain meadows such as Squirrel Meadows near Ashton, Camas Meadows near Kilgore and Bechler Meadows in Yellowstone National Park. There the cranes will build an inconspicuous ground nest and lay two eggs among the blue camas, white wyethia and slender-beaked sedge, often on the edge of lodgepole pine forests.

Sandhill cranes are indeterminate layers, meaning that they will continue to lay eggs for some time into the spring should one be lost. A few oldtimers from Squirrel, Idaho, once told how they used to take advantage of this fact. They would locate a crane nest and mark the first egg laid. After the second egg was laid, they would remove the marked (first) egg and then repeat the process. This would go on for a few weeks until their pantries were filled with fresh, large eggs.

I have also heard vague stories of eating the "tough ole birds." Most people didn't encourage this activity after trying it once.

In October cranes return to Teton Valley, which is the single most important area used by the Rocky Mountain cranes each fall for staging. They regroup here, feeding voraciously in cut barley fields in preparation for their migration to winter homes. Most of the fall cranes winter in western New Mexico, southeastern Arizona and northern Mexico. Their 1,000-mile trip will start together in Teton Valley and continue southward across southwestern Wyoming, across the tip of Utah to the San Luis Valley in Colorado where they will stop over again for up to six weeks. From there they travel across New Mexico to their final winter destinations.

Crane activity gives me a vivid perspective on the seasons. My assurance that spring has arrived is based solely upon the sound of returning sandhill cranes. I am not fooled by 50-degree temperatures nor rain and sleet in April. Cranes are the only gauge I trust.

Aldo Leopold, the father of wildlife management, once wrote this about cranes:

> Our ability to perceive nature begins, as in art, with the pretty. It expands through successive stages of beautiful to values as yet to be captured by language. The quality of cranes lies, I think, in the highest gamut, as yet beyond the reach of words. This much, though, can be said: our appreciation of the crane grows with the slow unraveling of earthly history. His tribe, we know, stems out of the remote Eocene. The other members of the fauna in which he originated are long since entombed within the hills. When we hear his call, we hear no mere bird. He is a symbol of our untamable past, of that incredible sweep of millennia which underlies and conditions the daily affairs of birds and man. [The cranes'] annual return is the ticking of the geologic clock. Upon the place of return they confer a peculiar distinction.

And so, in this place of distinction, I hope you too enjoy and share the excitement and dancing of the returning spring in Teton Valley.

Grullas, Señales de Primavera
Translated by Gloria Gomez Whitfield
and Aaron Leigh Whitfield

RECIENTEMENTE ESTABA SENTADA AL LADO DEL RÍO TETON escuchando y viendo la resonante llegada de las grullas Sandhill. Las grullas estaban alimentándose vigorosamente a la orilla del río y recorriendo la orilla buscando bichos y raíces. Usan sus largos y delgados picos para penetrar el profundo suelo, analizar excremento en ocasiones y forragear los residuos de las plantas que crecieron el año anterior. Las grullas parecen poder mezclar su alimentación con el baile y el canto a sus posibles parejas y compañeros de viaje.

Las grullas que descansan en este valle en la primavera y el otoño se llaman en inglés "Greater Sandhill Cranes," las más larga subespecie de grullas encontradas en el centro y oeste de América del Norte. Las aves del Valle de Teton son parte de la población de las Montañas Rocosas.

Las grullas que observaba llegaban a mediados de marzo. Solo pocas de ellas permanecen en parejas y anidan en el valle, alrededor de la pradera. Las grullas se dispersan extensamente en el verano y por lo tanto es difícil contarlas. Sin embargo, un conteo realizado en 1969 localizó cincuenta parejas veraneando en el valle.

La mayoría de nuestras grullas de primaveras se dispersaron en parejas a las praderas y a las vegas de las montañas altas como Squirrel Meadows cerca de Ashton, Camas Meadows cerca de Kilgore y Belcher Meadows en el parque nacional de Yellowstone. Ahí las grullas construyen sus no muy conspicuos nidos en el suelo e incuban los huevos entre las flores azules, wyethia blanca, juncias, a menudo a la orilla de los bosques de pino.

Las grullas Sandhill ponen huevos ilimitadamente lo cual quiere decir que continúan poniendo huevos hasta la primavera si uno se pierde. Algunos ancianos de Squirrel, Idaho, alguna vez me dijeron que se aprovecharon de este hecho. Encontraban un nido de grulla, marcaban el primer huevo puesto y después de que el segundo huevo fue puesto tomaban el huevo marcado, es decir el primer huevo, y repetían el proceso. Hacían eso por semanas hasta que sus despensas se llenaban de huevos grandes.

También he oído algunos interminables cuentos de comer los "pájaros viejos y duros." La mayoría de la gente no recomienda probar esta actividad.

En octubre las grullas vuelven al Valle de Teton, el cual es el área mas importante de descanso para las grullas de las Montañas Rocosas cada otoño. Aquí, se juntan para comer con voracidad en los campos de cebada en preparación para la migración a sus hogares de invierno. La mayoría de las grullas pasan el invierno en el oeste de Nuevo México, el sur este de Arizona y el norte de México.

Su viaje de mil millas empieza en el Valle Teton y continúa al sur cruzando el Suroeste de Wyoming, cruzando la punta de Utah al Valle de San Luis en Colorado, donde descansan otra vez hasta por seis semanas. De allí viajan a través de Nuevo México para llegar a sus destinos finales del invierno.

La actividad de las grullas me da una perspectiva vívida de las estaciones. Solamente me asegura que la primavera ha venido cuando escucho el retorno de las grullas Sandhill. No me engaño por las temperaturas de cincuenta grados ni la lluvia cellisca de abril. Las grullas son la única señal en que confío.

Aldo Leopold, el padre de las administraciones de la vida salvaje, escribió esto de las grullas:

> Nuestra habilidad de percibir la naturaleza empieza, como en arte, con lo bonito. Se expanda a través de pasos sucesivos de lo bonito a lo valioso, lo cual no ha sido capturado por el lenguaje. La calidad de grullas consiste, pienso yo, en la más alta gama que las palabras no pueden describir. Sin embargo esto se puedo decir: Nuestra apreciación de la grulla, crece conjuntamente con el descubrimiento del desarrollo de las historia del mundo. Sabemos que su tribu sale del Eoceno distante. Los otros miembros de la fauna de lo cual se originan hace tiempo se enterraron dentro de los cerros. Cuando escuchamos su grito, no escuchamos simplemente un ave. El es un símbolo del pasado indomable, la parte del milenio que se esconde y que coincide con las condiciones y hechos de ave y hombre. Su retorno anual es el tic toc del reloj geológico. Otorgan una distinción peculiar al lugar donde regresan.

Entonces es en este lugar de distinción que espero que gocen y que compartan la emoción y el baile del retorno de la primavera al Valle Teton.

J. M. SPENCER

The Witness

THE WOODEN STEPS ARE BUFFED WITH BLUE FROST, but the hillsides are tapestries of cadmium yellow, pale gold, sienna and fir-green. This morning carries a message in its splendor, that I live on the substance of the ephemeral. I already know the inclined tectonics of the present moment, how it slides its relinquished seconds beneath the heavy slab of an ever weightier past. The sun rises over the mountain late, nearly eight o'clock.

The tip of Fossil Mountain glows like an alabaster lamp; the sun has jumped the canyon. Above, a fine last paring of moon wavers and fades in the daylight. Finally I surrender and understand that one lives only to be a witness to this day.

Now the thin sunlight is brushed across the mountain's flanks, a spare autumnal light as thin as the soils it kindles. This is a hard-scrabble place, with a minimalist soul that speaks to the reductions in my own.

In these mountains abundance is always guarded and spare, as if the land is waiting in this interlude for the next ice age to come, or a great sea to rush in and cover. all, or for the mountains to fall—again. It's spare because it does not take its present configuration seriously, but knows that everything that has been given—that makes it what it is—will be taken. It would be a waste of time to invest in self-importance when the next geologic event is perhaps a tick of time away.

But there is love, a word that can be spoken without irony when speaking of geology. This land so loved the sun that it rose miles in the air to meet it. And whoever loves this kind of land is a lover of few ideas, but such big ideas, though only one or two. The biggest ideas require few words, few thoughts and few dreams, but all of them are big. Whoever loves this land is made a simpleton who can only say, "I love you."

Exuberance is sucked out of all youth quickly here, and the skin withers in the dry, sun-filled, spare air, goes thin as the begrudged soils. Blue eyes are burned out of skulls by the hot claws of the aching, eternal sky, and fingers go feeble when they fail to scrabble a purchase on the vastness, which never can be held. Those who love this land and give over a lifetime to it, will die and hit the ground already half dust.

It's evening now, and the flake of moon holds its own again in the darkness, with Jupiter following fast behind as if towed in its wake.

Unseen, restless animal life passes through the brush like an errant wind, never known, so not forgotten, but simply as if it never had been. In the dim light the yellowed trees look like plumes of luminescent smoke. The whole earth rolls over, sending the moon onto the Pacific and across another continent. Only big thoughts for this vast place, and only the kind of time that stars have.

JEAN LIEBENTHAL

Two Haiku

Pale, tenacious,
one dry blade of wild grass
reaches through snow

Suddenly, at night,
four white-tailed deer alert
by the hay shed

MARILYN ELLIOTT MEYER

Fox Creek

FOX CREEK RUNS THROUGH MY BACKYARD.

It begins as melting snow high in the Tetons, the droplets gathering into tiny rivulets, merging into channels, gathering momentum and mass as they tumble 10 miles down Fox Creek canyon. I hardly have time to finish my lunch while those billions of water droplets now called Fox Creek pass by my house, cross the valley and lose themselves in the Teton River. From there they travel to the Snake River and across the vast Snake River plain into the Columbia River and on to the Pacific Ocean. For a moment or two, though, their amazing journey passes by my house and I marvel at my good fortune to be able to watch its passage, free of charge, from my chair on the back porch.

I was born half a century ago downstream from here in a farming town built on the banks of the Snake River in the middle of the plains. I grew up catching garter snakes and frogs along the ditch banks that diverted water from the river to the fields of potatoes and sugar beets that surrounded town. I swam in the big canals on hot August days. My father sold tractors from a store built on the river's bank. Through my growing up, the river ran by my town always on the way to somewhere. I wanted to be on my way somewhere, too; I longed for something bigger, something grander, something new and different. When I was old enough, I left the river and its country and set out looking for adventure. I covered thousands of miles through jungles and deserts, mountains and seas. Ten years into my journey, I sat alone in a one-room house built on stilts above the sand, staring out my open window past the outhouse at the end of the dock to a turquoise sea. On my lap were photos of sagebrush and autumn-dead grasses along a dry creek bed. I was thinking that building a home among the sage-brush along that creek would be the grandest thing in my life. While the sounds of the sea lapping at the shore came in my window, I scribbled house plans into a tattered notebook.

A few months later I returned to the river's country and began building my home on the banks of Fox Creek. That summer, more than 20 years ago now, I lived in a tiny trailer across the creek from the house site. The creek sounds filled my ears at night while I slept; they drowned out the noise of the hammers as we put up the walls. I waded across the frigid water in the morning to work on my house and waded across it in the afternoon at the end of my day. I bathed in it, rested beside it, wove it into my dreams of the future. I swore that when my new home was finished and I moved in, I would still spend most of my time outside of it, on the banks of the creek which defined the place I had chosen to live. Then I moved into the house and closed the door.

Fox Creek slid into the background of my life. Its wild sounds came in through my bedroom windows during the night. When I went to work in town, I walked over it on a rickety footbridge and walked over it again on my way home. I saw it grow wide with melting snow in the spring and then slowly shrink over the summer months until fall when the rocks in the creek turned dry and dusty. In the winter the creek disappeared beneath the deep snows.

One early spring day I left my home on the creek and when I returned I was married and now two people lived in the house on the banks of Fox Creek. Months later, in the still-yellow days of fall, my husband and I stood silently at the edge of the tiny trickle that was the creek and scattered the ashes of our baby daughter; our dreams of sharing our home with her floating down the creek to the river on the plains and out to the sea. The cottonwoods filled the creek beds with a blanket of fallen leaves, the snow covered the ground, the spring beauties bloomed again, and brook trout returned to hide in the shadows of the willows. Fox Creek continued its journey through my backyard. One summer day a new note was added to the music of the creek: the laughter of two young boys.

The boys built forts on the island where their father and I had stood to scatter the ashes of their sister. They threw rocks at sticks rushing by during high water and waded in the cold waters when it ran quietly. They gathered rocks and built dams. In the fall when the brook trout were stranded in deep pools by the receding waters, they caught them in their bare hands and carried them across the road above the headgate to safe haven. They named their favorite places: the tree hole, the waterfall, the big rock. They dragged me from the house and demanded that I see the delights I was missing. I returned to the banks of the creek that runs through my back yard.

It was my sons who discovered the fossils. They showed me rocks etched with delicate patterns. My neighbor, the geologist, said they were shellfish and corals that lived here when the valley was beneath a vast sea, about 500 million years ago. The numbers scattered weightless in my head. Not just before man lived along the creek, but longer ago than the dinosaurs, longer ago than the mountains themselves. I now saw, not just the passage of melted snowflakes in the creek behind my house, but a story of life bigger than the grandest of journeys.

The sea receded about 200 million years ago, and what is now my home became part of a dry coastal plain. For millions of years the desert stretched from southern Montana to Arizona. After that, swamps and bogs covered the land. Around 50 million years ago the Big Hole Mountains were formed. The Tetons pushed thousands of feet above the earth's surface just 15 million years ago. According to my neighbor, they are still growing. Just 12,000 years ago, glaciers covered the valley and the mountains around it. Fox Creek didn't appear until the glaciers began melting. Now I am adding my short story to the land.

Through many summers my sons brought their rocks up to the house from the creek and piled them on the deck. I began to think they were endless. The deck seemed to sag with their weight. Then the novelty wore off; the boys grew older and turned away from the creek looking for things grander and more exciting. The creek flowed behind the house on its way to the sea unaccompanied by their shouts and their splashing. Over the years I grew weary of the rocks on my porch and threw them one by one out to the edge of the lawn.

One recent fall day my dog and I walked along the dry creek bed, crunching the fallen yellow leaves beneath our feet. I stood in the silence, letting memories play through my head. On a whim, I leaned over and looked between the leaves among the rocks for a fossil. Nothing but gray water-rounded stones lay beneath my hands. With a sense of urgency then I began searching harder. I walked bent over up and down the creek bed and back and forth until my back grew stiff and I grew bored. I found not one fossil. Perhaps it takes the eyes of a child to find the magic among the stones. I walked, a bit anxious now, to the edge of the yard, and poked among the tall dry grasses, the bitterbrush and sagebrush, for the rocks I had thrown there years ago. I found one. Only one. I carried the lone fossil to the deck and carefully placed it there. Maybe one day I will have grandchildren who will drag me down to the creek demanding I see the delights I am missing. Maybe they will show me how to find fossils. But just in case, I will keep the one I found.

Sometimes when I sit on my back porch above the creek catching the evening sun, I imagine the days when Fox Creek was 300 yards across or more, roaring down from the melting snows high in the Tetons and into the valley below. I think it was that wide because that is the distance from the bench in front of my house to its twin across the creek on the other side of the road. The Indians probably knew better than to set up camp on this creek bottom in the spring. The trappers knew better too. Today the creek seems tamer and the houses, like mine, inch closer and closer to the edge of the waters.

The stream no longer follows its own path but has been forced to flow where it is needed for irrigation. The first water right on Fox Creek was filed in May of 1889, and the creek soon became a tool for the people who lived here. Today the creek is divided into north and south channels at the canyon's mouth. Before the south channel reaches my house, it is divided by two headgates and a few small old ditches. After it passes my house, it is divided at least a half a dozen more times before it reaches the Teton River. The north channel has even more diversions. Fox Creek is split about 20 times before its various selves reach the river. Some old canals have been here so long they have riparian areas of their own. A few are nearly forgotten and unused. Still, Fox Creek's ancient route remains visible. When I climb into the foothills of the Tetons and turn to look down at the valley, I can see the thick line of cottonwoods that runs through my backyard marking the creek's original path.

The canals and streambeds formed from the valley's creeks look harmless most of the year but often overflow in the spring, flooding yards and washing out new driveways. Those that manage the canal companies are increasingly asked to provide water when there is none and to take the water away when there is too much. The creek has not changed itself to fit the new lifestyles in the valley; it still runs heavy with snowmelt in the spring when the ground is wet and slows to a trickle in the fall when the grasses turn brown and dry. I am lucky to live where the creek still speaks of its true nature.

The summer that I built my house, I carried countless buckets of water from the creek to a hundred tiny trees I had purchased from the Soil Conservation Service and planted across my 10 acres of land. Every day all that summer I carried buckets of water two by two to each of the trees. In the fall the creek dried up, my well wasn't finished and the trees died; all but one lone pine. That pine, now 22 years old, stands not quite five feet tall near my back deck along the creek. Since that summer I have been content to let the water flow as it will behind my house and down to the river.

None of the water that runs through my backyard belongs to me, despite my small attempt at irrigating that first summer. I own no shares in the Fox Creek Canal Company. When I built my house, only a few dozen people held shares of Fox Creek water. Since 1990 the number of people owning water rights has increased from 35 to at least 100. Land along the creek is being cut into smaller and smaller parcels, and the number of shareholders is increasing. In the late summer and early fall, I watch trucks pull up to the headgate at the edge of my property at all hours. People I recognize and people I've never seen add and remove boards, adjusting and readjusting the water's path, making sure they get all they own, then climb back into their trucks and drive away.

A few years ago when the winter snows fell deep in the Tetons and spring arrived wet and warm, Fox Creek rushed out of the mountains and over the tops of the headgates and around the sides of the culverts and across the roads. One culvert washed out, and the water flowed eight feet wide and four feet deep through our roadbed. Four households, including mine, were stranded. We had to ask our neighbor for permission to drive through his fields to get to and from our homes for several weeks. My neighbors said the culvert was inadequate and new precautions should be taken. When the waters receded, though, the culvert was replaced nearly the same as before. Since then the creek has flowed placidly between its banks every spring. I am glad we didn't try to tame the creek further. I was secretly happy to see it break through, to demand to be noticed, to proclaim some of its old power. Of course, if Fox Creek returned entirely to its old boundaries, became once again the 300 yard-wide creek of old, my house would be beneath the water.

I recently learned that the headgate at the edge of my property, the one that is so busy every fall, is known among the creek's shareholders as the "Meyer headgate." I was and still am, overwhelmed by a sense of belonging, a sense of grounding, here on the banks of Fox Creek. I have persevered long enough to become part of the geography along with the creek.

I sit on my back porch watching the creek flow by. I notice the heavy spring waters have widened an old channel and filled another in with gravel. I see dozens of new young cottonwoods sprouting along the banks. I can almost hear echoes of young boys' voices shouting over the noise of the creek. I imagine swamps and glaciers or a sea filled with corals and shellfish. I think about snow melting high in the Tetons and water flowing to the sea endlessly for hundreds of years. I remember moments of my life on the banks of Fox Creek, the beginnings and endings, the changes and the constants. Perhaps one day my children will live here, but I suspect they will leave, as I did, searching for something bigger and grander. Someday a stranger will live here and will wonder who "Meyer" was and why he got his name on the headgate. Someday the sea may again cover this valley, and then my bones will lie among the fossils beneath the water.

I watch the creek flow toward the setting sun and marvel at the journey.

LAURIE KUTCHINS

Still Life with Hawks and Storms

This was a good day for hawks:
storms, then lulls, then more storms.
I envied their eyesight and grace.
They buck and float the blue wind, are one with it
the way I would like to be one with the impalpable circle
of the unconscious.

I want to know how their wings
hold and hoist them against the brutal currents,
rain slats, the rumbles of thunder,
how they join the immeasurable intelligence of cumulo-nimbi,
so at home under them.

The storms stirred up their prey,
rockchucks and mice scrambling in and out of rocks and scrubs.
The hawks circled and waited, vigilant.
Then dove, snatched, glided from sight.

Beneath their voracious shadows, I was a random form,
an uncamouflaged lump,
a mere whistle in their chain of being.
I was the least of their concerns.

Five storms crossed over today.
Five storms like dreams, four of which I've brought with me,
into the clearing.
The fifth being the most elusive, the most charged,
the darkest. The one you wait for.

EARLE F. LAYSER

The Original Natural Setting of Pierre's Hole–A Changed and Changing Landscape

GAZING ACROSS TETON VALLEY'S PASTORAL SETTINGS, towards the timeless grandeur of those three mountain peaks, have you ever tried to imagine how Pierre's Hole must have appeared long ago?

In centuries past, the grunts and rattling dew claws of bison could be heard in the meadows. Herds of bison, antelope, elk and deer spread across the Valley's prairies. The echoing din of thousands of clamorous waterfowl and cranes reverberated from the river bottom and extensive beaver marshes. Aboriginal summer lodges stood amid giant cottonwoods, and wolves mournfully announced the moon rise over those same dramatic peaks—the peaks the Shoshone called the "hoary headed fathers." Back then, the Valley was a much different place.

Aldo Leopold said, "The difference between land and country is wildlife." Land is farms, fences, building lots, mortgages and such, but "country," in the sense with which Leopold spoke, is expansive natural settings, wildlife, adventure, and a freedom few of us may ever know or experience. Prior to European settlement, Pierre's Hole was Country.

Pierre Tevanitagon was a French-Iroquois who wandered into the Valley in 1818 and later returned with the Northwest Fur Company, and who, at the hands of the Blackfeet, had the tragic misfortune of becoming immortalized: *Trou á Pierre*, Peter's Hole.

What was it, despite the risks, that attracted the likes of Vieux Pierre, the Hudson Bay Company, the Astorians, the American Fur Company, the Rocky Mountain Fur Company, Ashley, Sublette, Wyeth, Bridger, Meek, Smith and a list of others reading like a mountain man's "Who's Who," to this Valley? Sure, abundant beaver and the fur trade. But, not unlike today, for some it was more than business or livelihood—it was the Country!

Few places elicited more glowing testimonials from mountain men and early explorers than Pierre's Hole. Quite a compliment from those crusty adventurers, who, as the historian Bernard DeVoto put it, "intimately knew every inch of the land and streams."

What invariably stands out in those early journals, and in the his-

Alan McKnight

torical research and novels that rely upon those accounts, are the repeated references to the Valley's dramatic setting and abundant wildlife.
A sampling of excerpts below provides insight into what it was like
through most of the 19th century.

In 1811 Wilson Hunt, leader of the overland Astorians, commented
on the "remarkable peaks" and named them the "Pilot Knobs." He also
took note of "numerous bands of antelope," "thickets of wild cherries,"
and Indian trails that existed across the passes (Teton Pass) leading into
the Valley.

In *Journal of a Trapper*, Osborne Russell states, "The East range resembles
mountains piled upon mountains and capped with three spiral peaks
which pierce the cloud. ... [The peaks] bear the French name Tetons.
... This is a beautiful valley consisting of a smooth plain intersected by
small streams and thickly clothed with grass and herbage and abounds
with buffaloe, elk, deer, antelopes."

In *Rocky Mountain Rendezvous*, Fred Gowans quotes mountain man
Joseph Meek's 1829 description of Pierre's Hole: "Found time to admire the magnificent scenery of the valley, which is bounded on two
sides by broken and picturesque ranges, and overlooked by that magnificent group of mountains, called the three Tetons. ... [It] was so
pleasant a sight to the mountain-men that camp was moved [to where
the peaks could be viewed] without delay."

Benjamin Bonneville, fur trader, journalized this 1832 account, as quoted by E.W. Todd in L.R. Hafen's *Mountain Men and Fur Traders of the
Far West*, "The Valley called Pierre's Hole is ... overlooked ... by three
lofty mountains ... which domineer as landmarks over a vast extent of

country. A fine stream ... pours through the valley ... dividing it into nearly equal parts. The meadows ... are broad and extensive ... [and their borders] covered with willows and cottonwood trees, so closely interlocked and matted together as to be nearly impassable."

Zenas Leonard, *Adventures of a Mountain Man*, describes the scene in 1832 , as a "valley ... situated on the river of the same name ... from 70-80 miles in length, with a high mountain on east and west—each so high that it is impossible to pass over them. ... The river runs immediately through the center, with a beautiful grove of timber along either bank; from this timber to the mountain, ... there is nothing but a smooth plain ... until the earth and sky appear to meet."

It was a place where, in Howard Driggs's tale *Nick Wilson—Pioneer Boy Among the Indians*, the Shoshone had their summer camps because of "the abundant game and berries," and "Indians came to this valley for game [from] as far away as southern Utah."

Henry Jackson, photographer for the 1872 Hayden Expedition, noted that the Valley was a "game paradise. ... Their party was kept well supplied with fresh meat without having to hunt for it, ... deer, moose or mountain sheep being nearly always in sight. ... It was equally easy to get a mess of trout. ... Bears were abundant, ... one topographer working ... above timberline counted eleven ... during a day."

James Stevenson, 1872 Hayden Party, wrote, "We were ... reluctant to leave Teton Canyon's fine forests of spruce and pine, its foaming cascades, and its constantly changing views of the Grand Teton, ringed by clouds, veiled by falling snow, rosy in the flood of setting sun, or gray and awesome in early morning light."

Langford, also with the 1872 Hayden Party, remarked on the prairies "carpeted with the heaviest and largest bunchgrass" he had ever seen, and "meadows full of camas." Thomas Moran remarked in 1879 on the "large beaver dams that stretched across Teton Canyon."

Dick Leigh, mountain man, Beaver Dick—*The Honor and Heartbreak*, summarizes it all by saying, "Teton Basin was the beautifulest sight in the whole world."

Based on historical vignettes like those above, we can say with some certainty that 19th century Teton Valley epitomized what biologists call "natural habitat." Still, what did the Valley's original vegetational pattern or habitat actually look like back then? Today we can only speculate based on those early accounts and vegetation ecology.

Very little remains of the original mosaic of vegetation that once occurred on the valley floor. What is left are: those wetlands that stubbornly resisted draining; aspen stands that somehow escaped clearing; patches of willow and hawthorn thickets that survived concentrated grazing; here and there some old-growth cottonwoods, like those along South Leigh Creek; and small isolated remnants of foothill shrub-grasslands. Generally, the small remnant and fragmented habitats existing today are incapable of supporting the numbers and kinds of wildlife that occurred under the 19th century conditions.

Based on the historical descriptions and vegetation ecology, we can visualize the primeval landscape as expanses of highly productive shrub-grassland prairie occurring on the Valley's deep alluvial and wind-deposited soils, dominated by snowberry, sagebrush, bitterbrush and bunchgrasses, gloriously carpeted with wildflowers in spring, particularly balsam root.

The prairies were abruptly and frequently bisected by corridors of dense deciduous floodplain and riparian forest, which were dominated by huge cottonwood trees that stretched in linear patterns along drainages leading to the Teton River. The deciduous riparian forest intergraded with dense spruce forest at the canyon mouths and wetlands in the Valley lowlands. The understory of the riparian forest was structurally diverse and was comprised of thickets of alder, red-osier dogwood, water-birch, willows and intermingled aspen and interspersed with sedge meadows. Abundant migratory birds nested and sang within the riparian forests.

Flood paths of streams were broader than those of today. Channels were often ill-defined, and tributary streams approaching the river frequently fanned out or re-emerged as springs, resulting in abundant wetlands that attracted incredible numbers and kinds of waterfowl. Spring melt water rushing from the mountain canyons frequently resulted in overbank events. Aided by blockage from beaver colonies and downed trees, this periodic flooding created shrublands and wet meadows where water birch, shrubby cinquefoil, willows and blue camas grew.

From the forested mountain slopes, aspen inter-fingered onto the moister valley sites where deep silt loam soils occurred. Aspen clones extended from the foothills and about the prairie fringes, where they intergraded into stands of berry-producing tall shrubs, such as chokecherry, serviceberry and hawthorn, which then formed broad transitions into the prairie grasslands.

Frequent natural wildfires played a role in further contributing to plant community diversity and productivity. In 1879 Thomas Moran, whose purpose was to paint the Grand Teton, found the air so smoky that the peaks were obscured. T.S. Brandegee surveyed forest conditions in 1897 and reported that "fires had swept over the country... completely and persistently, ..." favoring aspen growth. Widespread fires between 1840-1890 are responsible for current extensive aspen and lodgepole pine stands on the mountain slopes around the Valley. Loope and Gruell, *Ecological Role of Fire in the Jackson Hole Area*, documented how wildfire suppression over the past 90 years has altered natural fire cycles and plant communities.

In the late 1800s miners prospected the Valley. And later, scenes of the "Wild West" were played out, as outlaws hid horses stolen from Fort Hall in the narrow canyons and escaped across Horse Thief Pass or other Indian trails leading over the Teton Range. One Teton Basin outlaw, Ed Trafton, gained national infamy when he held up numerous tourist stage coaches in Yellowstone National Park. Writer Owen Wister used the Teton Valley as part of his romanticized setting for *The Virginian*. A few scattered trappers roamed Teton Basin during the late 1800s.

Hiram C. Lapham and family are generally credited as being the first year-round settlers. They arrived in the 1870s. Others followed.

The first arriving Mormon pioneers, who settled near Driggs in 1883, undoubtedly found a valley that was still very much wild country. Somewhere around this time the name Pierre's Hole fell out of usage. Settlers began calling the area "Teton Basin." Cabins and wagon roads began to appear. B.W. Driggs, *History of Teton County*, states that "within a few years the best land was taken up."

But still, the Valley's broader natural landscape and abundant wildlife must have persisted mostly unchanged through the late 1880s, as evidenced by B.W. Driggs' statement: "[In 1891] there were numerous sage hens," and that settlers "never lacked for fresh [game] meat." The fact that sage grouse and game were abundant indicates that substantial native prairie and other natural habitats were still relatively intact at that time.

In 1889, the same year of Dick Leigh's passing, large companies of Mormon pioneers began arriving. In a collective burst of Herculean labor, irrigation canals were constructed, the virgin prairie soil plowed, aspen forests cleared, wetlands drained, sawmills built and operated, fences erected, and substantial farms carved from wild country.

The entire hydrology of the basin was altered through irrigation canal systems. Droves of horses, lowing cattle and bleating sheep suddenly appeared where only a short time before there had been herds of wild ungulates.

Aboriginal summer camps disappeared when Native Americans were moved to reservations. In startlingly short time Teton Basin became agricultural land. Farms and fences cut off the ancient migration routes of antelope, bison, deer and elk. Domestic sheep brought diseases to wild sheep. Foraging wild ungulates and large carnivores conflicted with the new agricultural economy and lifestyle. Vanished from the Valley were the once numerous antelope, bison, bighorn sheep, grizzly bear, wolf, sage grouse, and whooping cranes. Gone too was the habitat—the extensive "beaver swamps," camas meadows, aspen and cottonwood groves, shrub thickets, and once-expansive natural grasslands.

The decline of the remarkable wildlife populations were marked not only by loss of habitat, but also by year-round hunting. In *A Community of Scalawags, Renegades, Discharged Soldiers and Predestined Stinkers*, K. & L. Diem quote W. A. Hague, a turn of the century Teton Basin guide and outfitter, "Their arn't any game wardens on this side in Idaho."

Although the natural setting has been dramatically changed, Teton Valley still offers much to be thankful for—open space, clean water and air, small town and rural lifestyles, and the majestic and timeless backdrop of the Tetons, which still beckon with mountainous backcountry and outdoor adventure. For years, life in Teton Basin, pioneered by Mormon settlers, has been more or less stable and predictable—a good place to live and raise a family. To paraphrase Barry Lopez, *Crossing Open Ground*, one of the great challenges of mankind is to find someplace between the extremes of nature and civilization where it is possible to live without regret. That challenge seems particularly apropos for Teton Valley as we enter the 21st century.

KEN SMITH

Spring in Alaska Basin

Pillows of light fold over the mountain crest
preventing the billowing granite from escaping.
Deer are among the first to eat mountain lilies and
strawberry leaves breaking through the melting snow.
Glacier water pools in massive rock beds, metamorphic
evidence of the Ice Age when hard cold buried life.
But now life escapes all around, gobbling up mountain air
and blanketing the Valley with its hardy existence.

JEAN LIEBENTHAL

Hillside in June

Myriad trees have fallen
since November,
vast piles of aspens
with shallow roots upended,
and one pine bent to the ground.
New trunks are scattered
helter-skelter over old,
like crude cabins
built by hidden hands
on the bright grass
still wet from snow.

These woods seem haunted,
as if at any turn
a house may rise,
inhabited by unknown
but familiar occupants
of all my longings.
Always, my eye is ready
for unfolding amazement,
some forest offering,
unnamed, elusive.

I turn back —
pick wild clematis wound
through a stunted lodgepole,
gather a handful
of kindling wood,
pocket an anomalous rock
as meager evidence
of my untenable search.

BARBARA AGNEW

Keeping an Eye on the Flock

TETON VALLEY IS RICH. Its resources are glamorous. That in itself could explain our perilous rate of growth. The valley has qualities which make teaching here a lifetime's worth of learning. At first glance, studying "home" seems so commonplace for the children who grow up here. But what if "home" is the "hook" and it is integrated with the rest of the world?

Pretend you got a job here as a teacher. The first thing would be to check the shelves to see what great literature you are supposed to teach. Among the sets of books is *Sadako and a Thousand Paper Cranes,* by Eleanor Coerr. Oh, so you get to teach WWII and Japan. Can 10-year-olds relate? Wait. We have cranes here: upwards of 5,000 sandhill cranes "stage" in Teton Valley each fall. Our place is important to them. We feed them in our barley fields so they can make their long trip south. All summer long, if one lives anywhere near the Teton River, one can hear them calling. We have even had the privilege of hosting a whooping crane or two over the last ten years. It is hard to beat a whooper for spectacular. There is the local hook, which connects to the world. Our cranes are very like Japanese cranes and Siberian cranes. A field trip leads to questions, which leads to research so the students learn to use the library, so they can write papers. They can fold paper cranes and launch themselves into the world of origami.

Check the shelves again. There are 30 copies of *The Trumpet of the Swan,* by E.B. White. We have swans here too. Sometimes there are 50 swans, sometimes 300. If you teach it in December you can go to the river and watch the swans. They come here because our river usually does not freeze over and they can find food. The setting for this classic children's book is our neighborhood. Red Rock Lakes is right up the road.

Let's see. What else are we supposed to read? *Owls in the Family,* by Farley Mowat, means we can study Saskatchewan and their grain fields. You can read that book as a class in Tetonia, and every student in the room will have an owl story of their own. I once had a four-year-old and an eight-year-old in the truck with me. In a two-mile stretch we spotted 18 great grey owls, the biggest owl in North America. The four-year-old was learning to count and ran out of fingers. That may not happen this winter, but it did happen. What kind of a wildlife preserve is this?

1. Great blue heron (2)
2. American avocet
3. Sandhill cranes (11)
4. Black-crowned night heron
5. Moose
6. Beaver
7. American bittern
8. Long-billed curlew
9. Canvasback (2)
10. Northern pintail (2)
11. Mallard (2)
12. Goldeneye (10)
13. Ruddy duck (10)

So you're teaching landforms, and you arrive home to read an article in the local paper by Blair Baldwin explaining why we have such great powder snow to ski in. We live on the spot where the wind off the Snake River Plain has to drop its load to make it over the Tetons.

Or you're teaching about watersheds, and you realize we live at the top of the watershed. We start the Columbia River in the *Streams to the River, Rivers to the Sea* sense. We are the watershed of southern Idaho. Our snow is their irrigation water.

We have hydrologists who want to share what they know. We have fish biologists with the passion to teach.

We teach the continental divide, and some of our lucky fifth graders get to go to Yellowstone and discover it is not a rocky ridge like they may have imagined.

I did a presentation recently for a library science class. The subject of the presentation was "How can the librarian work with the classroom teacher so there are two teachers in the classroom?" My professor wanted me to demonstrate what kinds of materials I could make or gather to support the classroom teacher in a given subject area. I borrowed a science trunk from the Teton Regional Land Trust, the one they call "Big Birds of Teton Valley." During the presentation, as I demonstrated the mating dance of the sandhill crane for the video camera, in the crane costumes from the trunk, I suggested that teachers teach science by inviting the experts into the classroom.

The professor was quite surprised. I roared when he said, "How can you get scientists to go all the way up to your little valley?"

"The place is crawling with scientists," I said. "Honest." We even have a scientist who has specialized in one particular kind of tree. The foremost authority on cranes in the Rocky Mountain area comes every fall. The swan expert must keep an eye on the flock.

We are rich in natural history in Teton Valley; therefore, we are also rich in people studying those resources. The scientists have taught me that although their work is important and they are awfully busy doing it, unless at least some of that information filters down to the children, all their work is for naught. What good is that knowledge if no one knows about it? Students feed the spirit of the scientist in ways that no one else can. Support in this community, time to share what you know with the children, has been 100 percent, and that includes the areas of history and business as well as natural history.

To borrow a line from Emily Dickenson, "Hope is the thing with feathers." Or possibly the thing out there following the sound of the frog. Or hope is the student with hungry ears, listening to the story of the life cycle of the stone fly.

ALAN MCKNIGHT

In a Glass House

I was sweating, arms itching, sneezing pollen,
when my neighbor hailed me from his lot's edge:
"I've been watching you pull thistles all day.
You know there'll be a thousand more next year.
You can't win. 'Live and let live' is my song."
His strategy was clear to see in thick stands
of musk, Canadian and bull
throughout his field upwind of mine.
I paused to gather thoughts, choose words
less spined than my weedy antagonists.
"Let's save the native plants these aliens
displace. Let's save the animals they host.
The thistles over-breed, are prey to none,
and multiply till nothing else can thrive."
"That's it," he smiled. "They can't be all that bad;
they're more like us than anything alive."

LAURIE KUTCHINS

Poems to the Quaking Aspen

1.
Each evening, I walk down to you to listen.
Your youngest
who were too young to know me
last summer,
now hover about my face and sing to me.
They are just learning to sing with their small green skirts
flapping on the updrafts,
quivering and lifting their song
toward the elders;
with leaflets so perfect I hesitate
to touch them.

Their sapling bark—
soft as first velvet on the antlers
of the elk who will wait
until I have gone
to come down,
rub their secret necks
against you, and feed.

2.
Though I do not completely belong,
I meander and bend among your whispers.
I embrace the smell of summer in your house.
You are more alive to me

you who understand things
about fear
I am afraid to learn.

What's here?
Chartreuse eyes, undersides of voices.
Is it the porcupine waiting for nightfall
to lift your dead,
or the bear nosing a carcass,
or the great horned owl who makes its night watch
over you, whose eyes move
only when I move?

3.
I wrap my arms around you, my cheeks against your slashes,
and cower under a sudden storm.
I hold the strong, delicate sound of you
breathing in the lightning
and hard rain.

I have shrunk back
but you, while I held on,
have grown.

4.
Until I found you, I could not have told you
I would like to become an eye
in the white bark
where a limb fell.

5.
Until I found you, I thought you stood still.
But I have followed, and know
you drift and lean,
loving the wide grassy slopes
that smell mysteriously
of rain and elk
though neither are here.

CAROLE LUSSER
A Bit of History in a Flower Bed

A LITTLE SOIL MIXED WITH GRAVEL AND COBBLESTONE seemed to be the main composition of the spot I chose for a flower bed one fall. A shovel was useless, and I had to resort to a pick. My plan had been to remove the turf, loosen the soil, add compost and plant tulips and daffodils. Ha! How did I ever think it would be that easy? As I loosened the soil, my pick struck rock after rock, shaking my forearms to the bone. Our neighbor's incredible flower beds have always been an inspiration to me. Our yard, down a little slope from hers, might as well be a river bed! In the distant past, it probably was part of a larger Teton Creek.

When performing a task which takes lots of elbow grease, time and very little thought process, the mind wanders and plays. My meanderings of thought muddled through the forces of nature and geologic time which brought the soil beneath my feet into existence. "My flower bed is on the periphery of an old Teton Creek. Creek bed equals alluvial soil. Alluvial soil deposited in the middle of a valley surrounded by young jagged peaks (*aka* The Teton Range) on the east and older, somewhat rounded mountains to the south and west. Jagged peaks with U-shaped canyons say, 'glacial work done here.'

"Mountains, tectonic plate action, fault lines and earthquakes. Oh brother! The Snake River Plain lava beds to the west and to the northeast, Yellowstone National Park ... volcano factories of the past.

"Wow! I am standing in the middle of some pretty impressive geologic happenings!"

Work progressed and an old trash and burn pile emerged with each swing of my pick. I felt like an archeologist as the dig revealed broken crockery, shards of green, brown, pink and blue glass. Bits of china and a mangled fork and spoon appeared. Car battery parts, spark plugs and windshield glass surfaced. Pieces of iron farm machinery, nails, screws, bolts. ... "Geez, flowers will never grow in this junk," I groaned. And so began the painstaking process of removing the chosen area and replacing the hole with soil compatible with plant life.

At the end of about three weeks, working approximately two to four hours a day, I finished the flower bed. Forty tulip bulbs of various colors and ten daffodil bulbs went into well-decomposed cow, horse and sheep manure. A pile of this wonderful organic matter lies behind our barn and has filled our vegetable garden over the years. Weeds and small rocks had to be picked out, but at least I could dig it with a shovel. I stood before my labor and realized abundant flower beds would probably not exist around our property. I patted the ground and sweetly admonished the bulbs below the surface, "You guys better come up with a big smile next spring!"

The tulips and daffodils were stretching their stems toward the sky and the flower buds were still hiding all their colors when I first saw my fall handiwork. My husband and I had been out of town for spring planting on the family farm in Illinois. In our two-day travel home, I started getting nervous in Colorado when I saw tulips in full bloom.

"I'm going to miss my flowers coming up!" I thought to myself.

Almost in unison, my husband and I said, "Teton Valley is a lot farther north. We'll be home before the tulips bloom."

We drove down our driveway before twilight had faded, and I could see the flower buds nodding in a gentle breeze. The next day and for a couple of weeks, the daffodils and tulips bloomed one color at a time. Red, pink and yellow tulips smiled and waved throughout that lovely spring. For every bulb that bloomed, I had hauled out ten times as many cobblestones and pieces of burn-pile junk. Every toilsome hour had turned into many more hours of pleasure and enjoyment.

CAROLE LUSSER

Avalanche Run

On a hike this spring, I came to realize
the power of an avalanche.
The snow was still piled and packed
along the banks of Coal Creek.
As I stumbled along, I climbed over
huge, gashed trees lying silently.
Their trunks were spiked with broken,
shredded, nubby branches.
Bark was hanging in strips.
Cones, pine branches and needles
were crammed in the snow.
There was a lump in my throat

and a tremble in my knees as
I stood in the narrow canyon.
The energy that ripped the trees
from their roots was still palpable.
I found myself suddenly sitting
as if I were tossed there.

MICHAEL WHITFIELD

Bright-eyed Gneiss

"I may not know who I am, but I do know where I am from."
—Wallace Stegner

MY TRIP TO MOOSE BASIN THIS YEAR BEGINS MUCH LATER than in most years
past. I travel under threat of snow in late September. And I travel much
more casually than usual, no students in tow. My pace has no race in
it, no need to be up front of the swell. This journey is mine alone, to escape, to heal.

I walk the long trail in with a beautiful woman. From the meadows
to Bear Creek she is a sweating beast of burden on the trail behind me,
bent beneath a crimson pack over half her height. In the narrows she
is Oread, flitting up the slope above me, dark green spruce caught in
her wild black hair. I reconcile to her absence, then startle from day-
dream at the sudden flash of her smiling black eyes.

I walk in a personal vacuum, slowly shedding the must-be-done details of the other life, drinking in the calls of jay and raven, the smell
of pine and autumn aspen, the tumble and splash of Bitch Creek. My
feet are hot, my hips hurt, I count the miles, but my mind drifts over
the high passes. Far ahead I hear the footfalls of pilgrims, crossing the
crest, going into the light of the alpine wild.

I lay down my pack in the opening north of Camp Lake and set up
camp in the alpine glow, Moose Mountain and Glacier's western faces
burning red in the evening light. My back trail is empty, and tonight

Alan McKnight

upper Bitch is quiet except for my sputtering camp stove. Tomorrow I will rise early. The pass into Moose Basin lies directly above me, a mere hour of pounding heart, a quick rush of sweaty back in cold air.

Pretzel Egbert still gets misty eyes when he tells of the ride up from Camp Lake, 50 years back. Pretzel came for meat, and those crisp nights in camp with the good old boys, mostly long gone, Dode and Jerry, Nate, Jim, Les. A little JD at sunset took the stiffness out of the knees. Later the piss fir campfire smoked, the skillet sizzled with onions and fresh liver. Martin told me that when the rangers were around, the pack-horses sometimes found their own way home to the barn, panniers full of winter's meat.

At dawn I make my crossing, climbing from shadow into daylight. Just over the crest, out of the wind, I warm water for breakfast, and glass the far ridges.

On earlier trips I have found the poacher's camp tucked into the whitebark forest on the east side of upper Moose Basin. From the west rim my spotting scope leads my eyes to the distant trees where the horses were tied, where rusty tin cans peek out beneath the brush. Crystal water flows nearby. Around that camp in September, the elk bugle all day and into the night.

If I pause long enough, I can hear the horses whinny, smell the sweat of long-legged sorrels, blacks shiny on summer feed. The aroma of cowboy coffee hangs in the still air under the trees, with the tall tales and belly laughs.

Lawrence P. Hatch was one of the old-timers I listed as potential sources for my research into the history of the wild sheep of these mountains. I worked through the list too slowly—LP died before I could record his story firsthand. His sons tell me of late fall hunts, long rides in new snow.

Dave Beard was here in the '20s, worked the rock in upper Moran, came for copper ore. Dave saw the wild sheep crossing the high ridge between Bitch and Moose Basin. I listen for the echo of rockfall high on the sheep trails, for the echo of Dave's work in the rocky ledges.

Leigh Fullmer came here as a young man in the teens. "We didn't intend to break the laws, we just weren't sure where Wyoming was." He found "little bunches of sheep in the ledges, and lots of elk." He still remembered a group of bighorns down at the stream below Moose Divide.

The early climbers skirted the basin's edges, topographers searching for summits and the joy of first discovery. Rolling Thunder Mountain, Eagles Rest Peak, Anniversary, Doane, Ranger. The later climbers came more for difficult routes to the summits, and finding few, gravitated south into the center of the range.

In 1912, Professor Eliot Blackwelder and his assistant ascended the high, rounded mountain that would bear his name from the Middle Fork of Bitch Creek. Blackwelder's Point on the Teton Crest was a good place to leave a name, a weathered stony sentinel at the intersection of canyons and basins. Today the mapmakers call this point Glacier. Deep, perennial snow glitters in the recesses of the mountain's sheltered north face, dripping snowmelt into the stream at my feet.

I have found the lithic scatter, chips of obsidian, from aboriginal hunters on such high points and in the passes. They too came for meat and insight. The delicately scalloped red chirt of a bird point found a few miles north, on the edge of Berry Creek, suggested art more than function.

I imagine a wind-burned man, passing time in his wait for the wild sheep. His weathered dark hands are those of a master artisan, crouched with an ache in his bent legs. I see the tension build around his intently focused eyes. He slowly catches his breath. Then he strikes, risking one more deliberate blow, one more tiny flake to perfection or failure.

In the watery light of autumn morning, the Oread and I wander down into the basin, stirring the senses. This is a place for alert eyes and ears. The grizzlies still come here, as they have for centuries, for whitebark pine nuts and lomatium, the omnivores' "mountain parsley."

The great bears search out pine nuts when they can be found, often in squirrel caches. But in this season the nuts are most available as the cones disintegrate and fall to the ground. In the whitebark forest, I find tall piles of grizzly dung filled with the scales of whitebark cones. The evidence suggests that the bears are nearly single-minded in their search for the nutritious pine nuts this fall. The grizzly scat is everywhere under the trees, and I imagine an ill-tempered bear dozing under each shadowy grove I approach.

In the open fields of finely leaved lomatium the scat is different, black and piled deep. I scan the gullies carefully as I traverse into the limestone. In August two years earlier Mary Maj and half of our students watched a large male grizzly strip-mining the lomatium below a snowfield. The plant, also known as "wild carrots," is typically an early spring food for the bears, but spring might be found somewhere in Moose Basin any time between June and September. Mary's big bear ripped trenches two feet deep through the limestone embedded soil, gorging on the thick, fleshy roots and wet earth.

The whitebark pine are the tallest live pilgrims in the Basin. Their wayfaring is far too timeless for us to reckon, but I believe they come for solitude. The fossil evidence suggests that the five-needled pine have been in the region for 50,000 years. Only the glaciers have periodically ripped them from the Basin.

To walk among the stocky pale trunks, twisted limbs, and deep green needles of a whitebark forest is to enter church, sanctum. The seniors among these silent old monks are centuries old. Growth is slow in the cold and wind. Some of the older trees live only by a thin sliver of live cambium, the bulk of the trunk dead as stone.

I find the whitened relics of dead whitebark standing among the living trees like tombstones. The twisted old wooden bones cling to the bedrock, the gnarl of long-dead roots wrapped around broken flakes of the gneiss itself, like a compulsive lover's grasp. I imagine that some of these ancient pioneers died in the age of Ulysses, lived when human history was first written.

In an open carex meadow, I find a huge, black boulder, a glacial erratic left in the ebb line of an icy tide. The cubical stone, eight feet or more on each side, seems otherworldly, out of place in this field of green sedges and gray gneiss. I approach it expecting an ancient script or the mechanical whirrings of internal engines about to propel it into the darkness of space.

This is a young mountain range on the geologic time scale. To the north and south of the crystalline peaks, the hills are lower, covered still in limestone clothing taken from Paleozoic seas, clothing that once covered the entire range. In the ends of the range I walk among ancient corals and brachiopods. At elevations of 10,000 feet and higher I trace the shorelines of restless ocean beds now dry for 60 million years.

Here, in the upper end of Moose Basin, the ancient Precambrian bedrock itself is exposed, scraped clean by the combination of mountain upthrust and valley glaciers. The center of the range was uplifted at least a mile and a half along its eastern edge in the Pliocene, a mere ten million years ago. The uplift, and the exposure of the bedrock, continue. The interglacial in which we now live allows us to see the art of the millenia in these rocks; the glacial period to come will again bury the canvas in ice, and resculpt the scene.

I walk the weathered belly of the Precambrian bedrock, three or four billion years of history exposed everywhere around me. Here is home, in this era, of the oldest gnomes of all: wind, rain, freeze-melt ice. I lie on the rock and count my breaths, the heartbeats in my ears. How many times does a human heart beat in three billion years? How many human hearts?

Later I climb up the slopes of Glacier Point for a better look at Ranger and Doane on the far side of the Basin. My personal friends of greatest duration in this locale are the sheep, the bighorns I have followed over the high ridges for half of my life. In the slanting light of late afternoon I finally see two groups. Eight rams of quarter curl to nearly full are bedded down near the krummholz trees under Ranger Peak's shoulder. A young ram rubs its horns on the face of the group's heavy-bodied oldster, tempting a clash.

Farther up at the ridge crest ten ewes, yearlings and lambs skip over a sedge meadow greened by melting snow. The entire group is up, feeding in their usual rapid meander. It was the sheep that gave me this place, and all of the friends who have camped here with me. My memories tumble down the slope before me as I seek my tent in fading light.

Our second camp is a cathedral with a floor of gneiss and schist and a roof studded with the broad sweep of countless stars, a thousand Milky Ways. The circle is full, 210 degrees of pitch blackness, 150 degrees of diamonds.

Deep in the night I dream. Laughing artists, two beautiful sisters, have come to decorate the Basin's floor. Their long, wild hair—gray streaks in the black—flows over bare sinewy shoulders. The painters dance on their toes, then ladle from spattered buckets paints of feldspar, muscovite, biotite. The powerful women giggle as they spill rich white swirls of quartz over the dark green of hornblende, splashing indelicate caricatures of animals and men.

In the early dawn I rise from a frosty tent and begin to heat water to boiling. The pale sky slowly evolves from blue-black to gray to pink. In the growing light, this landscape—this home of my history—begins to take form. Mentally I have already begun the circular trip back toward the valley along the northern rim of Bitch Creek. I am ready for another turn of the wheel. Only then, in the ledge next to my tent, do I see the real business of my pilgrimage.

I waken to the bright-eyed gneiss, dark magnetite pupils, surrounded by the white gneiss of quartz and feldspar. The finest creation from earth's oldest kettle stares unblinking into yellowing sky. The dark eyes. I spoon down my oatmeal, and bow to the east.

HARD ROAD TO TRAVEL

WILLIE PREACHER, WITH KATE WEST

Indian Legends

"MY GRANDMOM AND MY MOM TOLD ME the Tetons were used as navigational mountains. They always talked about it. When they camped under the Tetons, it was always windy, howling in the canyon.

"My mother's grandmother mentioned that one of the Tetons used to be taller. People respect the fact that the Grand Teton is tallest, but at one time there was a rock shaped like a steeple that was taller.

"One night people were camped. There was a thunder storm. Lightning struck the steeple-like rock. In the morning, when the people got up, it was gone, and the Grand Teton was the highest.

"My grandmom used to tell me that if I wasn't good, they'd take me outside and the owl would carry me away. Then later I read *Little Owl Boy*, [a story] of how a boy was taken by an owl and used as a slave. The lady that was with the owl told the boy how to get away.

"If the owl makes an appearance, something will happen. [Once] an owl kept coming in. It sat on my mom's deck. That was a scary thing. Then a grandson died.

"An owl is treated as an omen.

"The Tetons were used for their spiritual value. Young men would make vision quests in the area. The mountains and the springs were used for healing. All living things are used harmoniously with human life in the Native American tradition."

Willie Preacher is a Shoshone-Bannock from the Fort Hall area. Willie cautions that these are stories handed down in the oral tradition, and may not be considered scientifically true.

KATE WEST   FICTION

Story I Cannot Tell

I HAVE TO WRITE THIS STORY IN MY HEAD. I can't tell anyone the special thing that happened because I would get in trouble, and I can't write it because I no longer have my pen, ink, and paper.

I am twelve years old. My name is Julia. I live here in Teton Basin and I am the oldest of seven children. I help my mother as much as I can here in our cabin, and help Father when I have to in the fields or with the cows. I try hard to be good, but I have felt my childhood slipping away from me this summer, and more than ever I want to be outside, exploring in the fields and woods and hills and stream beds. So when I have done my jobs, sometimes even before Mother can find something else for me to do, I wander off for a quick adventure.

Ever since I can remember, my parents and all of the other grownups in my life have told me,"Watch out for the Indians. They are dirty. They might hurt you, or even kill you, or take you away." And every time they come over the Pass and into our valley, we children scramble up onto the sod roof and watch them go past.

People say they are Blackfeet and Shoshone. They are here to hunt elk, deer, antelope, or bison. Or to fish, or gather chokecherries, huckleberries, elderberries, currants, and other plants. Except for not raising cattle and planting, they are using the valley about the same as we do. Sometimes they are dirty, just like we are, and sometimes not. I could never figure out how they could be so bad, or so much different from us. We've always found their shiny black arrows when we've plowed or picked in the fields. And I have always watched and wondered and wanted to know them.

The horses drag travois loaded with red and black painted tepee skins, parfleche boxes, blankets, and other things. Sometimes small children are loaded into cages made of bent willow branches, where they will be safe on the travois. Some of the horses are painted with spots, stripes, or zigzag lines. The men wear upstanding headdresses, bead necklaces, and fringed pants. The women and girls wear white skin dresses with long fringes, and beads. Sometimes they wear cloth dresses with the top covered with shells. Blankets and fringes and ribbons flutter, dogs bark and bells jingle, and dust follows their trail.

Yesterday was one of the times a band crossed the Pass and headed north toward Montana. "Blackfeet," Father said.

Alan McKnight

I was hanging wet clothes on the bushes and raced to the roof of the cabin. "Julia, please get down here and finish what you were doing!" called Mother.

Last night I could see little triangles of light in the cottonwoods to the north of us, and could smell their fires, and could sometimes even hear shouts. I imagined running away to join them and wander free in the sun and wind forever. But I knew I couldn't.

When I got up this morning and went out, there were no signs of them except a smudge of dust far to the north. I worked hard, but all day I was in a dream of imagining. I grabbed a basket and asked Mother if I could go pick huckleberries near the stream about a mile south of our place. She said "I guess you can. We can use them and you have worked hard these past few days." I think she felt bad for not letting me watch the Blackfeet yesterday. She works so hard. She needs me, but she knows I am still not a grownup yet. Maybe she wishes she was able to wander outside too.

I got to the huckleberries under the tall pine trees. I picked for a long time. The sun was getting lower. I drank water from the stream and sat down. My dress was dusty, my legs scratched, my feet downright dirty. I remembered that I hadn't even combed my hair. I reached into my pocket and pulled out my most important treasures, a feather pen and a little jar of ink. And a scrap of paper. I wrote about Indians. I closed my eyes and imagined myself with them.

Then I heard soft voices and splashing in the stream. Two Indian girls were coming toward me. I froze. What should I do? Was I going to be hurt? But before I had much time to worry, they came over to me and held out their cone-shaped basket. It had a strap and a slanted black design woven into it. "Do' na' mbe," said the bigger girl, and handed me a bunch of chokecherries.

"Huckleberries," I said to them, and held out my basket.

They looked at my paper and writing. I wrote JULIA and FRIEND on a piece and gave them the pen, ink, and paper. The smaller girl took her necklace of blue beads from her neck and gave it to me. She pointed to the two of them and said, "Ne' we."

The sun was low behind the cottonwoods. I knew I had to get home. I stood up and pointed to the sun. I hugged each girl and started walking fast out of the canyon and towards home. When I looked back, they were gone. I ran as far as I could, then walked to catch my breath. I carried my blue beads in my hand. Before I got all of the way home, I hid them under a rock. I got home in time to splash water over my face and hands and help set the table.

And here I am in the loft under the quilt, holding my story in my heart forever.

VERLENE GREEN, WITH JOSH WELTMAN

Heda Rosella Johnson

VERL BAGLEY'S MOTHER, Heda Rosella Johnson, was born in 1890. She is said to have been the second white child born in Teton Valley.

One day during her childhood her father Joseph Johnson set her on the dirt roof of their house so she could see the Indians marched out of Teton Valley to the reservation in Blackfoot.

"The army came in here and they camped up at the mouth of Game Creek," Verl said. "And they were there part of one winter and all summer. They gathered up all the Indians that were left in here and didn't want to stay on the reservation. There were soldiers all around them. And they took them North down through the Valley.

"When I grew up you'd see those Indians come up quite a bit. They'd come by in a wagon and a team and they'd camp up there along Trail Creek and where Moose Creek and Trail Creek come together. You'd see tepees in there in the summertime."

JEANNE ANDERSON

Proving Up

IN FALL 1881, two trappers, David Breckenridge and Frank Sumers, settled into an isolated camp on Canyon Creek at the gateway of the mountain valley known for decades as Pierre's Hole. The men dug a place between some rocks and hung a tarp down the front and on top for protection from the cold. David and Frank turned their horses loose to rustle in the bottom of the canyon.

Their camp, according to David's grandson Dale Breckenridge, a 60-something rancher in the Cache/Packsaddle area, was just south of where the narrow bridge of Highway 33 now crosses the steep walls of Canyon Creek.

After that first winter, David Breckenridge headed to Jackson's Hole to trap for the next two years. As family lore tells it, during at least one of those winters (likely 1883-84) David was the only white person living there.

While on the east side of the Tetons, David split a lodgepole pine to make himself a pair of 10-foot-long skis. One of the skis is part of the collection of the Teton Valley Historical Society, now headed up by Dale.

David Breckenridge moved back to the west side of the Tetons for the winter of 1884-85. He trapped that season with a partner named Jim Goodwin. The two men shipped more than $1,000 worth of furs to New York City, and soon thereafter David bought a bachelor's squatters rights' cabin in what was becoming called "Teton Basin."

He was here to stay.

IN JUNE 1882, Hiram C. Lapham and his family moved to the head of Spring Creek. According to Dale Breckenridge, that's where the Royce Riley family lives now. Prior to this time, those who lived in Teton Basin were short-time residents who either came here for the abundant hunting and trapping or to escape the law. The Laphams are considered the first permanent white settlers of Teton Valley.

It wasn't an easy life, pioneering in Teton Basin. Settlement in the west meant some family members were out of touch for years.

A bible brought into the Valley in 1883 contained this quote: "We present this Bible to our children, Edward B. and Elizabeth C. Seymour, as they are about to leave this part of the country for the fair West with their family and we never expect to see them again in this world. There-fore, we bid them God's speed, hoping this book will be their guide. — Lyman and Elmeda Dunklee.

The Hubbards, another early pioneering family, left a collection of letters describing the adventures of settling in Teton Basin, both in terms of human interaction and the tough job to survive. Some of the Hubbards eventually decided to move away when more LDS settlers came to stay, thus being the originators of the "more isn't necessarily better" phenomenon as far as population goes.

In one letter, marked "Teton Basin, April the 30, 1892" at the top, William Hubbard wrote Jack Lyon, his son-in-law, asking if there was anyone in Jefferson Valley, Montana, willing to trade a ranch for hors-es and cattle. Although he'd formed several fast friendships with his neighbors in Teton Basin, William added this about the population here: "This country is getting to Dam thick with Mormons ..." along with this note about the weather, "Frank is getting sick of staying here. The winters are to dam long. It is too much work to take care of stock."

DAVID BRECKENRIDGE MOVED the original squatter's cabin from the mouth of South Leigh Creek north to a site on the Teton River that would even-tually become the Breckenridge homestead (land still owned by the fam-ily). On August 6, 1885, he filed for a cattle brand in Blackfoot, the coun-ty seat of Bingham County, which had been formed the previous January. Teton Basin was listed as David Breckenridge's cattle range, and his post office address was Rexburg.

Other settlers soon followed and scattered here, choosing creek-side, protected spots as prime real estate. The pioneers' life was diversified, but the need for bare essentials—food and water—took first priority. Where grass grew, it was high, "to the wagon hounds" or the top of the wheels, one Breckenridge account says. Game was plentiful, and winters were harsh. The creeks were full in early summer but often ran dry later. Like today, the valley was beautiful.

Trapping provided a welcome source of income to early settlers in this area, even though as an industry it had lost much of its ready prof-itability half a century earlier. A few good years of trapping, however, could provide enough money for what was called a "grubstake," used to set up and stock a homestead. Historical records say trapping re-mained a viable source of extra cash (and fresh game) for pioneers over the years.

David, however, turned his attention to his new herd of registered short-horn cattle, elected office and a visit by a woman who became Haden's schoolteacher.

BY 1889, THE ALINE WARD WAS ORGANIZED by the LDS Church, the first in this area. It included 60 Mormon families consisting of some "300 souls" living on both sides of what would become the next year the state border between Idaho and Wyoming.

About this time, the Moffat and the Letham families moved to Teton Basin by team and wagon from Beaver, Utah. These two families are Dale Breckenridge's predecessors on his maternal side. In 1891, Margaret Keyes of Beaver came to visit her sister, valley resident Kate Blair, and their friends, the Moffat girls. Margaret had been living in Menan with her brothers after her father died earlier that year.

Margaret Keyes must have liked what she saw here. She stayed in Teton Basin and taught school in Haden for three months in the fall of 1891. For Columbus Day, the schoolteacher and three of her friends (Maggie Little, Nora Little and Maggie Moffat) donated dresses so that a flag could be sewn and flown from the schoolhouse. (This flag is currently on display at the Teton Valley Museum, Dale Breckenridge notes proudly.)

Margaret Keyes, who by then was also called "Maggie," soon became acquainted with an up-and-coming rancher named David Breckenridge.

By this time, David was becoming increasingly active in political circles and rising to prominence in the community. He was elected county commissioner of Bingham County in 1890; in 1892, he was also appointed special deputy sheriff.

IT WAS PAST TIME, however, to make things official on his land.

The Homestead Act, first passed in 1862 and then modified several times beginning in 1873, granted 160 acres of land to anyone over 21 who would "prove up" the ground—live on it and make improvements. The five-year process was a method to weed out those without the muscle or determination to make a go of showing they deserved the "free land" offered by the federal government. Ideally, the homestead would show it provided enough sustenance to support a family; this could take as long as eight years.

David Breckenridge was among those who hoped to prove up in the minimum time because he already had at least one improvement, the simple squatter's shelter he'd bought with his earnings from trapping.

Homesteaders with structures could focus on the chores of taking care of livestock and growing a garden. With a protected living space in place, David was well on his way to proving up.

Before homesteads could be filed, however, the territory needed to be surveyed. The original survey of Teton Basin stopped at Badger (now Felt). Even though the whole region had been surveyed in 1890, the documents weren't turned in to the federal government until 1891. The paperwork took some time to be processed in Washington, D.C., and then returned to the Blackfoot Land Office.

However, it didn't take long for citizens here to be in the thick of making their land-claims legal. On July 8, 1892, Frank Hubbard filed on the head of Spring Creek (the site where the Basin's original white settlers, the Lapham family, had settled a decade earlier). On July 16, both David Breckenridge of Haden and Charles M. Smith of Fox Creek filed for their homesteads.

David's original homestead filing was signed by President Grover Cleveland and is dated 1893. In 1894, David paid $1.25 an acre for another 120 acres of ground under the federal "Desert Act;" the low price was because that land needed irrigation.

The thick paper of these two documents is now graying. The ink is fading but still legible. They're tucked away in a trunk at Dale Breckenridge's house, part of the family legacy, a treasure that includes piles of letters, copies of newspaper articles and typed remembrances by family members. They are tangible proof of the Breckenridge participation in an enormous part of Teton Basin history.

MARGARET KEYES AND DAVID BRECKENRIDGE were married in 1893.

The soon-to-be family man David served as road overseer for Fremont County. About this time, he and Sam Swanner (another Valley pioneer who "held all kinds of offices," Dale says) surveyed the road from Teton River to Canyon Creek—not too far from the place where David originally camped with Frank Sumers more than ten years earlier. Another fellow, Ed Little, plowed a furrow with a hand plow to mark the route.

David also surveyed irrigation ditches and was asked by the State of Idaho to check and report on approving water decrees.

"He weren't one to stay idle," Dale notes.

He was also busy at the ranch. The original squatter's cabin belonging to David was moved again to serve as a bunkhouse. The Breckenridge family eventually built a four-room log house, in a T-forma-

The Breckenridge homestead, with Margaret and David (seated), their daughter Davida (second from left) and son Jim (right). Fred Hunter stands by the doorway and Emma Crow (a friend of Davida's) stands far left.

tion with a dirt roof, on a high spot of ground. Thick willows protected this new building from winter blizzards. Ultimately, the logs from this structure were used to build the ten-room, double-story house where Dale was raised.

The far part of the Breckenridge land did not quite reach the town of Haden, considered a big community for what was then Fremont County. It eventually had three stores, a church, school, dance hall, hotel, livery stable, pool hall and butcher shop.

COMMUNICATION WITH THE OUTSIDE WORLD was not easily or quickly accomplished. People took turns going to Rexburg to pick up the mail for all of Teton Basin's residents. Dale Breckenridge says most of these early couriers would make the 40-mile trip out to Rexburg one day ("that's where we started callin' it out below," he explains) and come back the next.

The exception, Dale notes, was the infamous Tim Hibbert, a fellow who had reportedly escaped from jail in Kansas, stolen the horse of an Indian leader named Chief Yellow Face, and vamoosed west, riding 100 miles in a stretch. When Tim's turn would come round to collect the mail from Rexburg, he'd ride for it "between suns"—all in one day.

THE VALLEY GREW IN POPULATION, with small communities forming around a school, church and sometimes a post office. By 1901, LDS wards in the Teton Stake included Chapin, Clawson, Darby, Driggs, Haden, Victor and Pratt, church records say.

The Breckenridge family started to grow as well, with five children born by 1905, including Dale's father, Bill.

The first-born, Lucy, lived just a little more than two years. Within two weeks after her death, Haden Cemetery had been platted on high ground behind the original site of Jack and Kathleen Blair's place (Kate Blair was Margaret Breckenridge's sister.). Two meetings had already been held to discuss necessary materials and cost of fencing for what was originally called "Lucy's cemetery." The minutes of the meetings— another Breckenridge family keepsake—were written on the back of a newspaper page printed on just one side.

Eventually, David installed scales at the Breckenridge ranch, which was the center of activity at cattle market time in Teton Basin. In typical frontier hospitality, meals were furnished free—but it cost a dime per head for the use of the scales.

In 1903 and 1904, the "Fremont County Oil, Gas and Coal Company" drilled for oil on David's ranch. An industrial issue of the *Teton Peak Chronicle* reported that drilling had progressed to 650 feet. The project was never finished, reportedly due to the death of the man with the most money, Dale Breckenridge says.

Besides the Breckenridge children, the family welcomed another important member in 1902, when David's nephew Fred Hunter (then a 26-year-old "Ioway farm-boy" as Dale calls him) came to spend the summer in Teton Valley. He'd been experiencing poor health but had already helped his mother raise his siblings, so being around the growing Breckenridge brood made him feel right at home.

As available open range was diminished, the Breckenridge family expanded its spread by purchasing more land. A few milk cows were added as well. Horses continued to provide a major source of income for the family until farmers started using gas-driven tractors.

When the Oregon Short Line Railroad built a spur line to Driggs in 1912, the route was laid out to run some two miles north of the town of Haden. The townsite of Tetonia was created next to the tracks, and several structures from Haden were moved there.

"It took 48 horses to pull the Campbell store," Dale Breckenridge says. "The dance hall became a storage area for General Mills."

Haden is now nothing but memories and a ghost of a building's foundation.

By 1913, the railroad ran all the way to Victor. A mini-boom took place in Teton Basin, with tourists journeying through on their way to Jackson Hole and farther north to Yellowstone.

. THE BRECKENRIDGE CLAN had enjoyed a three-decade run of good fortune, but that luck was also about to change. In January 1915, David Breckenridge's appendix burst, reportedly at a political meeting in Felt. He died during the unsuccessful appendectomy operation.

Less than two months later, Margaret Keyes Breckenridge died as well ("grandma had the dropsy, ya know," Dale says). Their oldest son, Preston, was not yet 19.

David's nephew Fred Hunter assumed the guardianship of the kids and the care of the Breckenridge ranch. He worked diligently to hold things together—another time of proving up.

TETON BASIN CONTINUED TO GROW. By 1918, several more LDS wards were established (in Cache, Bates, Valview and Cedron). However, folks began to have their share of "real bad years"—World War I, the flu epidemic and the drought in 1919 were especially difficult. Some people were starved out, Dale Breckenridge says.

Written-down records are scarce for the most part. But in 1919, only 22 students in just five schools took the eighth-grade tests, according to a school record Dale Breckenridge compiled when the current school district (#401) was organized. For comparison, an average of 90 students each year took the eighth-grade tests between the years of 1916 and 1948, excluding 1919; Teton High School's class of 2000 graduated 99 students.

As many as 18 elementary schools operated in Teton County during those 32 years, including now-vanished schoolhouses in Judkins, North Leigh, Breezy Hill, Richvale, Sam-Brown Bear, Palisade, Clementsville, Hunnidale and Badger.

The 1920s brought Prohibition and the 1930s brought more hard work and more hard times. To survive economically, the Breckenridge ranch diversified, becoming more of a farm than a cattle operation. Dale's parents, Bill and Isabella Letham Breckenridge, were married in 1929, and Dale was born in 1930. Bill's sister Davida Breckenridge married Lynn Wade, while brothers Preston and Jim Breckenridge remained bachelors, as did Fred Hunter.

By the Depression years, the Breckenridge property now included land for grain and hay. Beef cattle, shorthorn milk cows, hogs and sheep were raised. The county absorbed some of the land in payment for back-taxes.

Very little was cultivated the summer of 1934 after only light snow fell in the winter of '33-34. One year the Breckenridge cattle, along with those belonging to neighbor Frank Harrops, were trailed to Roberts to find hay; the next year, the cows went to Hamer to be fed. Family records say those areas had stockpiled three years of hay before the worst of the drought.

Times got even tougher. In 1935, the drought deepened. The main issue: who would receive what little water there was, farmers and ranchers here or those farther downstream. At the time, about 2,000 Mexican migrant workers and other foreign laborers came to the Basin to pick the green-pea crop in the southern part of the Valley. They mostly lived in large camp near Cottonwood Corner. When they went on strike, the trouble provided a ready reason to seek "outside" help.

"It was the sheriff's idea to call

Important Jurisdictional Dates

SOURCE OF RECORDS: Dale Breckenridge's personal collection.

March 3, 1863 Idaho Territory is organized, includes Teton Basin;

Jan. 22, 1864 Teton Basin is part of Oneida County, with a county seat of Soda Springs; coaches begin bringing mail from Salt Lake via Fort Hall to Boise;

1865 Territorial capitol moves from Lewiston to Boise;

Jan. 5, 1866 County seat is moved to Malad;

Jan. 13, 1885 Bingham County is created with Blackfoot as the county seat (Teton Basin now part of Bingham County);

July 3, 1890 Idaho is admitted into the Union as the 43rd state;

Dec. 8, 1890 The first session of the Idaho Legislature meets in Boise;

March 4, 1893 Fremont County is created with St. Anthony as the county seat (Teton Basin is now part of Fremont County);

Nov. 4, 1893 Madison County is created with Rexburg as the county seat (Teton Basin is part of Madison County); Jefferson County also created at the same time;

Jan. 26, 1915 Teton County is established with Driggs as the county seat.

in the state militia," Dale says. Under martial law, guards were posted at the headgates of irrigation channels to control the flow of water. Common sentiment at the time was that "they (would) only need one body to start a war in Teton County."

Somehow the Breckenridges made it through the lean years. The first purebred Herefords were brought to the Breckenridge ranch in 1939, and the place slowly regained its cattle and hay emphasis, something it continues to this day.

The outbreak of World War II "changed everything," Dale says. There may have been nine to 13 men working a hay-crew at the end of the summer of 1941, and in the next harvest, just women and kids were doing it.

"Everyone who was old enough went to the war. There was no labor left behind to do what needed to be done," Dale says.

The Breckenridge family survived those days with few workers to accomplish all the chores. Fred Hunter's influence was to be felt on the ranch until he died in 1969.

Today, Dale and his wife, Ronell (another descendant of pioneer Teton Valley families), operate the family partnership with their son David, who is named after the clan's patriarch. Among them, Dale and Ronell's six children have produced another flock of Breckenridge kids, the fifth generation to enjoy the country life here.

Dale currently serves as president of the Teton County Historical Society, and has been instrumental in building the County Museum north of Driggs near the fairgrounds to eventually house at least some of the Breckenridge memorabilia. Dale's taking it just a bit easier around his place nowadays after heart by-pass surgery this spring.

His family's background is something he's clearly proud of. This is his home, where his roots are, where he hopes his descendants will live and prosper.

History is more than faded documents packed away in a trunk—it's something he lives and breathes, the stories he tells.

The questions roll out: What would it take to last a winter in Canyon Creek? How difficult must it have been to create a sustainable homestead in this inhospitable but beautiful place? What did David and Maggie think as they saw Teton Basin change over the years? And what would it take to keep a large family and spread together after both of them died? The courage needed by young Fred Hunter rings through Dale's account.

Proving up was a lifetime venture, not a five-year ordeal.

DICK EGBERT OF TETONIA, a 94-year-old family friend who now lives in Rexburg, was asked this winter, "What do you think identifies the spirit of Teton Valley?"

His reply: "Well, I think people like Dale Breckenridge. He represents a love of the past and yet he's progressive."

David Breckenridge, who once carved a pair of skis from a lodgepole pine and passed them on to the care of his descendents, might have appreciated this answer. Maggie Keyes Breckenridge, who buried a baby, built a family and died so soon after her husband, would likely nod in agreement.

If the spirit of Teton Valley today is epitomized by Dale, the legacy of his grandparents is indeed secure.

GWEN DALLEY CRANDALL

Rob and Lou

MY EARLIEST MEMORIES are of living in the home of my grandparents, Robert and Louella (Uncle Rob and Aunt Lou) Dalley, on the west side of State Line Road (now Teton Creek Resort).

One of 44 children, Rob was born September 24, 1862, and grew up in Summit, Utah, a Mormon community settled by his father.

One of 15 children, Lou was born January 1, 1867, and also grew up in Summit.

Rob married Sophia Farrow in 1883. Six years later, he was asked by the leaders of the LDS (Mormon) Church to take a second wife, so in April of 1889, he married Louella Hulet.

In 1890 the church discontinued the practice of plural marriage; the Government said a man must abandon all wives and children subsequent to the first marriage, and most men were unwilling to do that. At the time, plural marriage carried a penalty imposed by the United States Government for up to three years in the Utah State Penitentiary.

In the fall of 1893, Rob and Lou were arrested. Lou was released, but Rob was sentenced to 18 months in the Penitentiary. He served eight months before he was pardoned, but he still had the problem of two families.

Lehi Pratt, who had married two of Rob's sisters, had moved to a

The Dalley cabin at the present site of Teton Creek Resort.

small valley on the Idaho-Wyoming border that was settled by polygamous families in 1889. He encouraged Rob and his families to join them, so on October 10, 1894, Rob and Lou loaded their wagon and began the 600-mile trek to Teton Valley. Lou had two little boys and expected a third baby in four months.

After 26 days and two tipovers, they reached the Valley. When they reached Canyon Creek (of course there was no bridge), Lou refused to ride, so she and the two little boys climbed down and back up the steep canyon walls. I remember this every time I cross Canyon Creek Bridge.

The next spring, Rob returned to Summit for Sophia and her two children.

By summer, Sophia and her *three* children lived in a log home on the Wyoming side above the "dug way" (now Marion Butler's property), and Lou and her *three* children lived in her log home on the Idaho side, above Teton Creek. Rob spent alternate weeks with each family.

By the time I came along, Sophia had passed away, and Rob and Lou lived in the "new" house built about 1917 (it now belongs to the Melehes family) just south of the log home on the Wyoming side of the state line.

At one time, the family owned three 160-acre homesteads—Rob's, west of "Greenville" in Wyoming, Sophia's and Lou's—but ended up with just Lou's.

When I was six, we moved into our new log home north of Teton Canal (now the Doris Moss home).

Rob at various times raised sheep, milk cows and chickens (for eggs) and farmed the land with a team of horses. They never owned a car, a refrigerator or had indoor plumbing, but they did have a telephone. Lou had many lilac bushes, beautiful flower gardens, big golden willow trees and a huge raspberry patch. The grandchildren living nearby had the "privilege" of picking the raspberries.

I spent many happy hours playing in the "crick bottom," and swimming in the icy creek and the "subby ponds" which were much warmer, especially if the cows had passed by earlier!

Rob and Lou were at one time the oldest married couple in the Valley. They had numerous descendants, some of which still live in Teton Valley.

Rob passed away November 29, 1953, at age 91. Lou passed away June 15, 1962, at age 95. They are buried in the Pratt (Alta) Cemetery, beside many other pioneers to this beautiful Valley.

DONALD F. COBURN

Our Mountain Home So Dear

OUR BEAUTIFUL TETON VALLEY was one of the later areas to be settled, perhaps because it was far off the wagon train routes and quite secluded; perhaps also because of the reports of the terrible winters. Although several early families settled in the early 1880s, the real migrations into the valley began around 1888 with the advent of the "Mormons," the members of the Church of Jesus Christ of Latter Day Saints (LDS).

There was no mass organized movement by LDS settlers into the valley. Rather the Mormon immigration was by small groups of families or associates, lured by the prospect of land open for homesteading and lush grazing for sheep and cattle. Most of these early LDS settlers came to Teton Valley from Utah or other parts of Idaho, although many were originally from Denmark, England, Switzerland, Germany and other countries.

After hearing the wonderful reports of this valley, an early group made up of Don C. Driggs, Ben Driggs, Issac Waddell, Thomas Wilson, Mathoni Pratt and Henry Wallace, guided by E.B. Edlefsen, came to the valley in July 1888. Don Driggs wrote in his journal:

"I shall never forget our reaching the summit beyond Canyon Creek where we could look over into the Valley. The vision we beheld was overpowering. It indeed looked like a Promised Land. It was a beautiful Valley over 30 miles in length, from 8 to 12 miles in width, with the towering Tetons on the east range ... a scene untouched by man. It is true there was some sort of trail or road into the Valley which had been made by the venturous trapper and frontiersman, who had preferred to get as far away as possible from the haunts of man and who had found his Paradise within the confines of these. The Valley is almost totally surrounded by mountains, making it truly one of the 'Valleys of the Mountains'."

These travelers returned to Utah and made preparations to move to Teton Valley, arriving April 4, 1889. The Wilson family, typical of others, took advantage of the Homestead Act, which gave each adult 160 acres, and the Desert Act that allowed 640 acres by means of reclamation at a cost of $1.00 per acre. The Wilsons built a log cabin about 3/4 mile north of Driggs.

When early LDS immigrants beheld this beautiful valley covered with a waving sea of grass, its abundant streams of clear water, its forests of timber and good soil, they paraphrased an earlier expression, "This is the place." By August 1889 there were 60 LDS families comprising about 300 settlers in Teton Valley. These early pioneers were mainly sons and daughters of a people who were driven at gunpoint from Missouri and Illinois. Their ecclesiastical organization followed them closely.

Mary Hulet Coburn, Donald Coburn's mother, wrote of her family's movement to Teton Valley from Snowflake, Arizona: "In 1896 we decided to move to Teton Valley. We had two covered wagons all fitted out and left about June first. It was quite a lark for us children. Mother drove one team and father the other. We camped out and made our beds on the ground. After riding all day we were glad to run around and play games. One night while we were playing, a train came tooting down the track, and the smaller children thought it was coming after us, and we were frightened to death." The family drove their sheep and cattle along the way. It took all summer to make the trek. This was typical of the many families that migrated into the valley during this time.

When the LDS Church established organizations in Teton Valley, they were a part of the Bannock Stake (1884), and later part of the Fremont Stake (1888). The first LDS ward in Teton Valley, named Aline, was organized in the Driggs area in August 1889 with Mathoni Pratt as Bishop and Thomas Wilson and Apollos Driggs as counselors. When Pratt and Wilson moved from the Driggs area to Alta, Wyoming, they took the Aline Ward organization with them. The name of the Aline Ward was changed to Pratt Ward in honor of Mathoni's famous father, Parley P. Pratt. This continued to be the LDS religious center in the valley until other wards were organized in the next few years.

The first permanent settlers in the Alta area were William Rigby and Austin Green in 1889-90. These families settled in Wyoming because of the LDS doctrine of plural marriage, or polygamy. At that time Idaho had placed a bounty on polygamists, and there was a vigorous effort by Idaho sheriffs and marshals to arrest and prosecute them. The U.S. Supreme Court had upheld an Idaho test oath that disenfranchised Mormon polygamists. Wyoming did not have such desires or any personnel in the Alta area, and therefore that corner of Wyoming became a safe haven for LDS members who had more than one wife.

Sheriff Sam Swanner of the Haden (Tetonia) area was notably active in pursuit of polygamists, and William Rigby was a favorite target. As an LDS official, Brother Rigby traveled throughout the region, and when word came that Brother Rigby was headed for Alta to be with his wife and family, Sheriff Swanner was determined to catch him. Both men had fast horses, but Brother Rigby usually managed to get across the state line without being caught. Apparently fast horses became a tradition for the Rigby family early in their Teton Valley history.

The LDS members who settled in the Victor area came primarily from Utah in 1889. They too enjoyed the beauty of the mountains, meadows and flowers, and their histories tell of the wild game, antelope, deer, elk, sage hens, grouse and fish. As these settlers traveled to the valley, they strictly observed the Sabbath as a day of rest. It took seven years to found the city of Victor, but only a few days to organize into a religious body. In August 1892 the Raymond Ward was created, and later changed to the Victor Ward. In 1896 a log building 28 by 45 feet was built for a meetinghouse. On December 31, 1900, the Victor Ward had 317 members.

The first LDS settlers in the Darby area were the John and Henry Todd families in the fall of 1891. Half of the Darby settlers were Scandinavian. The Darby branch of the Church was organized as a ward in August 1895. The first church building was a log structure that later burned down.

Chapin became a ward in 1897 with 111 families in the area centered around the mouth of Fox Creek Canyon. Ebeneezer Beesley, Jr. was the first Bishop.

The Tetonia Ward was first organized as the Haden Ward in June 1898. It consisted of 34 families whose first meetinghouse was near Harrop's bridge on the river. The Haden Ward and the entire town were moved east to Tetonia when the railroad arrived and the name was changed to the Tetonia Ward. Other branches of the church organized at Clementsville, Palisades and Richvale joined with the Tetonia Ward, as did Cache later on.

The Driggs area was also mostly settled by LDS families, and the ward organization took place in June 1901. D.C. Driggs was the first Bishop, but when he was called to be Stake President two months later, he was succeeded as Bishop by Hyrum Crandall. The Driggs Ward served 627 members in 1930.

The Bates Ward on the west side of the valley was organized in August 1908 with Alma Hansen as Bishop and Thomas Bates and Samuel Kunz as counselors. The Cedron Ward was split off from the Bates Ward due to travel distances in 1922. By 1930 the Cedron Ward had increased to 99 members, and the Bates Ward had 130 members.

Of necessity the early LDS ward buildings were usually small and were primarily built and paid for by the members. Given that horses were the primary means of travel at the time, these wards were widely scattered, and served a wonderful purpose for those members in the isolated areas of the valley. Most of the meeting houses were actually one large main room with a raised area at one end where the speakers and choir would be located. Benches for the congregation filled the main floor. Wires criss-crossed the room so that curtains could be drawn to separate the area into gospel classes. The buildings were plain, rustic and functional.

This was where the members came each Sunday to worship and partake of the Sacrament. This was where funeral services were held, where wedding receptions took place, and where the young people met on Tuesday evenings for activities. Relief Society sisters met here to receive spiritual lessons, sew quilts and perform charitable work. Here the ward Priesthood brethren met. When necessary, the church buildings also doubled as schools. Many winter nights the pot-bellied stove would be glowing, the lanterns lit, and the local musicians warming up their strain of the Virginia reel for a ward dance. The church houses housed the ward family and were a vital part of their lives.

Leigh Fullmer remembers a Christmas Eve miracle when he was about seven years old in the Leigh Ward church house. The Leigh area was near what is now Clawson between Tetonia and Driggs. "The church house was a high building. The committee that cut the tree chose a very tall one. It seemed to me, then, that it reached up to the sky. I expect it was about 15 or 20 feet tall."

A base was built for the tree, and it was decorated for the ward Christmas tree. The final step as the event began was to light the candles, which burned in little brass cups clipped to the tree branches. As the program neared completion and gifts were about to be handed out, the huge tree burst into flames.

"That tree just took fire," said Leigh. "Two of the cowboys had their lariats on their saddles outside. … Quicker than you could think, they ran out and came in with those lariats and tossed them. They made a loop around the tree and drug that burning tree right down the center of the church and out the door. It just happened so quick. They covered the tree with snow and it lay there all winter. I've always had such respect for those cowboys.

"During the confusion I found out that Santa Claus was my father, Halsey Dean Fullmer. I saw Santa measure the base of that tree after the fire."

Later that night when Leigh's family got home and put the team in the stable, they had a family prayer during which "my dad remembered those cowboys, and he thanked the Lord that whoever made the tree stand hadn't made it an inch wider or it wouldn't have gone out the door."

On September 2, 1901, the Teton Stake was established with Don C. Driggs as the first Stake President. Two LDS apostles were present at its organization, Joseph F. Smith and John Henry Smith. During this time a Stake tabernacle was built at a cost of $5,000. In 1930 the LDS church membership had grown to 3,052. The present stake building was dedicated in 1943, and has been added to and remodeled in subsequent years. Stake Presidents over the years have included Albert Choules, William Strong, LaGrande Larsen, Leonard Jensen, Donald Coburn, Stephen Hoopes and John McKellar.

In the early days of the valley, attending the Stake Meetings was often a real challenge. Many stories were told of the sisters swimming their horses across the Teton River to get to a meeting when the river was running high in the spring. Members fought through blizzards in their sleighs, quilts thrown over the families and hot rocks covered with towels added to provide some warmth. Stake Conferences usually featured prominent church leaders, apostles or members of the First Presidency from Salt Lake City. These leaders drew faithful members into Driggs from all over the Teton Valley and from over the hill in the Jackson Valley, often an arduous trip.

The leaders from Utah visited each Stake often when the LDS church was much smaller than it is today, and some took time to enjoy the area's fishing. A later member of the Stake Presidency, Leigh Fullmer, told of fishing with revered LDS Church President and Prophet David O. McKay. Fullmer asked the Church President to "hold this string of fish [and] let me get a picture."

President McKay said, "Oh, I'll be tickled to death to hold the fish." He stood up and displayed a beautiful stringer of fish, but just as President Fullmer was ready to snap a picture, he dropped the fish and said, "No, I won't have my picture taken with them. People would have a right to feel that I caught them, and I didn't. I won't have my picture taken with them. I'd like my picture taken with the string I did catch." He had caught one lonely little fish. So President Fullmer settled for a picture of a grinning President McKay with one little fish.

Because of the isolation and distance from hospitals, medical care often came back to the people themselves. Often times there was no doctor in the valley. A group of dedicated women played an important role in the early years. Ruby Schiess tells of that early history.

"Mrs. Ellis Shipp, a medical doctor, was sent here by the LDS Church to train women to serve as midwives. The customary fee for the delivery and three days of care was $5, but many could not pay even that, and gave eggs or meat or vegetables or could pay nothing. My mother, Clara Miller, a mid-wife, delivered 150 babies and never lost a baby or a mother."

Ruby remembers her mother coming home from one delivery and telling her father that the new mother and her family had no money, not even any milk for the baby. The next morning Ruby saw her father going up the road with a wagon load of hay and a new little heifer tied on behind.

This was the welfare system, people helping people. The church also had a more structured system. Every family fasted two meals the first Sunday of each month and gave the money saved to the Bishop to help the needy. Most of the wards had a welfare farm where the members grew grain or hay to give to the church welfare fund. The LDS people of necessity had learned to take care of their own.

Not all of the medical help was provided by women. Among others, Thomas Wilson of Pratt Ward was noted for his natural ability to set broken bones, sew up cuts, and take care of the injured and sick. In one recollection, two Jackson Hole men were on their way over the Teton Pass to collect the mail for Jackson when one of the men broke his ankle. The men walked all the way to Haden on their snowshoes, the injured man on a splinted ankle. Thomas Wilson was summoned to come through the deep snow, and he was able to reduce the injured man's swelling and set his bones.

In the isolated valley communities, the residents had to find their own entertainment. Fortunately, many of the Mormon settlers were talented musically. Music, dance and acting were all part of the church activities—as one settler recalled, there was a dance going on somewhere in a valley ward every week. Each ward also produced their own road show and presented it to the other wards in the valley.

Thomas Wilson told of a special musical contest in 1895. All of the wards in the region were invited to participate in a choir contest to be held in Rexburg. "At that time Teton Valley was divided into four wards: Driggs, Haden (later Tetonia), Raymond (later Victor), and Pratt. Only one, Pratt, entered the contest.

"An intensive practice campaign was begun. A fine of ten cents was agreed upon for each failure to attend practice, with the result that owing to the shortage of dimes, it never became necessary to assess a fine. No body of people could have thrown more enthusiasm into an undertaking than did these 20 men and women. It was drill, drill, drill. Well did they realize the handicaps that were to be overcome.

"As the great day of departure neared, preparations had to be made. Transportation over some 50 miles of unimproved roads presented a problem. The only vehicles available were farm wagons, ... so with four horses and the same number of spring seats to the wagon, the line of lumbering vehicles with its earnest passengers set out on the morning of October 4, 1895, all determined to bring back the grand prize of $50.00.

"The hour of battle nears. The several choirs were assigned seats. The judges were placed in a position where they could hear, but not see the choir that was in action. Place was determined by drawing lots. The Pratt choir drew third place. As the choirs would sing, their hearts would beat faster, and hope was not always at the highest. But what a thrill

The Teton Stake House dedication Feb. 17, 1907. Apostle George Albert Smith, seated in buggy wearing a white suit, performed the dedication.

came over them when at the conclusion of the contest Pratt was declared the winner! Fifty dollars! The money itself was regarded merely a symbol of success."

These people, early LDS settlers, were never wealthy. They were mostly deeply religious, proud of who they were and of their heritage, and fiercely independent. The early settlers in Teton Valley loved this valley so deeply it almost had a spiritual quality. We sing of "our mountain home so dear" and of "firm as the mountains around us."

On the 24th of July all the businesses in the valley would close their doors and there was a general exodus to the campground in Teton Canyon for an event termed Stake Day. Most everyone camped over one night in the canyon, and what a breakfast! Mormon cooking is wonderful. Most church socials are built around some of the best cooking ever tasted.

For about 80 years this valley was "Mormon Country." The Church, the schools, and the civic leaders were intermingled and worked together as one. I believe this would be typical of any region that was 95 percent of one faith. The Church leaders could be the doctors or the schoolteachers and administrators and the business leaders. Mormon ranchers and farmers owned most of the land. The elected officials were also LDS. The school choir would sing at Stake Conference. The high school orchestra would perform at church functions and no one questioned or worried about separation of church and state.

Things have changed. The changes began with the second immigration as people were again lured by the beauty of Teton Valley. People came seeking the seclusion and peace that the early settlers had found. Let's hope that we don't destroy those things that have attracted us here in the first place.

We now have a diversity in the valley of the Tetons undreamed of just a few years ago, a diversity of race, of background, of religion with new houses of worship so that every one might worship according to their own wishes. LDS Church President and Prophet Gordon B. Hinckley has counseled, "Be respectful of the opinions and feelings of other people. Recognize their virtues; don't look for their faults. Look for their strengths and virtues, and you will find strengths and virtues that will be helpful in your own life."

BEN WINSHIP

Harry Had a Pontiac

Harry had a Pontiac car
but he never drove it all that far
it was the first car in the town
and people gathered round
just to watch him drive

I wonder where he got the gas
it must have been a lot to ask
you couldn't fill 'er up on Main
people went by horse and train
just to get around

Refrain: Oh Harry pick me up and take me back
          back to a time when time alone
          stood nearly still or so it seems
          it seems we've come so far
          so far so good so I've been told
          but the wheel keeps spinning around
          oh pick me up and take me back
          I long to hear that sound
          the sound of the wagon wheel
          hoof beats and the wagon wheel roll by

Harry had a Pontiac
some folks say he was a maniac
some say he had a heart of gold
until the bottle made him old
and tired

Harry's in another land
but now his home is in my hand
at night the wind blows through the wall
I wonder if I hear him call
my name

Long-time Valley resident Harry Scott was a former owner of my house. Though he passed on before my time, neighbors and old-timers filled me in on his life. He used to drive the mail from Victor to Jackson by horse team. Later he owned one of the first cars in Victor. I found one his Pontiac hubcaps stuffed in a wall when I was remodeling the house.

1927

Tetonia: 1910-1930

THE IDEA FOR THIS MAP was conceived during conversations with Dale Breckenridge, in which I realized that it would be considerably easier to understand Tetonia's local history if there were a picture to go with the story. The first interview with Marge and Bob O'Brien turned out to be pure fun. Prodding from Dale to "get it right" resulted in later interviews with Elmoyne Hansen Hanks and Wright C. Hanks. Both Marge and Elmoyne were teachers in Tetonia.

Adults who have seen this map remark, "I didn't know Tetonia was such a thriving place!" As Julia Hibbert keeps saying, "The landscape is constantly changing. We've got to record what we have now." Our map, opposite, is an attempt to record the important businesses in Tetonia over a 20-year period.

Respectfully submitted, knowing full well that I probably did not get it quite right,   —Barbara Agnew

1   Hibbert's Hotel
2   LDS Church
3   Protestant Church
4   3-Room School
5   Pete Christensen's Car Garage
6   Home of Parley & Lettie Rammell
7   Mrs. Hoopes' Bed & Breakfast
8   Luke Hastings' Hardware Store
9   Walt Hastings' Drug Store
10   Service Station
11   Barber Shop
12   Floyd's Cream Station
13   Post Office
14   A.C. Miner's General Merchandise
15   Farmers State Bank
16   Livery Stable
17   Main Pool Hall
18   Barber Shop
19   Mrs. Cherry's Millinery
20   C. Earl Harris Meat & General Merchandise
21   Pool Hall/Auto & Axel Munson Meat & Groceries
22   Alderman's Garage
23   Cheese Factory
24   Service Station
25   Blacksmith Shop
26   Hank's Livery Stable
27   Midland Elevator
28   Johnny Hanigan's Lumber Yard
29   Farmers Grain Elevator
30   Train Depot

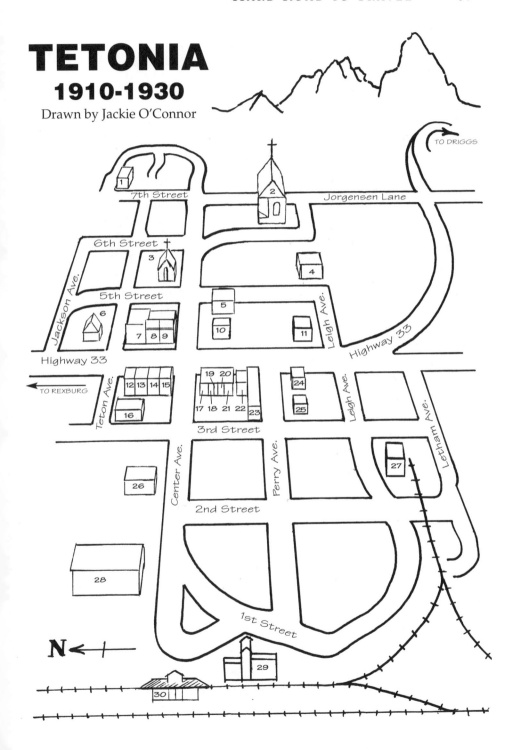

TETONIA
1910-1930
Drawn by Jackie O'Connor

VERL BAGLEY, WITH JOSH WELTMAN

Whoa! Whoa! Whoa!

THE ARRIVAL OF A MODEL T AT THE BAGLEY HOUSE is a famous family story.
That was a great time when you got to ride in that Model T. It sure
was faster going to town than hooking up the buggy. Right after we
bought that car, somebody had a small building uptown they wanted
to sell. We jacked it up and put logs under it. We hooked it up to two
teams so we had four head of horses and then pulled it down to the
farm. The building was too short for the car, so we made it a little bit
longer and jacked it up and put it up on logs or some blocks of wood
so it would be a little bit higher and put some doors on it. Dad went
out to drive the Model T into it. It fit pretty good but when dad drove
it into the garage, he got nervous and scared and he hit the end of the
building. He tore the end out of it, and why, the building rolled on the
blocks a little ways, and he was hollering, "Whoa! Whoa! Whoa!" Finally he got it stopped and backed it out. We put it back up on the blocks,
then put the end of the building back in. Mother was standing out there
watching. She really laughed at him. We all laughed at Dad going
down through the field, taking the garage with him.

BERTHA CHAMBERS GILLETTE

Moving from Wyoming to Idaho

THE WINTER OF 1936-37 WAS AN UNUSUAL ONE, partly warm and sunny.
My husband Wendell Gillette, our little one-year, eight-month old son
Glen, and I were very happy and comfortable living in our little three-
room apartment, which was upstairs over the Ford Garage in downtown Jackson, Wyoming. Wendell was employed in the Garage, which
was owned by his brother Francis Gillette, and Francis's partner Walt
Hynes.
    One day Wendell got a telephone call from Francis, who was living
in Victor, Idaho. Francis's message to my husband was, "Wendell, I want

to come to Jackson this evening to talk with you and Bertha."

We were happy to have him come, and I prepared a nice dinner. While we were eating, Wendell said, "Fran, what did you come over to talk about tonight?"

"Well," Francis answered, "I am moving you and Bertha to Victor."

I immediately replied,"Fran, you are not moving me to Victor. My mother is dying with cancer, and she needs me here to help with her little ones. Three of us girls are married, but she still has three teenage boys, a little girl of eight, a boy six, and a boy four. They are depending on me to help, and so is my mother."

Francis replied, "I have been elected to go to Boise as a legislator, and will be leaving in January to be gone for the winter. I have no one else to turn the Garage business over to while I am gone. I am leaving Eugene and Jeannette here in Jackson to manage the Garage here."

I answered, "How can you do this to me? Please take them and leave us here."

Francis was firm and said, "No, Eugene can manage this business, but I need Wendell to keep the books, and sell automobiles over there."

I left the table crying big tears, and took my baby into the bedroom. I felt that I had a broken heart. Francis and Wendell talked matters over, and as I listened, I knew that Francis was determined for us to make the move.

After he left, Wendell came in to talk with me. "Honey," he said, "I have to go where my business calls me. I have no way out."

The next day I took my baby, and we went to break the news to my mother. I thought that she would say, "You tell Francis and Wendell you don't have to move. You can come home and live with us."

I was very mistaken. When I opened the door and went inside, still crying, Mother knew something was wrong. She asked me, "Why all the tears?" I told her my troubles, still crying so hard that she could hardly understand me. Mother hugged me tight, and when I regained my composure, she began to share her reasoning. "Dear, you have to go with your husband, and you will just love Victor. You know that I lived there in my younger days, and I felt just like you do when I had to leave Victor and move to Jackson. The people there are just as good as they are here." That wasn't what I wanted to hear, but I knew that she was right.

Francis told us if we were in Victor by New Year's Day, it would be all right. I was happy we could stay for Christmas with my family. No snow had fallen by Christmas, which was very unusual. It was warm and sunny most of the daylight hours, which enabled Wendell to move all of our furniture and belongings to Victor in good weather.

We had a most happy Christmas with my family. Father tried hard to find the most perfect tree, and Mother and my sisters Margaret and Erma took great pains to beautifully decorate the tree. I tried hard all day to hold back the tears, knowing that this Christmas might be our last one to have all of the family together.

When we got up the next morning, we were so surprised to find that four inches of snow had fallen during the night. We didn't stop for breakfast, because the snow was getting deeper all at once.

We said our goodbyes in a hurry and got into our 1936 Ford car. We thought we were making good time and that we would be in Victor by ten o'clock that morning. But to our surprise, when we reached the place known as 'the Water Hole' on Teton Pass, we could go no farther. We were stuck in deep snow.

We could see three other cars stuck ahead of us. Wendell thought that if he put the chains on the back tires, we could possibly get around the other cars and keep going. Just then a man from the car ahead of us came back to talk. He told us two brothers, Benny and Eugene Daniels, were pulling cars to the top of Teton Pass with their two teams of horses. He said it might take several hours to get to us because as they got a car to the summit, they had to change to a fresh team and let the team that had just worked take a rest.

I was so thankful our baby slept all the while we were waiting. We had received a one-pound box of chocolates for Christmas, and we nibbled on the candy until it was all gone. That was one of the most beautiful snowstorms we had ever seen. The snow fell quietly and peacefully like big white feathers.

Just as we knew we were next in line, anxiously waiting our turn to be pulled to the top, another car came up behind us. The two men in the car were trying to get to St. Anthony, Idaho, to attend a funeral, so what was there to do but to push our car nearer the side of the road and push the funeral goers ahead of us. By this time it was two o'clock in the afternoon, but there wasn't anything to do but wait another hour.

When the Daniels brothers got to us, we could tell that they and their teams were tired. Just the same they hooked the doubletrees underneath our car, climbed onto the hood of the car, and started the horses to pulling. We knew this was true punishment to both the brothers and the horses.

When we reached the summit of Teton Pass, they unhooked our car and informed us that we were the last ones they were going to pull that day. They only charged $10 per car, but in that day $40 to $50 was a big wage.

Francis and his wife Ora were relieved to see us, and we were so glad we were safe in their home with a delicious dinner waiting for us. Victor, Idaho looked pretty good to us.

It didn't take us long to get acquainted with some of the dearest people on earth, and to love Idaho as much as Wyoming.

HELEN NELSON RICHINS KUNZ AND
ELLA NELSON GRIGGS, AS TOLD TO JON RICHINS

A Christmas Story

IN THE WINTER OF 1934 Clad and Viola Nelson were farming and ranching and raising their ten children in Teton Valley very near the Wyoming border. The day after Thanksgiving, 13-year-old Guy, child number six, said he was sick. Of course he was sick, the family thought—too much goose, dressing and other Thanksgiving fixings. But when Guy continued to complain, Dr. Redner was called.

The ranch was about six miles from the doctor's quarters in Driggs; Dr. Redner had to come to the ranch by horse and sleigh. When the doctor examined Guy, he said, "Scarlet fever," dreaded words as the ailment was considered serious. The Nelson family feared for Guy. Scarlet fever was sweeping through the valley; Lillian Lyons had just died from the disease, and Reed Durtschi was very ill.

Because scarlet fever was thought to be very contagious, the doctor put the family under quarantine. There would be no coming or going allowed from the ranch until the doctor gave an "all clear." Guy's symptoms were sore throat, aches and a very red rash over his body.

Dr. Redner gave permission for two of the older kids, Ella and Phyllis, to be "fumigated out" immediately, to leave the home and live elsewhere until it was safe to return. The two older children were bathed in a number-three tub in very hot water generously dosed with liquid Lysol. Ella remembers climbing out of the tub, hurriedly dressing, and still steaming as she climbed into the sleigh for the hasty ride into town.

The oldest of the 10 children, Nola, was married and living over on Teton Creek near the Pratt Ward church. Phyllis stayed with her. Two other older Nelson children, Leona and Wells, were living in an apartment in Driggs so that they could go to high school. Ella went to stay with them. This left a quarantine around Guy and his parents, plus Helen age 11, Rex age 9, Arlo age 6, and Bonnie age 4.

Guy was banished from human contact and put into the southwest room of the ranch house. A sheet dampened in Lysol water was hung in the doorway. Thus, Guy's isolation began.

The children who remained at the ranch didn't find the quarantine so bad. In fact they found missing school to be fun. But times were tough. Due to the hard times the family was preparing to move from their ranch, and this quarantine only added to the many challenges.

The estimated time for quarantine was 21 days, provided that no one else contracted the disease. Thankfully no one did. But the good doctor never made it back out to the ranch to check on Guy until the morning of December 24th, Christmas Eve day!

Apparently when Dr. Redner got to his sick patient, Guy was just returning from the foothills where the family had cut a Christmas tree. When the doctor looked at Guy he said, "I cannot lift the quarantine as Guy's hands are still scaling." No one had been able or would be allowed to go to town to Christmas shop.

Ella was sent a message to come to the ranch and get some money to do the shopping. The news was a heartbreaker for the older children who couldn't come home for Christmas. Ella pondered on how she might make the trek to the ranch for the money?

At this time of her life Ella was fascinated by a very handsome, debonair young man from the Driggs area, Robert E. Griggs, Jr. Robert wanted to take Ella to the ranch but couldn't as he was assigned to be Santa's helper in the Driggs town square. Of course that duty could not be put off as Santa had so much to do on Christmas Eve. So Robert graciously hoisted Ella aboard his riding horse and Ella was off on her important errand.

Ella traveled the road that went up through what was called "Calmer's Property" straight east past the cemetery. Of course, there were no plowed roads in those years. The day was clear but very windy.

When Ella arrived at home, the family was happy to see her but could exchange no hugs or kisses as they were still dangerous. Mom had put some money in a box and heated it in the oven to kill the germs. Mom passed the money out the door, and Ella was on her way back to town.

It was a small amount of money, but Ella did her best. The next problem was the trip back to the ranch. By the time Robert's assignment was over and the shopping was done, a full-scale Teton Valley blizzard was in progress.

Robert had the cutest little green bumper sleigh with a seat and a dashboard. He was also in good standing with Frank Knight and his team. So Robert said he would take the things up to the ranch with that outfit. Of course, Ella wouldn't hear of Robert going without her. So he put the beautiful-sounding Swedish bells on the horses and stored the treasures under the seat. Then he wrapped Ella and himself in a quilt and faced the storm.

By the time Robert and Ella got underway, there was no sign of a road in the drifting snow. Robert chose a path near the more sheltered creek bottom. Since the sleigh was light, the horses could break trail easier than with a large outfit, but the going was slow. Robert sang whenever he thought Ella was getting nervous.

Meanwhile, back at the ranch, Clad, Viola, Helen and Guy were up sitting around the warm and cozy stove. Every few moments Clad got up and paced the floor. He was feeling all the disappointment of leaving the ranch and the prospect of an empty Christmas morning. "They're not coming. They're not coming," he murmured.

But the sweet mother Viola tried to reassure her frustrated husband, saying, "Dad, they will come. I know Ella won't let us down!"

Occasionally Clad would go outside to look and listen into the darkness and then return to pace in the kitchen. Finally he said, "I am hitching up the horses and going to town."

His patient wife simply said, "Dad, they'll make it." But Clad was out of patience. He went outside to hitch the team.

When Ella and Robert hit the state line road, the horses broke into a trot. Boy, did those sleigh bells ever ring out that Christmas was on its way!

When Clad heard the bells his feelings of frustration seemed to magically melt into relief, excitement and joy. He returned to the house, announcing, "Well, I hear the bells," acting as though he never had any doubt.

Ella felt a lump in her throat when she saw the lights of her home. She knew the relief her Mom and Dad would be feeling. Robert and Ella still couldn't go into the nice, warm house. But they gestured and talked to the family through the frosted window as the firelight shown on their faces. They exchanged love and Christmas greetings while Robert unloaded the Christmas gifts.

With their mission accomplished, Ella and Robert hopped into the little green sleigh and headed back into town. The storm had stopped. The night was quiet and beautiful. The horses broke into a brisk trot as the bells of Christmas rang out.

Ella gazed back at the two-story ranch house with a dim light showing in the windows and smoke rising in a lazy curl from the chimney. Ella still remembers the beautiful scene and the feeling of being wrapped in a mantle of love and Christmas spirit as she and her beau rode through the snow. She felt a great appreciation and love for Robert, who would later become her husband and the father of her six children.

Helen says, "I had a wonderful Christmas. I got a brown purse with a chain handle and a blue ever-sharp pencil. Mother made me a coat with a big fur collar." But the most lasting gifts were those of love, the memory and heritage that remain to this day.

VERL BAGLEY, with JOSH WELTMAN

Watching Sheep

I WASN'T VERY OLD WHEN I FIRST STARTED HERDING SHEEP. I had to keep them on about 200 acres. On the south side was alfalfa fields. Had to keep them out of that. On the west side, why there was another family there, the McBrides. They had a few sheep, but there was a road between us. We had to watch them, keep them from going back and forth. I don't think we ever did get them mixed up. On the east were more alfalfa fields I had to keep them out of. On the north was another road, the Cedron Road.

I spent a lot of time out there alone. I made flippers out of the rubber from car inner tubes and a good forked willow branch, and I'd shoot ground squirrels. That's how I'd entertain myself.

About the second year I was working the sheep, I had an old horse I rode. When I wanted to get on her, I'd put her in the ditch so I could climb on, then I'd go home or go around the sheep. The ditch was kind of a central spot, and there was water there, so that was where I'd eat my lunch. A lot of times I'd bring a sandwich, but I usually brought a potato too. I'd put the potato in the fire and let it cook for a while, and that would cook it, but it would get kind of charred on the outside. I usually brought my scout book with me, and I'd read that a lot. That book said to put sand in a bucket and put the potato in the sand and build the fire around the bucket. I found me an old gallon bucket and some sand, and I started cooking it that way. Usually in about an hour it would be done, and I'd cut it open, and sometimes I had some butter with me on the sandwich, and I'd put butter on it. Sometimes I'd have some pepper on it, and sometimes I didn't put anything on it. That's what I'd have for lunch.

The McBrides had a great big barn over on the west side of the road where they had their sheep. We'd climb up into the hayloft of that big barn and play and swing on ropes. On the south end of the barn they had a little hole in the wall in the top, and if you climbed a ladder and looked out, you could keep track of where their sheep was and where our sheep was.

We had a lot of times it would be stormy weather. I'd take me a coat and watch for the storm coming over the mountain. When it started to rain, I'd watch, and when it really got white over in Pine Creek, I would know that was a heavy storm and I'd better head for some shelter. I'd jump on a horse and go for home. I'd put the horse in the barn and run to the house until it was over. Then I'd have go back out and see what the sheep was doing. One time I went out and saw that lightning had hit a post on the fence that ran through the field. It was on fire and burning. It was only a few hundred feet from where I usually had my lunch, so I was glad I wasn't there.

One time I had a dog with me that started chasing squirrels. This was the last of May, and the young squirrels were coming out. The little ones would stick their heads out of the hole and look at me, and I'd shoot at them with the flipper, then they'd duck back down. I made a loop in a piece of wire about a foot long and put it on the end of a string, and I put that loop around a hole, and I'd sit back and watch for the squirrel. When he'd get his head out, I'd jerk that string and I'd snare me a squirrel. One day this dog got between me and that squirrel and laid down on that string. He was a-barkin' and a-snappin' at that little bit of a squirrel, and he was really having a time. I jerked a squirrel right under him one time. He went in the air about four feet and let a yip out of him. He never would get around a squirrel after that. He just stayed clear. I laughed about that for an hour. I learned how to teach a dog not to chase squirrels. Problem was they'd get to chasing squirrels or rabbits and get into the sheep and scare them. Then I'd have to go get the sheep.

It was always quite an experience when I'd be out there in the spring, about the middle or the last of May, and it would start to warm up. We would take the sheep over to the sheds and shear them, shear all that wool off of them. Sometimes it would take a couple or three days to shear the sheep. If it rained, we couldn't shear them; we had to wait until the sheep dried out again.

We had a big woolsack about seven or eight feet long that would hold the fleece off of about 30 sheep. We'd put a ring around the rim of the sack and hook it up on a stand. We would hang three bags of wool and then get in and tromp it. When I got a little older, that was my job. After we tromped the wool, we would take the ring off the sack and sew up the bag just like you'd sew a sack of grain. They'd weigh about 300 pounds, sometimes more, depending on how fast you tromped them. We'd take the woolsacks to a warehouse. All the guys who had sheep formed a "wool pool." The pool would sell the wool to a company that would load the wool into boxcars and ship it out. Several times I got a job helping them load that wool into the woolsacks. At night we'd always bring the sheep back over by the house and put them in the corral we had. One night some dogs got into them, and the sheep ran against the fence, broke it all down and went out through the fields. We had to get up in the night to bring them back. We kind of made the dogs scarce after that.

It was my job to herd the sheep in the spring after I got out of school. In the fall I'd have to herd on weekends and after school. We had a few more sheep in 1928, so we rented a place north and put the sheep on about 160 acres there. I fixed a corral fence to put the sheep in and stayed with them night and day. Slept in a tepee. I'd cook my own lunch, dinner and breakfast. Sometimes I'd have somebody sleep with me at night.

I remember once in 1928 a circus came to town. The hired man and I got on a horse and rode to town to the circus. It was a two-ring circus in a big tent. They had a big African lion that was the last act of the show. The trainer got that lion out of a cage and made it go through its performance. The lion got mad and grabbed that trainer by the knee. He kept shooting the lion in the face with blanks, but it wouldn't let go. A fella went into the ring with a two-by-four and raised it way up high and come down and hit that lion between the eyes and kind of knocked him cold for a minute. It let go of the trainer and went into its cage, and they shut the door. They took the trainer to Driggs to the doctor. He died the next morning. That circus never come back through here after that. Before then they'd come through every two years.

Coming home that night in the dark both of us was kind of scared. We had to ride about a mile down through the dark until we got the sheep back where the camp was. We crawled into that tepee to go to sleep. It was kind of a spooky night for both of us. That lion kind of bothered us.

The next year we got some BLM ground at Mud Lake east of Victor. I only went up with the sheep for a week or two that year. The next year my dad and I and three other guys spent about a month up there. We built a corral at Mud Lake and sheared the sheep right there. Mother came up to cook lunch for the guys when we sheared the sheep. It took about a week because it kept raining on us. It was pretty up there on that lake. I got my picture up there leaning against a tree with my initials in 1930 or '31. I spent five springs herding sheep there. That lake had quite a lot of water and lots of frogs. They'd sing all night to us. I never seen that many frogs. About that time the frogs started to disappear. You don't see them or hear them anymore.

LORI McCUNE

Hearty Hymns Were Sung

I ARRIVED IN TETON BASIN WITH MY FAMILY IN JUNE 1995. My husband, Ken, came to work for Fred Reed of Western Air Research, tracking the radio-collared grizzlies and wolves. A few short months after our arrival, Fred lost his life in a flying accident. We soon sensed God's call to work as Protestant missionaries to the Hispanics of the valley, the same work we had done in Peru and Bolivia for 13 years prior to coming to Driggs.

As time went by, listening to older ladies in my church congregation speak of past preachers and church events, I became curious about the history of Protestantism in the valley. I read the work of the Teton Valley Community Bible Church historians, and Grace Reece of Tetonia shared with me the history of the valley Protestants as she remembered it.

Rev. Parker arrived in Teton Valley for the very first Pierre's Hole Rendezvous in July 1832 to minister to the trappers and Indians. Rev. Jason Lee, a Methodist missionary, preached the first documented Gospel sermon west of the Rocky Mountains at Fort Hall and points north and south, very possibly ministering to the Indians and mountain men in the Teton Valley as well, especially at rendezvous time.

Little is known about the early valley Protestants. We do know that in 1910 the Rev. Rankin, a Presbyterian missionary, organized the first Protestant Sunday School in Teton Basin. Many Protestant families had begun moving into the Teton Valley area to homestead 160-acre farms. In 1912 a building was erected on the Ernest Cowles ranch, on the west side of the Tetonia-Ashton highway (now Highway 32), across from the residence of Cliff and Grace Cowles. Later that year, the church building was moved into the town of Felt where services were held regularly for a number of years. The concrete door stoop was left behind on the ranch and presently lies at the entrance to the Cowles' old home with "Welcome 1912" inscribed on it.

Helen Cowles Cochrane (Mrs. William Cochrane) remembers the Sunday School classes assembled in the four corners of the rooms, trying to talk quietly to avoid interrupting the other classes. Memorizing substantial portions of the Bible was a major part of the lessons. The students were presented with a certificate upon completion of each segment of Scripture memory. Summer picnics were a common occurrence. The church families would meet at a pre-arranged spot along Badger or Bitch Creeks or the Reiley Bridge to eat a noon meal together.

Felt Community Church was re-built in the 1920s by Rev. Charles Hawley. It was a white, one-story building. Rev. George Peacock ministered in the church during the summers and boarded with various families in the area. The late 1920s and the first half of the 1930s brought drought and falling farm prices. Many families were forced from their farms, and numbers at the church declined. Services were limited to once a month when a pastor was sent from Ashton. More of the congregation was lost to Seventh Day Adventist revivals, and finally the church building was sold. A snowmobile left inside one night caused the building to burn to the ground, but the original pulpit was still in use in the Driggs congregation many years later.

Activity in the Bible church apparently did not increase until the 1960s when Jim and Beverly Williams moved to the Driggs area to manage Van Gas. According to church minutes, the two persuaded Rev. Hard-en Young from Swan Valley to preach regularly here in the Basin. An LDS bishop provided Rev. Young with a list of non-LDS families in the area. From this list, a new Protestant congregation was begun.

Bible classes and services were held in the homes of members because they had no church building. The Briggs and Robson families were especially generous in offering the use of their homes. As the group became larger, it began holding meetings at the American Legion Hall in Driggs. Several well-known Teton Valley families were in regular attendance, including the Robsons, Fonnie Jones, Reeces, Ella May Hatch, Andersons, Ecks, Briggs and Stulls.

Over the years, the group saved their tithes and offerings until in 1964 they were able to buy a piece of property from Mr. and Mrs. Leo Davis, just east of the present-day Teton Valley Hospital. The first step toward the actual building process was in 1965 when the Driggs firemen, for practice, burned the old building on the lot. The Eck family, which owned the necessary equipment, excavated the site in 1967. Church members raised funds for each step of the construction before it was begun, believing God would not have them go into debt for the building.

Grace Reece recalls her husband, Orville, standing on top of his pickup to reach the tall window frames while Grace covered her eyes in fear of his falling. Orville spent much time finishing the walls, floors and windows with his carpentry skills and "can-do" attitude.

"The ladies of the church were there working nearly every day. Young Kurt Reece, Bonnie and Clinton's son, was about two then. I remember his lisping comment as his mama brought him to the church for yet another workday. 'Shursh, shursh...all we do is go to the shursh.' To this day it bring tears to my eyes to think of the laughter we shared over that."

Pastors came and went, but Cindy Reece Croft most remembers the pastor with the booming voice and strong command of God's Word, Pastor Walter Scott. He and his wife began traveling over Teton Pass from Jackson each Sunday to lead worship services. Later, they came on Wednesday for Bible study and on Tuesday evening for youth group meetings held in the home of Max and Haddie Jorgensen.

After a chilly first winter in the building, Orville and Grace Reece spent considerable time in the crawl space putting insulation under the sanctuary floor. Their sweaty, itchy arms and faces were rewarded with much warmer church services that second winter!

The pastor that led the church in 1973 had not a musical bone in his body, so Orville Wolfe, who started the Good Samaritan mission in Jackson, would come over each week to lead the congregational singing.

"And, oh, what hearty hymns were sung!" Grace reminisced.

Emil Hein of Badger Creek, logger and sawmill operator, began studying the Scripture in earnest in 1977 and came to faith in the Lord Jesus Christ the next year. Later, he was ordained as an elder, or spiritual leader, of the congregation and then pastored the flock during the late 1980s after Pastor Harvey moved to Heyburn.

"I enjoyed being the pastor. It was a very busy time, running the sawmill and logging operation, working with the church, teaching mid-week Bible studies and Sunday School. Somehow it all got done."

Emil also saw to it that the outside of the church was re-sided in logs, making the structure much more attractive.

By this time there was another Protestant group meeting in the valley as well. This second group, led by Ron Derrick, met at the Pines Motel and later, in the Legion Hall. A turning point for both congregations was when Lance and Karen Eisele moved to Driggs in 1989. Eisele's first Christmas Eve service was held jointly with Ron Derrick's congregation from the Legion Hall. The marvelous result of the two assemblies' coming together that night was that they agreed to merge into one body.

The Eiseles' contributions to the Protestant traditions of the valley have been many. They helped bring Christian radio to the valley in 1994. Along with other Protestant families, they started the Teton Christian Academy in 1995. Eighteen students began studying there that fall and thus far all graduates have gone on to college.

Besides the Teton Valley Community Bible church, today there are three congregations in Victor, all started in the mid to late 1990s: Sonrise Christian Fellowship, led by Bob Fogelquist; Teton Valley Christian Center, pastored by Scott Prindle; Teton Valley Independent Baptist, pastored by Dave Mullenex; and in Alta, St. Francis of the Tetons Episcopal Church, pastored by Sandy Casey-Martus.

STANFORD PETER SORENSEN

Darby

FROM THE FIRST DAY AFTER I HAD ARRIVED at my parents' ranch on Spring Creek in Teton Valley, I had been aware of a feeling—not troubling, really, but persistent and growing steadily stronger. I was on one of my annual visits from California. The feeling that plagued me was disquieting and defied logical explanation. It grew steadily stronger. One bright, Sunday afternoon it became too compelling, defeating any attempts at being ignored. I had to go back.

My parents' house was cocooned in its usual Sunday afternoon peace and quiet which always followed our return from church and my mother's incomparable Sunday dinners. Slipping out unnoticed, I got into my car and drove off. Leaving in this manner required making no explanations to kindly questioning or offers to accompany me. It also allowed me to avoid the embarrassment of attempting to answer the unanswerable:

"Where are you going?"

"Darby."

"Sunday afternoon driving over to Darby. What on earth for?"

I could not explain this strange desire to revisit Darby. Many times during past summers I might easily have returned. The distance there from my father's home was short, calculated by today's transportation methods. But years had passed and Darby had faded into a quiet dimness among my memories.

Darby was a small farming community nestled peacefully alongside gently slopping Rocky Mountain foothills. We had moved from there when I was entering my teens. It was just before electricity had come to the community. Only a year earlier Darby citizens had voted to consolidate their school, busing the children to a nearby town. It was a time before the final encroachment of big farm machinery replaced more manual and horse-powered farming methods. Changed it would be. Perhaps it was to see this difference that compelled me.

I turned my car onto a dusty dirt road. When I was young a large handsome red-brick school had once stood with quiet elegance across the road from our house. It had burned, I had been told, mysteriously catching fire one night just like our small wooden church had years earlier. After the church burned, our school had become the hub of our community. Sunday school, Sacrament Meetings, water and potato committees met there. Parties, funerals, dances all took place under this one roof.

The school had an enormous basement with a hardwood floor. Upstairs were two rooms: the big one and the little one. Both rooms were exactly the same size but one was for bigger students, grades five through eight, the other one for younger children. The schoolrooms were reached by climbing two short flights of stairs that put them half a story above ground level. Each was furnished with the appropriate-sized wooden pupils' desks, a teacher's desk, back and front blackboards, and cloakrooms. Along the eastern wall in the little room and the western wall in the big room were high windows, filling almost the entire wall. One of my most vivid memories of the big room was entering it one day after school hours and finding light from the setting sun streaming through those tall windows, flooding the entire room with a beautiful, golden radiance and transforming it into a wonderful, magical kingdom.

In the earlier years a furnace located in the basement had heated the school. Later this had changed. I don't know why. The furnace heat was replaced with large cast-iron potbellied stoves placed in one corner of each room. A galvanized reflector encircled the back of each stove to throw more heat out into the rooms. It was not an effective heating system. On exceptionally cold days, ink could remain frozen in the bottles at our desks while everyone huddled close as possible to the stoves for comfort. Boys needed to exercise caution. The copper rivets securing overall seams and pockets conducted heat faster than heavy denim.

We grew up liking school no more or less than children all over America, but many basic lessons were learned in those two rooms. Darby alumni have become lawyers, dentists, teachers, nurses, engineers, outstanding farmers, scientists, army officers and respected citizens in communities thousands of miles removed from Darby.

The basement beneath the schoolrooms was large, equal in length and width to the entire upstairs. Its wooden floor was smooth and polished. This basement was our theater, dance hall and the place for larger community gatherings. There, generally found leaning against one wall, was a rough wooden platform we graciously referred to as our stage. Before the performance of plays this stage was lowered behind sheets pinned along a stout wire stretched across the room. Benches constructed of finished pine two-by-fours were arranged for seating, completing the theater. Our theater did not lack pre-curtain excitement. It grew tense, noisy

too, with friendly chatter. Frequently theatrical performances were followed by a dance. Young boys competed to see who could push the most benches along the walls, leaving plenty of space for dancing. The orchestra, consisting of two and three musicians, played without printed music. Popular tunes were intermingled with Virginia reels and other older favorites. Homemade pies, cakes and ice cream were served, or sold if it was a fundraising event. Those happened frequently.

Along the front edge of the schoolyard had once been a row of majestic tall cottonwood trees, their elegance and beauty creating an impressive border. I had thought of them as utterly indestructible and timeless, but they, too, had disappeared. Nor was there any sign of a small barn that had been in back of the school for sheltering horses ridden by those students living long-distance from the school. Gone also were two state-of-the-art outhouses, which, at the time, were great advancements over the mere two-holers found throughout the community.

Following a smooth, earthen foothill road, I approached the farm that had once belonged to my grandfather. Its large, brick farmhouse was built entirely under my grandfather's supervision, even to the making and baking of his own bricks. This dwelling's second story was one large, wonderful room, an unexcelled pleasure for the family's younger generation. The original design was a floor of bedrooms but for some reason the carpentry work was never completed. Wooden supports stood exposed, scarcely interrupting progress from one area to another, yet clearly marking where each room was to have been. Through large windows we could see miles out into the valley or gaze down at a well-kept raspberry patch and garden that took on a mysterious glamour induced by the unaccustomed height.

The room contained a profusion of treasures: a small harp decorated with shamrocks which we hooked over one shoulder to play, ancient catalogs made from heavy, unbending paper showing styles long out of fashion, toys collected through many years, books and magazines. Some of the magazines were forbidden literature, secreted away in a never-ending plot to thwart adult authority. I don't believe any of us ever fully realized just why we weren't supposed to read certain publications, but the fact they were banned heightened many exceedingly dull pages.

Three enormous wild fruit trees, a serviceberry and two chokecherry, had grown along the road directly in front of the house. They produced abundant, delicious harvest nearly every fall. On Sunday afternoons, when the fruit had ripened, we interrupted our perpetual games of cops and robbers. Climbing among the stout branches we ate until our hands turned purple. Our mouths became stained and puckering from the tart pungency of wild cherries.

I noticed that the road had been improved, some curves removed. Along with the curves, many wild rose bushes, natural trees and shrubbery had disappeared. Then I saw that the house, too, had been improved—not beyond recognition, but changed nonetheless. I paused only a moment, glad that I did not know the people who were now its occupants. I might have been tempted to go inside although an inner voice told me that upstairs ordinary rooms were now set aside, each in its own sphere, where once had been a vast land complete with castles, dungeons and Nordic halls.

Driving on, between green fields, I saw other transformations wrought by time and men. Fences had been built or removed. Many houses were delightfully familiar, but conspicuous gaps appeared in the landscape where there had once been a home. Even sadder were the abandoned dwellings with broken windows staring like lifeless eyes and roofs sagging in mournful neglect. One fine, newer building did stand out, a red brick church built in more recent years. Even it had been converted to private use.

What had been our farm was greatly altered, I knew. None of the original buildings had survived long after we sold. Besides the buildings, an immense yellow rose bush, lilacs which my mother had struggled to keep growing, a lawn, a small orchard, two huge willow trees that had sheltered the house from south winds, had all been swept away to make room for more efficient farming methods. A narrow sagebrush ridge where I had spent hours watching red ants building their mounds and gathering food, and a small pond with its surrounding willow grove, haven for my first reading of "Alice in Wonderland," had vanished.

Driving past the farm I scarcely even slowed down. A new farmhouse stood in a section of what had once been a hayfield. One of my most unique childhood experiences occurred in that field. For some now forgotten reason I had gone down into the field on a summer's evening after the hay was cut. I was startled to hear beautiful music: a symphony orchestra playing big and full, as if I were standing in front of it. This was not some condensed sound, which I often heard coming from battery-powered radios or a hand-operated phonograph. Moving more than three steps in any direction caused the music to disappear. Fascinated, I listened, until an older brother's repeated calling took me away.

One place I looked forward to visiting was the community cemetery. It was a plot of ground originally part of our farm. An earlier owner had donated the ground, located at the farthest possible point from all existing roads, against the farm's northern boundary. In order to reach the cemetery, a road was constructed past our house and farmyard, down a little knoll then on between hayfield, pasture and our vegetable garden.

Because of the cemetery's proximity I grew up with an unusual concept about death and burial. It never fostered the ghoulish or frightening. On the contrary, I felt that the cemetery was an intrinsic part of our farm, a focal point of unusual interest. On Memorial Day it brought exciting activity. Cars began arriving early in the morning with flowers; fragrant yellow roses, lilacs, apple blossoms, pinks, great bunches of colorful pansies, all from local gardens and orchards; delicate wildflowers gathered from roadsides and forests. There were homemade floral bouquets of crepe paper, sometimes dipped in wax. The mounds of earth were freshly raked and cleared before the flowers, arranged in fruit jars and tin cans covered with bright paper or paint, were placed on them. The cemetery changed from its half-cleared, weedy and sagebrush existence into a garden. Occasionally there would be a wreath of hothouse plants, but those expensive carnations, calla lilies and red roses were seldom present except during burial services.

The graves were decorated early because everyone wanted them looking their best before the American Legion arrived to honor deceased veterans. Several men from World War I, dressed in uniforms complete with leg wrappings and carrying old Army rifles, formed a single line beside Darby's one veteran's grave. A musical number was rendered. I recall most clearly a ladies' trio singing "Flag Without a Stain," which was lost to those not standing in a favorable wind position. Taps sounded clearly and mournfully across the cemetery. On command the Legionnaires lifted their rifles and fired a volley of honor. A few moments of seemingly endless silence followed before the company of performers immediately began piling into cars, driving off to another nearby community where the service was repeated.

My favorite time at the cemetery, however, was not Memorial Day, but the latter weeks of June. At that season, in sagebrush areas around the farm, large, slow-flying brown beetles, known locally as June bugs, began appearing. In early evening they began their flight. A small boy, sighting one on the wing, could run and intercept it in the air with his bare hands. Although found on many parts of the farm, they were most prevalent about the cemetery. Marked-off rows between graves made the best and longest running space. From the time I was allowed to wander about by myself, almost until the year we moved, I practiced my secret sport during the few short weeks June bugs were in flight. My rules of sportsmanship were strict. They had to be sighted only while on the wing and were never to be injured. To prod into flight or harm the insect counted as a foul and invalidated any score.

The road no longer entered where our house had stood. A new one ran along the north fence, conserving farmland. I parked my car outside, along the main road and walked in. I could see the cemetery fence was now in excellent repair, which was not always the case. Wild morning glory, a curse to farmers, had entwined itself around posts and through the wire mesh, forming a delicate wall of white trumpet flowers and rich green leaves. At least there was one useful purpose for this beautiful weed. I was surprised to see that the western half of the cemetery, never cleared for burial purposes in the days of my childhood, was now planted in grain.

I walked on, nothing preparing me for what I was to see. I stopped in shock. From fence to grain patch stretched a green, velvety lawn, gently watered by a modern, built-in sprinkler system. All the distinctive grave mounds of my childhood had been leveled. None of the natural sagebrush, wild grasses and plants were there. I took a hasty tour. Some of the gravestones were familiar, that was all. Hurriedly I left, wishing I had known and never come.

When I stepped over a small wooden bridge crossing an irrigation ditch I looked down at the water, thinking of times when I had lain flat along similar muddy banks to quench my thirst. The water probably could not pass a health inspector's test-tube scrutiny, but to me it appeared only cool and inviting. The water flowed half-hidden beneath the shade of tall grasses growing along the banks, humming softly over rocks and gliding through gently waving clusters of dark, green moss. Scooping up double hands full, I drank eagerly as water seeped through my fingers to run down my arms. One thing was unchanged. The humble ditch water was as wonderfully refreshing as it had been across the years of memory.

I drove away, letting dust from my wheels wave goodbye. I noticed a little boy playing intently at the edge of a new farmhouse's lawn. What changes would he find as a grown man when my memories ceased to be even memories?

MICHAEL B. WHITFIELD
The Grand Old Man

I saw the Old Man of the Teton
in a green boat, catching trout,
red-plaid shirt and rosey cheeks
framed in the river willows.

Have you seen him in the meadow,
Spencer's pasture by the slough;
rough, broad hands that smoothed boat poles
checking trap lines in the mist?

Clouds were forming over Fox Creek
where I glimpsed his flashing smile;
a spray of sunlight crossed his face,
I'd say he's poling Foster's now.

BARBARA BOHM-BECKER
Roosevelt's Tree Army

FIFTY YEARS AGO, Teton Valley was deep in the grip of the Great Depression.
Jobs and money were scarce. Week after week, the local newspaper contained column-long lists of ranches and homes that were to be auctioned
off at tax sales.

The federal government placed advertisements for the Civilian Conservation Corps in the *Teton Valley News*: "Young men are eligible, if
they are U.S. citizens, between the ages of 17 and 23, inclusive, unmarried,
unemployed, and in need of employment."

Many local men gratefully enrolled in the CCC.

Art Kearsley of Victor joined up in June of 1933. He said, "We did-
n't buy anything. They took us naked, you might say. They furnished
the clothes, shoes and all. You didn't have to buy even a handkerchief."

Each man earned $30 per month, $25 of which was sent to the man's dependents.

Many different types of projects were undertaken, from roadbuilding to fighting forest fires. "They put me on timber because I was a native, and I knew how to handle an axe and saw and horses," Art said.

One day the U.S. Forest Service ranger in Victor, Claude Shannon, asked Art to look for a flagpole. "The flagpole that I chose and got out was the longest flagpole that the Targhee National Forest ever had," Art said. "We cut it in two to get it out, and they got irons on it and bolted it together to get it up." That same pole was later used at the Forest Service Supervisor's Office in St. Anthony.

Art drove the horses on a grader when the corps built the Packsaddle Road. The actual grader man was Bri Campbell, some of whose children still live in Teton Valley.

The local CCC camp was located next to the Mike Harris Campground. Over 200 men lived there in tents, many of them Teton Valley natives. Some of the local men Art remembered were Reno Williams, Dean Wilkie, Russ Allen, Revere Roberson, Ed Roberson, Percy Roberson, Tad Bircher, Floyd Fisher, Hiles Fisher, Orville Peterson, Marion Weeks, Ray Ballard, Whitey Dodd, Doc Holgarth, Calvin Kyte, Rex Fairbanks and Al Deveraux.

Warm friendships often formed. "You had to be close when times were rough. You had to think the world of those people you were working with and living with, or you had to get out of there," Art said. A group of New Yorkers were sent to his camp, "but they shipped them out early."

Ron White was another local CCC enrollee, though he worked out of Osborne Springs near Ashton. He worked with other local enrollees, including Alan Egbert, Lyle Smith, Ray Reiley, Byron Reiley, Bob Hillman and Keith Arnold. These men cleared trees to widen the road from Ashton to Island Park. Projects like this gave the CCC its nickname: Roosevelt's Tree Army.

Ron said that his group also built the airport at West Yellowstone.

Ray Moss' father, Francis Moss, was the ranger at the Rapid Creek Ranger Station north of Darby Creek, and Ray lived at the station during those days. Ray remembered the CCC doing some work up at the Treasure Mountain Scout Camp, at the Teton Canyon Campground, and at his father's ranger station.

Jim McDonald, archeologist for the Targhee National Forest, said that the CCC reconstructed the house and office at Rapid Creek, and built a new washhouse, garage and barn there. McDonald said that the old Victor Ranger Station was probably also reconstructed by these men and that the new barn and other outbuildings that were built in the 1930s were also probably done by them.

The Forest Service used the CCC to do quite a bit of reconstruction in the 1930s. McDonald said that before then, the construction of Forest Service buildings was often the responsibility of each local ranger since the U.S. Government didn't release sufficient funds to hire other labor. The quality of the construction was often a function of how much talent each ranger had. When the CCC program came along with such an abundance of labor, many of these buildings were rebuilt using the buildings' original materials.

When the local camp was dismantled in the mid-1930s, many of the local enrollees went on to work at camps in other parts of Idaho. According to Forest Service records, during the nine-year life span of the CCC, there were 82 camps in other parts of Idaho.

Ray Moss said that the corps seemed "kind of Army-oriented." Actually, the Army had the administrative control of the program, while the Department of Labor selected the enrollees. The Departments of Agriculture and the Interior both provided technical supervision. The Soil Conservation Service and the old Grazing Service (forerunner of the Bureau of Land Management) also had roles.

Throughout the small communities of the west, projects built by the Civilian Conservation Corps, many of them still in use today, grace Main Streets and back streets. As those whose memories hold the stories of Roosevelt's Tree Army pass away, these projects remind us of those hard times and the creativity that was needed for survival.

SUSAN AUSTIN

Tailings

So much seems to be failing—
the bluebird nest in the sauna,
the aspens with their red blush,
the peasant road ...

What was the idea anyway
scooping pit-run off the county road
and shoveling it into mud-hole ruts?

I hear bluebird chicks peeping in the sauna,
all the mistakes I made come back to me
but it's only the wind hissing over roofing tin
torn loose, I lived here once.

Empty cabin full of emptiness,
hewn logs without the job of keeping in the heat,
no one to leave crumbs for the mice—
Who nailed the tuna can over the hole in the floor?

You think you see our shadows
disembodied, two brothers and me
hunting windmill blades
through barley silvered in the moonlight

but it was never more than the wind
pulling up out of the earth
the smell of sweet carrots on our breath.

I am down on my knees in the nettle patch
ferreting out some reason for
three transparent chicks in the tailings of a nest.

The mourning doves are after me every day:
Go ahead, let go, they say,
Go ahead, let go.

MARILYN ELLIOTT MEYER

An Essential Life

"WHEN I GET TO HEAVEN, God is going to ask me how I liked the Earth which He created. I'm going to look him in the eye," Chet Miller said in an interview in 1981, "and I'm going to tell him what a wondrous place it is. That is the key to heaven. Those who have gone through life with their eyes closed and their ears clogged aren't going to be admitted."

The youngest of 11 children born to a farming family in Teton Valley, Chet spent his life avoiding farm work and exploring the mountains and waterways around him. There wasn't much he didn't see or hear.

He had been described as a man who fished for a living, but making a living had nothing to do with fishing as far as Chet was concerned. Fishing and running rivers and collecting rocks and listening to the sounds in the forest were much more important than money to Chet.

"I maintain that though the average person may live 70 years, only once a year or so does he feel totally vibrant and totally aware—and that's living. Half of that time he spends sleeping and much more than that he spends drooping around. The average person spends perhaps six months of his life living," Chet said.

Chet pursued the thrill that made him feel totally alive, the challenge of attaining excellence in an old activity or adequacy in a new one. In his life he was a trapper, a rancher, a sheepherder, a construction worker, and a schoolteacher. He had been a whitewater river guide, a fishing guide, a hunter, a rockhound, a boat builder, and a modest expert on the life in the woods around him.

From his childhood, Chet showed little aptitude for farm work.

"I wasn't worth a damn on the farm. If there were any excuse to get away from milking a cow, I would use it. I was only good for herding sheep and fishing and hunting." So while his brothers and sisters helped with the farm work, Chet became his mother's "little breadbasket," supplying the family with food from his fishing and hunting forays.

He started fishing when he was just two or three years old on a private pond his parents had on their ranch. The pond was part of an ill-fated business venture. At that time the government was providing free fish for those who wanted to raise them; so the Millers built a pond and hauled the fish in wooden barrels over 70 miles from Ashton, the nearest train station at the time. Chet thought they were the first to bring rainbows into the valley, along with some Eastern Brook thrown in by the government workers.

The venture never got off the ground as a business. The Millers were about 40 years too soon, Chet said. At that time there was practically no limit on the fish you could catch and they were abundant in the rivers and streams of the valley. The pond and its fish remained and were Chet's learning ground.

Chet served as unofficial guide for friends and relatives in Eastern Idaho for 30 or 40 years. He worked as a fishing guide at the Teton Valley Lodge but eventually quit and took up guiding whitewater raft trips in Jackson Hole because the frustrations of trying to make poor fishermen catch fish were more than he wanted to put up with.

In all his years of guiding fishermen, there was only one man that got skunked. "That fellow couldn't cast further than I could spit and he stood in the bow of the boat wearing a white shirt all day long," Chet said.

Usually he could help even the poorest fisherman make a catch by zigzagging the boat down the river over just the right spots, at just the right time and in such a manner that even a poor cast could net the client a fish. He could also use those talents to prevent a catch.

One day Chet guided a "fish hog," who had been fishing the Teton River for quite a while, catching more fish than he or anyone could possibly use but refusing to release any of them. Chet told the other guides that he could guarantee the man would not catch a single fish all day. They were doubtful he could carry out his pledge, but he did—the man caught not a single fish all day.

The lure or the fly isn't the important thing when fishing, Chet said. Despite owning a collection of over 2000 flies, he said he could probably catch all the fish he wanted with just six of them.

"There's no way I ever fish just throwing the line out. I have a target every time I cast—about a six-inch target. It's not the lure, not the fly, but how it's presented to the fish that brings success," he said. "I take it as a personal insult when I miss the right target."

Chet said he was "totally ambidextrous" as to whether he fished with flies or lures. The first fish he caught was, in fact, with a rifle. He progressed to a willow pole, then a big cane pole, and finally more "modern" equipment.

"That's where my money has gone," he said. "I have violent likes and dislikes in equipment. I want the best and I don't care what I have to pay."

In 1981 when he was interviewed, Chet was 64 and living in Driggs in an old log cabin which he had built himself. He refused to have a phone. He was running whitewater trips on the Snake River for a company in Jackson Hole and making twice the money he had made as a fishing guide. He'd been doing the trips for a friend's company for many years. The low water that year was a disappointment but his challenge was to make sure everyone on the boat got a thrill and got wet.

"I always go back to the rivers because that's where the thrill is," he said. "And it's one of the few things I can still do better than the kids."

Chet was one of the pioneers of the white waters in the Salmon and the Middle Fork of the Salmon. He first floated the Salmon in 1946 to recover the body of a friend who had drowned while trying to cross the river on horseback. He and his brother-in-law ran the river in a six-man army surplus raft with one set of small aluminum oars.

Though he was "getting quite cocky at the time," Chet admitted that there were times on the river during that trip when he would have backed out if there had been any way to do so. They recovered the body and returned home safely, but the nightmares from the trip stayed with him for many years.

"The ultimate thrill in life is to bet your life that you can do something and then give it a try. Basically I'm afraid of the water—I have a lot of respect for the water. The nightmares have left," he said, "I don't know why; but the thrill is still there."

Chet met his wife, Lila, on his first out-of-state fishing trip. He was ostensibly on a mission for the LDS Church in Minnesota, Chet said, but he managed to work a lot of fishing into it. For several months he was based on an Indian reservation, and during that time there was hardly a day that he didn't find time to go fishing with the local Indian youths.

He and those young Indians took canoes into just about every stream in the area and fished every day. He remembered those as fun, care-free days—"You just didn't care where you were." They saw a lot of wildlife, practiced their tracking skills and got lost more than once. Each learned a little from the other. Chet said that as a child he had read all the Indian legends and lore he could put his hands on and prided himself on his tracking skills. He felt very at home on that reservation.

Lila, whom he met in Minneapolis, was one quarter Chippewa. The two corresponded for several months after Chet returned to the Teton Valley following his mission, and then he sent for her to come to the valley and to be his wife.

Chet spent a couple of winters trapping rabbits for a living after the Depression and then worked for many years with his father on his ranch. He was prone, in those years, to just stop in the middle of haying and take off fishing when the thought entered his head or the time felt right. Eventually he rented the farm to a friend and began doing construction work in the valley. He spent 13 years at the job and had a hand in building many of the schools, a church, several homes and some dormitories at Ricks College before he was through.

A lackadaisical student at Teton High School, Chet said he spent only about one week out of one particular six-week period actually attending classes. He would be distracted on his way to school by his trap lines on the river or by the fish that were biting that day. He had no real pressure from home to attend. His father thought he should get an education, but his mother, Chet said, didn't think it was very important. Chet himself couldn't quite see the value of sitting in the classroom. The principal told him he might find he was a genius if he would start coming to classes, "But who wanted to be a genius?" Chet said. No one would have expected at that time that Chet would eventually spend 17 years teaching science at the Middle School in Driggs.

After high school he took some correspondence courses and did some studying on his own, learning "a little of everything from arts to zoology," he said. Then he began wondering if the people who had gone on to college "had something I didn't." At the age of 49 he enrolled in Ricks College, working a full-time construction job at the same time. Eventually he attended college at Brigham Young University and the University of Idaho, too.

Chet naturally turned to something practical and earthy in his studies. From a set of bird encyclopedias belonging to his father, he had already come to know all the birds in the area. He said he could tell every bird in the Rocky Mountains just by watching its wing beats. Because he knew the flora and fauna of his mountain home so well, he turned to the study of geology because he didn't know the rocks and minerals. It was after he taught a 4-H group a few lessons on area rocks and had so much fun that he went into teaching.

Chet was drawn to the mountains all his life. He learned to listen and he learned to watch. He learned to appreciate the beauty and admire the life there. In his lifetime he saw many changes. Streams were being fished out; many were being polluted. So many people were looking for the wilderness experience that much of the wildness was gone from the state's wild rivers. The times when he could spend days without seeing anyone were gone. The problem with all these people, he said, was that "humans are always dropping or dribbling something here or there."

He refused, however, to wish for "the good old days."

"Wishing," he said, "is a waste of time."

KERRY GEE, WITH ADAM EDWARDS
Little Spare Time

I WAS BORN ON JANUARY 29, 1937, IN ST. ANTHONY, IDAHO. That was the only hospital around. I was the first of the children in our family born in a hospital. I was born during the time my parents owned the farm. I lived on the farm from the time I was born up until the time I went on my mission when I was 20 years old. We came down to Sugar in the wintertime to go to school because up in Teton Basin the county would not plow out the roads. When we got old enough to go to school my parents had to move out. They had a choice of going either to Driggs or down to Sugar. They chose to come to Sugar because that way we could live at home and go to college when we got old enough.

I was probably five years old when I had to do chores. My dad woke me up at about six in the morning and gave me a piece of bread to kind of entice me. My job was to push the hay up to the manger while he did the milking, and from about that time on I was working every morning and night before and after school.

Probably the worst experiences stick out in my mind. For instance, we always had cows to milk, and our cows were always the meanest cows in the country. They would kick when you would try to milk them, and I was scared to death of them. In order to milk the cow I had to put a rope around the hind leg and tie her leg back, and then I could sit down and milk her. Just getting that rope on the hind leg was a major thing 'cause I started milking when I was about eight years old. So I was a little kid trying to handle one of those big cows. I always just dreaded that all of the time because they were so mean.

I had two homes that I lived in, one in the Basin and the other down here in Sugar City. (The home in Sugar City was destroyed in the Teton Dam flood and rebuilt on the same location. My dad lives there now.) Up in the Basin is a log home that my dad built. Bitch Creek is behind it, and the canyon goes down its side. It's about 300 feet before you come to the brink of the canyon. It's a two-bedroom with a living room and kitchen. My sisters had one bedroom, my parents had the other bedroom, and Jerald and I would just sleep in the living room. When [my brother] Jim came along, my dad bought a sheep camp. I was seven years old. From that time on Jerald and I had the sheep camp as our bedroom.

We had 900 acres out on Bitch Creek, and we farmed the 410 acres that Jerald and I run now. On the west side of the valley across the Teton River we farmed another 360 acres. We were farming about 1,700 acres when I was growing up. On Bitch Creek and across the river it was all just wheat and summer fallow. It was a dry farm. [The place Jerald and I farmed] was irrigated. We raised hay and pasture as well as some grain.

We had six or seven milk cows and maybe 40 or 50 beef cows. I had very few pets while growing up. My grandfather was a sheep man, and he would give us some bum lambs, but they would always get eaten after they were grown up.

Up in Teton Basin, some years the snow would be higher than the eaves on the house, and so my dad would have to dig out around the windows in order to get light into the house. There were some severe, very severe, winters up in the Basin. In this house there was no electricity, no plumbing. The outhouse was down over the hill. I bathed in a round tub that wasn't very big or pleasant. We had two woodstoves: one in the kitchen that we cooked on and one in the living room to keep the rest of the house warm. We would heat up the water on the woodstove to pour into the tub to bathe.

When I was quite small, all we had was an International truck and that was our sole transportation for both the farm and the family. During the first three or four years of my life, we were just coming out of the Depression, and nobody had anything. If you had a truck you were fortunate. My parents would take the whole family in the truck from Sugar up to our farm. Later on, of course, the Second World War came along, and then prices got good, and my dad bought a car.

When I was about six years old or so, I started driving a tractor. Driving the tractors and combine was boring, very boring. They would break down, but that was my dad's problem, not mine. I didn't have to worry about it until I got in high school and my dad quit farming. Jerald and I did all the farming; we were responsible for the whole operation. Our brothers were too young to do much work on the farm, so they would just tag along and do what we wanted them to do.

I had seven brothers and sisters—four boys and four girls in our family. All the girls had to learn how to milk cows, and they all had to drive the tractor.

My dad grew up when horses were used for farming, and he thought his kids ought to know how to work with horses on the farm. Even though we had tractors, he bought an old dump rake (to make windrows), which was pulled by horses, and a horse-pulled mowing machine. Even though we had tractors, he made us get out there with that six-foot swather on the mowing machine and go around the 40-acre field. In order to take the hay to the harvester we would have to bunch it with a bunch rake and then go along with a pitchfork and pitch it onto a trailer.

During the years I was in high school, we had a drought. When I was a senior, I would go to Seminary, and the teacher would put up on the chalkboard the number of days without rain. I can remember him putting up 180 days without rain. That's six months. All summer we had not had any rain at all. Things were very tough on the farm that year because all the crops were dry.

A few years before, the snow came in September and never did go away. My dad didn't harvest any of his crops that fall. It was when I was six years old because he went out in the spring, [hoping to harvest the grain that was lying on the ground]. I was driving the tractor, and he was on the combine—we didn't have our self-propelled one then. We went about 20 feet, and we put the header too close to the ground, and it dug in the ground. By the time I saw what the problem was—a six-year-old doesn't think very fast—it had bent the header back around and against the side of the combine and ruined it. Dad just gave up and never did harvest that crop.

I had very little spare time when I was growing up. We didn't have any toys or anything to play with, but we had free access to a .22, so we'd go shooting ground squirrels. There were lots of ground squirrels around the farms at that time. And we spent a lot of our time along the creek just playing. We'd go swimming down there, fishing, whatever we wanted to do along the creek. There was a limit on how many fish, but the local people never paid any attention. I've never bought a fishing license in my life. In those creeks you don't get very big fish.

We didn't have a TV or radio; in fact, all we had was candles or a gas lantern for light. One thing that is interesting, we didn't have refrigerators. That is pretty essential. We didn't have running water either, but we did have a cistern. A cistern has a big hole about five to six feet in diameter and is dug about 12 to 15 feet into the ground. The sides are cemented. We put a top on it made out of wood and then filled it up with water.

We had three 100-gallon water tanks we'd put on the back of the truck. We'd go down to Bitch Creek and fill them with water. When I was a kid, my dad dipped it up by the bucket fulls. Five hundred gallons of water he'd dip up out of the creek and put in these tanks. Later on we got a gas engine with a pump on it, so when I came along, it wasn't quite so bad.

We would fill the cistern with 500 gallons of water and that was our source of water for the place. And to keep the milk or anything else cool we'd put it in a gallon pail with a lid on it, put it on a rope, and drop it down into the cistern until all but the top was down in the water. Then we'd tie it to a string on the side of the cistern. That would keep it cool because the water was always cool down in the ground.

The worst part of dry farming was all the hours you had to sit on a tractor with no cab or anything like that. If you were going the same way as the wind, you could become enveloped in a cloud of dust so thick you could hardly breathe, and you couldn't see where you were going. You'd have to stop the tractor, let the dust go away and then start up again. You would keep doing that until you came to a corner and turned so you weren't going the same direction as the wind. Just dealing with the boredom of sitting out on the tractor hour after hour, day after day, was the worst part of farming—especially for a young person. I don't even like it today.

My dad would send us out there for half a day and then trade off. Then Jerald and I finally rebelled and said, "We don't want to sit out there for four hours; let us go two-hour shifts." As long as we got the work done, he didn't care; so we'd trade off every two hours just so we wouldn't have to sit out there so long.

One other thing that was not particularly pleasant was, we had the cows to milk, even up in the Basin. We had them in a great big pasture that was probably about 200 to 300 acres and would extend maybe a half-mile along the bank of Bitch Creek. Every morning we'd have to go find them and bring them in, then milk them, and then turn them out. We'd get up in the morning, and the dew was pretty heavy, and it was very cold, so we'd be wet from our knees on down going through the sage brush and the trees, trying to find those cows so we could bring them in and milk them in the mornings. That was a real trial for us.

Sometimes we'd dry up all the cows but two of them because we needed that many for milk for the family. My dad was called to be in the Bishopric in Sugar City, and that meant that instead of going to Church up in the Basin, we had to start coming to Church in Sugar every Sunday. Every Saturday night we would have to load up those two cows, bring them down to Sugar, unload them so we could milk them here Saturday night and Sunday, and then early on Monday morning we'd load them back in the truck and take them back up to the farm. They got trained to the point that all we had to do was back the truck up to the loading shoot, and they just automatically would walk right in.

The only real entertainment we had after we started coming down to Sugar were the movies in Sugar City by the hardware store. That was our treat to come down and see a movie on Saturday night. The bad part was my dad wanted to always work us until six o'clock on Saturday night. The movies started at seven, and we were always wondering if we would make it down in time for the movies. Sometimes he'd work us until 6:30 or so, and we wouldn't make it. That was a great disappointment. Roy Rogers, Hop-Along Cassidy, Gene Autry were the movies we always liked to watch.

One thing I always enjoyed was hunting grouse in the fall up along the creek. They were what we called a rough grouse. They were more accessible in the fall because the leaves were gone and you could see more through the trees. We'd cook them up and eat them.

When I was a junior in high school, my dad hurt his back; well, he had always had a bad back, so he had to quit farming. He got a job working in a potato warehouse, and then my brother and I had to do all the farm work.

My folks would send one of my sisters up each summer to cook for us. The time came when they all graduated, went away to school and got married and stuff like that. My folks would just give Jerald and I a box of groceries on Monday morning and say, "See you next Saturday." So we'd have to do all our own cooking up there and taking care of everything, which trained me for being a good cook.

In the culture my father grew up in, you helped each other a lot. He never got over that. When we were teenagers, he would loan us out to people to help them. My uncle had a farm, and my dad would loan us out to my uncle every summer. We would go put up his hay because he didn't have any kids. We would do our hay, and then we would have to go do his hay. Then, when somebody else needed some help, well, he would loan us out to them. He sent me out to Mud Lake one summer to help one of my cousins with his hay because he needed a little help. I never got paid for it, ever. My dad never paid me a penny in all the time I worked for him.

We hauled hay with one guy on the ground and one guy on the truck with one of my sisters driving. The guy on the ground would throw the bales up, and the guy on the truck would just stack them. We loaded them as high as we do now. The tough part would be finishing off the stacks, when you had to throw the bales up just as high as you could.

The person on top would have to reach down and grab them and pull them up to finish the load out. We'd get two loads a day and bring them down to Sugar City. We had a goal to get our last load down in time so we could go to Barus' canal and jump in and go swimming.

I started driving when I was six years old and received my driver's license at age 14.

When I was seven years old, my dad had a practice of keeping me out of school in the fall. My job was to drive the truck in the field. When they got a hopper full of grain, I would drive the truck over where they were so they could dump it. I didn't start school until about a month after most kids. When I was in the second grade, my dad started doing that, keeping me out of school, and the local school board told him he had to stop doing that because it was illegal to keep me out of school. That ended my career helping with the harvest for many years.

I played sports. I lettered four years in track, three years in football, and three years in basketball. I set some records in track but they no longer stand. I had the record of the mile, the half-mile, the pole vault and the high jump. I also ran at Ricks College and Utah State. I went to Ricks on a football scholarship. I played at Ricks for two years. I was student body president at Sugar City High School.

Every winter we had to go onto the house, particularly when the snow was deep, to shovel the snow off the roof to ensure it wouldn't collapse the roof. Sometimes we had to ski out and sometimes we would snowshoe out from Highway 32, approximately four miles. Snowshoes were very difficult to use and very hard work. Skiing was pretty easy work. We did that every year.

We always went up there to get our Christmas trees because we owned the land along the creek bank. The trees grew on the north slope. Each year we'd go in and cut the trees. We'd just take the top off because the trees were all big ones. There weren't any small trees that you could cut for just Christmas trees. We would bring the tree to Sugar for our Christmas tree. That was an annual affair.

There was a main highway that went up to Teton Basin which was paved—that's Highway 33. The roads going from Teton Basin over past Felt were all dirt roads. Every time it rained we were in trouble. If it ever rained, you avoided traveling at all cost. After the rainstorms, there was a mud puddle in every hollow, and if you went slow, you'd get stuck in it. If you went fast, it would throw water up on your ignition system, and your car would stall on you sometimes right in the middle of the mud puddle.

You would try and work around the side of the mud puddle if you could; if not, you'd have to judge so you could go fast enough to get through the puddles but not so fast as to throw water up on the ignition system and stall your car. Traveling on those dirt roads was a real problem. If you ever had to, it was so muddy, we were never sure if we'd get where we wanted to go. Having gravel roads was a great improvement in all these rural areas.

BONNIE KRAFCHUK

Donita's Cinnamon Rolls

Fleshy, perspiring, out of breath body
Underarms sailing back and forth
Hands powerfully work the dough.
It's five a.m., the sun's not yet up
And someone's tapping at the door.
She wipes the sticky flour off her hands onto her apron
Unlocks the door and lets the northend farmer in.
She gets him coffee and lets him tell her
about his wife, his barley, his life
while she's elbow deep back in the dough
nodding, smiling encouragement.
Gradually it takes shape, stops taking flour
gets the right amount elastic.
She covers the living mass with a clean, damp cloth,
pushes it to the side of the counter and leaves it to grow.
A few more folks coming in now and she moves around
serving coffee, exchanging the small talk.
She knows who they are, what to say.
She knows them.

With daylight, the waitress arrives and takes over.
She's back in the kitchen, the griddle's warmed up
she mixes pancake batter, checks the bread dough.
It's about ready to beat down.
The waitress calls in two number ones over light
and she slaps bacon on the hot stainless, grates spuds.
The day with its chores is like any other
that flow together like a simple pleasure.
Folks wandering in to share news, gossip
while she's mashing (real) potatoes, or making a cream pie.
City folk might of thought it was a flat no-consequence life
not realizing she was a special kind of glue
stretchy, elastic as any good cinnamon roll dough
that helped to hold the little farming town together.

"Donita and I followed each other around Tetonia and Driggs cooking and working in cafés for over 30 years. I miss Donita; she was good company." —Wilma Hansen, left. Wilma, who says she's 39 and holding, plans to keep on cooking in the café as long as she can. Donita died in 1999.

COMING HOME

CHRISTINA ADAM   FICTION

Blue Skies

IN THE MORNING, there is a live wire fallen down across our driveway, lolling like a round, black jump rope, a walker's tight-wire, swinging two feet off the ground. The far end attaches still to a leaning utility pole, gray with age and pitted with holes. The other end, amazingly, remains connected to the corner of the house. A light wind barely shifts the weight of it, and sparks sizzle at the pole.

I think about safety films I've seen. What action to take in a gale, in an electrical storm. But there has been no storm, no rain, no lightning. And I can't remember whether one should stay in the car or run. Can the tires, no longer made of "rubber," save you?

I call in the dogs, and though we seldom have a visitor, I wonder if I should post a warning sign at the end of the drive. I call the electric company, but no one is in the office, and it takes several calls to reach a woman at home. She promises that her husband will bring a bucket truck "some time today."

My own husband is away working in Baggs, Wyoming, conducting an agricultural survey for the government. Every year, they mail forms, pages of questions to every land-owner in America asking, "How many acres are planted in hay, in corn, in oats? ... How many head of live-stock do you feed? ..." In the corner of the west where my husband works there's always some old-timer who refuses to answer the sur-vey, and our government actually sends out a roving team of house-wives and cash-poor ranchers to find out why.

Though we have only lived here a few months, my husband turns out to be very good at this job. He has a graduate degree in political science but has taken to the west as if he were a native. He can sit in the coffee shop for hours without saying one word. He begins his sen-tences with "If a fella wanted to, how would a fella go about. ..." He has a natural gift for never asking a direct question, and I picture him sitting for hours around kitchen tables, coaxing information out of ranchers who, in point of fact, simply hate the government.

I am from the city, from the suburbs, sunny places where it never even snows, and it makes sense to me to call the company when a live electric wire is hanging where anyone could walk or drive right into it. I'm still unpacking boxes from the move, scrubbing hand-sawn and many-times-painted cupboards in our plain, asbestos-shingled ranch house. From time

to time, I venture out and stare at the wire, keeping my distance as if it were a thick, black snake. I wonder if I should call again.

The weather, though not storming, is bleak. It is November and the hay fields that were golden stubble when we arrived are fading, large patches dampened to a lichen gray. The sky is blue, but so distant, the land seems abandoned, too exposed. I feel exposed, waiting in the tree-less yard.

Finally, a white truck with black lettering on the door and two heavy men in hard-hats in the cab pulls into the driveway. I can see a hydraulic bucket folded into the back of the truck and go out to stand on the steps. It is so cold, my nose begins to run, and I have to go back inside for tissue. When I return, one of the men has buckled cleats to his round-toed boots and climbed the rotting pole, which threatens to give under his weight. He descends the pole without touching anything and walks across the driveway, looking down, to me.

"It ain't our deal," he says.

"What?"

"Not our pole," he tells me.

I still don't understand. If it's not their pole, whose is it?

"I'm sorry ma'am," he says. "We didn't set that pole. I can't touch it."

It still takes me a while to understand that some previous owner owned the pole—and now we own it, and I'm supposed to somehow fix the wire myself.

The man is walking back to his truck, and I go after him.

"But the wire's live? Right? Isn't it?" I'm circling as far away from the wire as I can get and still be able to make him hear me. I realize, I'm terrified of the wire. I'm terrified of electricity.

"Isn't it dangerous?"

The two men stand beside their truck conferring. The older, his hair slicked back with some kind of oil, looks like the comic villain in a melo-drama. The younger, his hands and overalls actually black with soot or grease, reaches in the cab of the truck for a microphone and speaks into the radio.

"We're out here at the White Bridge. Lady's got a problem."

I have some trouble hearing myself spoken of as "Ma'am" and "lady," as if I were older than I am, dottering. I will be 35 this year. I think of myself as young, as strong. I've moved to eastern Idaho to live on a ranch. And I'm getting ready to beg this man to fix my wire.

And I do. "Please," I say to him. "I understand it's not your deal. But my husband isn't home. He's working. He won't be back until Saturday. That's a live wire, right? Please. Isn't there something you can do?"

I understand as I do it, that I've done the unforgivable. I've put someone in a position where he might have to say "No." I haven't said, "Well, if a woman wanted to, how would a woman go about getting someone to raise that goddamned killer wire off her driveway?"

"Well, I don't know, …" he says.

"Please," I say, and now, genuinely, I am crying.

I RETREAT TO THE PORCH, a good safe distance, while the men back up the truck and the younger man ascends in the hydraulic bucket. Enormous clippers and pliers hang from this leather belt. The afternoon has grown so cold I am shivering. I look over to the fallow field behind me just as a blanket of wild ducks takes flight. The same color as the earth, they fill the sky with tiny x's as if a thousand cloves have been tossed in the air.

The week we moved in, my husband drove me to the best sporting goods store in Jackson, Wyoming, and, during the off-season sales, bought me Sorrel pack-boots and a two-hundred dollar down jacket. But I don't have them on. In the hills surrounding the ranch, I can still see yellow, the leaves on aspen trees, which are brighter and more yellow against the blue November sky.

This is something Van Gogh knew. What happens when blue and yellow stand next to each other. The blue in the sky and the ochre on the ground. There is an emptiness between we can't explain, a hollow in the universe.

Standing on the porch, I can almost smell it on the air, that vast blue space, from which winter is coming.

JEAN LIEBENTHAL

Life in the Basin Selectively Recalled

MUD SEASON IS HERE, MY SECOND MUD SEASON. Deep ruts slice the driveway's surface, and the sturdiness of the footprints on my carpet would cause any detective to rejoice. But footprints don't bother me the way they did last year.

My husband's retirement brought to fruition my longtime wish to return to the Idaho countryside where I began. But city life must have made me soft while I wasn't looking. That and the fact that in my reveries of summer sunsets and browsing cows, I failed to remember certain aspects of country living.

For example, mud season and car washes. While there is a car wash 11 miles from our house, it is far from automatic, except for the part that takes car paint right off the body. Nevertheless, for a while I scrupulously followed the routine of zapping my car there once a week. I gradually realized that by the time I got back home my car looked pretty much as it had when I left. Rinsing with the hose on the gravel drive only splashed on a new coating of mud.

When mud season was over, I was soon reminded that mud turns into thick powdery dust that is only quenched by four or five feet of snow.

And while my memory had retained the scent of red clover in bloom, it had apparently blocked out the smells created by the browsing cows, particularly pungent in barnyards in the spring. Another thing I had forgotten was the way people leave vehicles in the traffic lane. Sometimes these vehicles—tractors, trucks, pickups, snowplows—are simply parked there with no sign of a driver or any lights. On other occasions, both lanes are blocked and the drivers of two vehicles are passing the time of day. They don't seem to realize they are making you late for an important appointment!

But as you pass them, another thing you had forgotten about happens: They smile and wave, whether they know you or not.

And now we approach the subject of flies. The flies here are huge beyond description, and it seems that nothing stops them or even slows them down. Indeed, they seem to relish imbibing Raid and Bug Bomb. I almost expected them to buzz back to the kitchen and ask for a second helping.

But in reality, it is birds who dine with us, just outside our window. Many of these beautiful and varied dinner companions are birds I have never seen before. Occasionally, white-tailed deer breakfast in our front yard, and we have seen moose across the lane on our neighbor's property.

These are the positives that soon began to outweigh mud and dust. And anyway, I've started buying clothes with muted—might as well face it—muddy colors, so that when my arm rubs against the car door, the dirty smear just looks like part of the cloth.

As for the car wash, well, I run my car through that in the big city—

regular as clockwork—about twice a year. I also dust off the license plates every month or so when the numbers are no longer legible.

And when I have an appointment, which is rare these days, I leave 10 minutes earlier than I used to. That way, if I see someone I know, I can stop the car in the traffic lane and chat for a minute.

Late last summer, when Jack and I were driving into town, we noticed that a good-sized fire had started at the sawmill. As we debated about whether we should report it, we spotted the fire truck coming toward us, its lights flashing.

We eased off the narrow road as far as we could and stopped. And as the firemen passed, all of them waved and grinned.

JULIA H. HIBBERT

The Question

What brought you to Teton Valley?
You not born here?

What reached out,
trapped you,
refusing to let you forget.

Did you give in soon,
did it take years
to get back?

Friends or relatives showed you,
chance or accident led you,
whim or curiosity
triggered by
a remark, photo or word.

What was it
brought you
to the valley?

Was it
wildflowers, birds
aspen and pines meeting the sagebrush,
mountain streams,
small private lakes.

Hanging valleys holding
moose, elk,
deer, lion, bear,
wolves, coyotes,
wolverines, goats,
bighorn sheep.

The possibility
of a buffalo
passing through.

Huckleberries, fishing,
ranches, farming,
family, people,
history.

Snow, mountains,
peace,
long winter nights,
choice short summers,

Or of course,
The Tetons.

RUSSELL JONES

Going "Out Below?"

COLLOQUIALISMS HAVE A WAY OF BEING SIMPLE for some and complicated for others. For example, new residents of Teton Valley should be aware of some of the peculiar forms of speech the hard-core residents use or they may encounter some frowns.

The other day I was renewing acquaintance with an old friend who has been living in the valley for the past several years. During the course of our conversation, I slipped up and mentioned that I had to drive down to St. Anthony. By the way he reacted, you would have thought that I had insulted his mother.

"You don't drive 'down' to St. Anthony," he said, "You drive 'out below.' Don't you know how to talk?"

I had forgotten all this, but I was in an argumentative mood, so I said, "I don't see what difference it makes. Besides, doesn't 'out below' mean anywhere from St. Anthony to Blackfoot? If I say I'm going 'down' to St. Anthony, I'm being more specific."

"You are dumb," he said. "Teton Valley residents like to be ambiguous. Anybody knows you can't drive 'down' to Idaho Falls. You drive 'out'."

"Then how come when you're in Idaho Falls, you drive 'up' to Teton Valley," I said. "You never hear anybody say they are going to drive 'in' to Teton Valley."

"I can see," he said, "that you need to be re-educated in Teton Valley customs and colloquialisms." With that he started in on his lecture.

"If you are in Driggs," he began, "you can drive 'up' to Victor, 'down' to Tetonia, and 'up' to Targhee. Tetonia is the only place you can drive 'down' to from Driggs in Teton Valley.

"But if you are in Victor, you can drive 'down' to Driggs and Tetonia. The only place you can drive 'up' to from Victor is Targhee.

"You have to go 'out' to Sugar City, West Jefferson, Firth and Ririe. But when you're coming back you had better go 'up.' You can't go 'down' to any of those places, but you can go 'down' to Pocatello or Salt Lake City."

He paused for a breath. "If you're in Cedron, Bates, Clawson, or Chapin, you can drive 'in' to Victor or Driggs, but those are the only places you can drive 'in' from. You can also drive 'down' to Driggs and Tetonia from Chapin and Cedron.

"If you are going to Swan Valley or Jackson you have to drive 'over.' You can drive 'over' from any place in the valley, but you don't drive 'across, up or down.' And finally, if you plan on going to any place from St. Anthony to Blackfoot, you had better say you are going 'out below' or you'll be sorry."

I had sat patiently through his little tirade, but his last comment got my back up. I said, "I am going to prove that a person can drive 'down' to Idaho Falls from Teton Valley."

"O.K." he said, "But I'm not going with you."

I got in my car and started driving. I drove about three miles, hit an icy spot on a turn and plowed into a snowbank. By the time I got out it was too late to go 'down' to Idaho Falls. Maybe next summer I'll try going 'down' to Idaho Falls. Until then I think I'll go 'out' because I hate being stuck in snowbanks.

JESSICA A. KERR

Shoppin' at the Mall

My dad said let's go to the mall,
We brought big bags and had a ball.

We hauled out boards, bikes and tires,
Heater ducts and chicken wires.

If you need a water pump,
Get it at the County Dump.

The County Dump has hidden treasures,
Things that bring me mighty pleasures.

The County Dump is really cool,
You just might find a swimming pool.

When we go there we fill our trunk,
With nothing but that good ol' junk.

Whether it's sun or rain or snow,
The County Dump's the place to go.

BONNIE KRAFCHUK

The Cultural Hub

ONE OF THE OLDEST BUSINESSES ON MAIN STREET in Driggs is Fred Mugler's Mountaineering Outfitters. Running a mountaineering business was not Fred's original intention. While back in New York, he trained to become a civil engineer and worked in this field for seven years. But he became restless and decided to learn about mountaineering retail enterprise. So he contacted the owners of a mountaineering store in Albany, New York, who agreed to allow him to work for them for several months in order to learn about their business.

Next, he researched where he wanted to live and chose Driggs. He had his reasons: "Jackson was a tourist trap even back in 1970, but Teton Valley hadn't been discovered. And when I tasted a Gladys Burger at the Spud Drive In, I knew the place had character!" On April 16, 1971, Fred opened his store and remembers D.J. Freese as his first customer buying bamboo ski poles for $7.50. Now his shop is something of a fixture in town. Valley folk check in with him and Lynda Oleson to learn the latest valley happenings and pass the time of day. Out-of-towners marvel at the clutter and diverse inventory. A popular item sold in the store is the Cultural Hub T-shirt, which facetiously features Driggs as the center of the universe.

Fred has never regretted choosing Teton Valley for his home. He likes the valley's rural features, his proximity to an airstrip and that there's a ski area. One memory that Fred still finds remarkable was the time two Mormon elders came to see him.

"Now these really were elders. They weren't young kids in their twenties but were in their sixties, and they always wore overalls. But setting up an appointment to talk with me about God and the Church was important, so they put on suits and ties to make a date." When they came for the visit, they were back in their overalls. They had flannel boards to help depict historical stories and the personages in them. Fred said that one elder would talk for 20 minutes and the other would nap; then they'd switch.

"They didn't really get anywhere with me. They wanted to come back, but I told them it probably wouldn't be worth their time." He explained, "I don't have much respect for organized religion. You take away a person's capacity to think for themselves, and it takes away the

great satisfaction of their learning to solve their own problems."

Fred saw one of the elders a few days later in town. He looked a little despondent and Fred asked him what was wrong. He responded that he'd been thinking about Fred's comments. "You know how to take the joy of living out of a guy," he told Fred.

In 1975, Fred went back to work as a civil engineer in Alaska. Although he found the work moderately interesting, he was homesick; he found he missed visiting with the steady stream of people in and out of his shop. Although Fred can be irreverent, his insights and strange sense of humor are appreciated; for 20 years people have chuckled over his classified advertisements in the *Teton Valley News*. The shop is definitely a center of sorts, a cultural hub. Surprisingly, he claims to pray a lot: "When I think of how rapid development has become in the valley, I pray for winters like we used to have—winters so severe they scare off some of the developers and their customers."

ANN-TOY BROUGHTON   FICTION

The Moon of the Mailbox Massacre

IN THE MOON OF THE MAILBOX MASSACRE, mailboxes that at other times of the year would stand firmly and confidently rooted on their patch of roadside, live their lives precariously awaiting the next swipe of the Killer Blade.

It is a difficult time for the Mailbox Nation. Their heads sink slowly into ever-growing mountains of snow, until for some of them, only a nosehole allows them to breathe. Others perch on vertiginous cliffs of dog-stained white, like lemmings ready to plummet to their deaths.

One by one they disappear in the night, or perhaps early dawn. No one hears their screams as heads are torn from bodies, arms and legs sent down street, never to be seen again until the Moon of the Shedding Ponies.

Survivors lay akimbo like fallen drunks, heads, seriously bashed from yet another brawl, thrown back with eyes staring crazily into the sky. Mouths hang open, twisted and gaping. Sometimes only a foot is seen dangling from its icy grave, or in one case on our road, a headless trunk, peeping from the snow, two twisted nails sticking out of the neck.

A rare member of the Mailbox Nation remains proud, dignified, pristine. If you were to stop and talk to his human relatives, you would find a family newly moved, and most likely a price tag still adhering to Mailbox's left cheek.

These are the innocent children, the ones who still watch with excitement the cars go by; who open their mouths willingly when the man comes to feed them. Sometimes they act prideful and look down their straight necks at their slanty tired-looking neighbors. I knew a couple like that—one had daisies painted on her face, but now she lives in whatever hole her people hurriedly dig for her in the day's redesigned snowbank. Another I know lives safe and cocooned an arm's length inside a snowcave.

MEN AND WOMEN OF THE HUMAN NATION have pitted their fine creative minds to help the people of the Mailbox Nation make it through the long valley winters. The incredible diversity of contrivances is wondrous to behold.

Neckwear that allows heads to pivot to the side (then becoming em-

bedded irrevocably in solid ice), huge cantilevered bodies with heads dangling from chains (usually only one still connected), feet propped in tire hubs (saw one of those sticking out of a snowpile today), mailboxes in neat snowblown eddies—like Beverly Hills entranceways—so perfect, until their owner goes away for a week.

I'm sorry our mailbox was murdered yesterday before the sun rose, and I mourn the funky yet appropriate aspen support it had; but, well, now we have a dented, crooked, bashed-up box whose door only opens with brute strength, mounted on a two-by-four stuck in the snow, and I feel like we belong.

CAROLE LUSSER

Huckleberries

NO DOUBT ABOUT IT, huckleberry pickin' is one of my favorite things to do. I'll have to be too old, crippled and blind in one eye and can't see out of the other before my huckleberry pickin' days are over.

Sure signs of a huckleberry picker fresh from the patch: purple stains on hands, tongue and behind. Grassy, dirt stains on knees. A big, silly grin on face and tall tales of the day's events.

I just can't imagine my life without huckleberries. Most Sunday mornings, my husband serves up his favorite recipe of huckleberry pancakes. It's a tradition in our household that is as solid as all the berry pickin' outings each summer. We pick enough to put up cases of jam, give away as gifts and then some to see us through the winter and into the summer until the berries come on again. In my experience, huckleberries ripen any time from late July with good pickin's clear through till the first week of September.

When I've read in the paper about there not being enough huckleberries to keep the bears busy up in the mountains, I chuckle. Or talk at the store, "Geez, there just aren't any berries out there this season!" I can honestly say there has never been a season that I have not found enough huckleberries to satisfy my family's craving for the tastiest wild berry known to man and bear in the Rocky Mountains.

I don't have just one favorite patch but three. They are all at different elevations. From one year to the next, one patch might be more pro-

ductive than the other. Each season, it seems there is at least one outing where I pick so many berries I have to go to the car and wash my
hands. It's critical to put the berries in the bucket. Sticky fingers lead
to some berries dropping to the ground and no picker worth his salt
would let that happen.

As all who have picked huckleberries know, the berries are small.
Most are about the size of an eraser head on a pencil. Some are smaller and if you find some as big as the tip of your little finger, that's a big
huckleberry! It takes a long time to pick a gallon of huckleberries. Between my husband and I, we usually pick a combined gallon in a day's
outing.

I've heard there are several species of huckleberries. I can believe it
because I've picked huckleberries with shades of purple, burgundy, cran-
berry, dusty blue or dark blue. Sometimes I wondered if I was picking
huckleberries. But the leaves looked right, the bushes looked right and
the taste was right. Huckleberries have a tangy, distinct taste that de-
fies description. You just have to put some in your mouth or open up
a jar and dig in with a spoon.

You wanna go pickin' with me?! Come on! Let's go. Put on your most
comfortable pair of jeans and a long-sleeve t-shirt. You're gonna get huckleberry stains on your clothes so wear something you don't mind get-
tin' dirty, stained and maybe ripped. I have one pair of jeans I save just
for huckleberry pickin'. Grab a gallon plastic milk jug, cut the top off
big enough to put your hand comfortably through and leave the handle. Wear your hiking boots and bring a rain jacket. Don't forget to pack
a lunch and bring plenty of water.

We're gonna drive up any forest road in the Teton foothills or the
Big Hole Mountains. Huckleberries love to grow in the partial shade
of lodgepole pine forests. I've found huckleberries from about 7,000-
to 9,000-foot elevation or there about. The bushes vary in height from
just one hand high to waist high. When you find a berry patch waist
high, you're in good pickin's. For the most part, bushes are such that
I'm sittin' on the ground, kneeling or perched on a log. Actually, the
best vantage point for spying huckleberries is sittin' on the ground. That
way you can look under all the leaves where those succulent wild delights like to hide.

The sounds, smells and sights of the forest make huckleberry picking special. The sunlight filters through the trees and dapples the
ground as the trees sway with a breeze. The birds and the critters chatter and admonish my presence. The moist dirt beneath me emits an

aroma that mixes with the heady pine scent. Flies drone and hum and flit about. An occasional rain shower will sprinkle through the forest adding the sparkle of water to reflect the sunlight.

A huckleberry outing always presents the opportunity for lots of time to think. I usually hum a tune or sing, but even still, thoughts and images roll through my head. I play back the previous week's events, or thoughts wander to family members far away. I have to be careful I don't get too quiet and focused on pickin' or daydreaming. More than once, I have suddenly realized how hush it is around me and quickly surveyed my surroundings for bear or any other goblins.

A season or two ago, one of my favorite berry patches donned a warning sign. The area was closed to overnight camping because a couple of radio-collared grizzly sows with their cubs were in the area. My ears and eyes were significantly alert for bear, and I never strayed but a few feet from my car. The berries from that patch held a significance unlike earlier years.

Huckleberries mean mountains to me. They sing of wildness and their roots are wilderness. Huckleberries speak of solitude in the forest and a weekend outing highlighted by lunch with a ridge-top vista. But I am not the only one who enjoys the berry. If I see signs of the bear, I quietly and respectfully retreat. There are more huckleberries than the bear or I will ever eat.

MICHAEL McCOY

Back in the Saddle Again

GEOGRAPHICALLY, TetonValley is just a mountain range away from tourist-filled Jackson Hole. By temperament, though, the high basins are as far apart as Mayberry and Malibu. Ever since we met at Grand Targhee, after both landing jobs there the winter of 1973-74, my wife Nancy and I have known that someday we would return to stay. We'll take Andy and Barney as neighbors any day.

In 1993, we purchased a couple of acres in the foothills of the Big Hole Mountains. Two years later, when an opportunity knocked, we jumped at the chance to leave our home of nearly two decades, the relative metropolis of Missoula, for our beloved Teton Basin.

Preparing for the big move is why, early in 1995, we were sitting in the offices of a Montana-based timberframe company. Thoughtfully, head-scratchingly, the staff architect and two key employees glanced about, at us and at one another. One alternately scribbled on a piece of paper and tapped the keys of a calculator. Suspense mounted.

"All right," the scribbler-tapper finally grinned. "This house fits your budget."

Nancy and I looked at each other with relief. For years we had dreamed of building a compact mountain home of traditional post-and-beam construction, but until this moment, we'd feared that such a house was beyond our means.

Building our house was a series of crash-course learning experiences. Blinded by enthusiasm and beguiled by builders, we were quickly several-thousand dollars over budget, even after trimming the master bedroom wing. And after moving in, we didn't stop learning things.

We were in the grip of a howling, blinding, weeklong January blizzard, snowbound. Nearly two feet of feathery powder sat on the roof. "You better move the car," Nancy cautioned.

"Nah. What can a little snow hurt?" I replied.

That night the temperature rose drastically, consolidating the snow into the consistency of pourable concrete. We huddled in bed as the goop thundered off the metal roof, first over here and then over there. In the morning, I ventured out to excavate the car and survey the damage. After twenty minutes of digging, here's what I found: a snapped-off rear windshield wiper, a sheared off front bug screen and a caved-in roof. Inside the car were eight fewer inches of headroom than it was designed to feature.

Bummer.

Now that we've been in our (still unfinished) mountain home for more than five years, the costly and aggravating trials of building it are fading memories. We love how the morning light pours through the windows to dance off beefy recycled-fir beams. We gaze eastward at the Teton crags, watching them change moods throughout the day and with the seasons. Deliciously crisp fall days bring the bugling of bull elk and the unfathomable beauty of aspen stands, spilling like quaking rainbows down the deep, damp creases in the sage-green foothills. The hushing snows of winter blanket the landscape like a giant comforter.

From December through April, our cross-country skis are either propped against the house or carrying us over the snowpack. Spring hints at greater warmth to come, with trickles of snowmelt meandering down the driveway. In summer, we kick back on our broad porch, enjoying the hot days and cool, high-country evenings. More hummingbirds than we can count battle for berths at the feeders, and more company than we hosted in 18 years in Missoula knocks at our door. ("There's only two seasons in the Tetons," a neighbor warned us early on. "Winter and relatives.") And the cows come home.

"The cows" are a herd of Bagley cattle that graze in the nearby Targhee National Forest canyons. Occasionally, a downed fence or open gate permits them to wander at large. Early one September morning three years ago, as I prepared to leave the valley on business, Nancy yelled, "Mac! Grab the bikes—the cows are out!"

I'd love to have it on videotape: Nancy zipping down the dirt road on her mountain bike to gain position beside the 10 wild-eyed beasts, her long, strawberry-blonde hair trailing back; and me, bouncing in bedroom slippers over a hay field to attack from the rear. After a half-hour of whistles, whoops, false starts, wrong turns and near bike-cow collisions, we drove the cattle through the open gate and back onto the forest. "Good job, cowhand," I said, high-fiving Nancy.

We won't be moving back to the city soon. It's way too boring there.

NEIL GLEICHMAN

Becoming Two

Framed in a summer of good climbing,
Before I moved away
I recall most clearly
A leisurely bike tour with a perceptive companion.

Looking past the trees for a view of the peaks
Esther brought my eyes lower,

To the calf only now alive.
Babe was not craving or seeking milk;
Just coming to, like an accident victim.
Momma sniffed once then got to the real business,
Eating the placenta.

She did this with as much focus
As I've ever seen in a bovine.
Was there anything else in that pasture?

Or that universe as she pressed on,
Devouring the bloody slather of her own insides,
With a jaw and teeth and guts
Designed for less gristly fare?

Vegetarian that she was:
There must be something about iron cravings,
After spilling so much to the earth...

Not to mention the pain,
For there she was a good twenty minutes,
Gnawing, sliding the thing down
and then licking the grass.

Only then did she turn on her baby
And lick him clean;
Ten minutes of tongue prodding....

Disturbing enough to the newborn
To inspire his first shaky steps.
At that moment when he gangled toward her,
Finding his way between the confusion of her legs,

She became a mother.

MARY CAROL STAIGER

Donkey Joe

YEARS AGO, my husband Dick and his best friend, Fred, won a donkey in a raffle. "Donkey Joe" was often the source of funny stories that we begged to hear over and over. Donkey Joe had a mind of his own! "He killed a horse once," or so they say.

According to Dick and Fred, they were packing out of hunting camp several years ago. They had each gotten their elk, which meant eight quarters of meat needed to be carried out of camp on horseback. It was

The Agnew Family—Barb, Ariana and Davey—with Donkey Joe.

raining and getting dark.

Donkey Joe was packed with two panniers, one on each side, which hung on a special pack saddle. Then a yellow slicker was tied over the top of this bulging mass. The donkey stood about three feet tall and he now had an additional three-foot yellow "halo" wrapped around his back! The horses were similarly packed, but they measure five feet tall and would carry their burdens on their sides, covered tightly with canvas.

Because of his independent nature, Donkey Joe broke loose from the line of pack animals and took off in the opposite direction. Dick went after him while Fred remained with the pack string. Unbeknownst to both of them, another hunter was just setting up camp down the trail from them. He had picketed one of his horses to the ground while attending to other details.

Along came our Donkey Joe with this huge yellow pack wobbling over his head. He frightened all the horses in camp. They scattered, except for one picketed near a tree. The donkey just kept barreling down towards the campsite, and the hunter watched as the tied horse tried to run away and instead slammed headfirst into the tree and dropped dead!

Dick cautiously approached the scene, not knowing what to say to the hunter whose horse had just gotten killed by Donkey Joe. Finally the tension was broken when the hunter said, "That was the funniest thing I ever saw. If I hadn't seen it, I wouldn't have believed it." Dick apologized as best he could and took the donkey back to the trail heading home.

That's my favorite Donkey Joe story.

DAN GERBER

Wild Horses

OUT MY WINDOW, WILD HORSES. Or they aren't really wild; they are my neighbor's horses wandering over the unfenced fields. They are wild to me. They touch something long before monoxodil and The World

Wide Web. *To see you naked is to see the earth swept clean of horses.* But not really; swept clean *for* horses maybe. My neighbor's daughter rolls down the car window to ask if I've seen her horses. One of them is black and white. Something in me wants her to ask me to saddle up and help her corral them. To ride down the scree slopes of canyons, to come into a wild country where the centaur still lives, to ride together till *the hills run away.* I tell her I saw them move off over Teton Ridge, southeast. Good luck I tell her. She backs on the shoulder and waves as she turns toward home. Wild horses. One of them a paint with a black fiddle head. I look back over my shoulder. I can smell the riders coming. I wait for them on the ridge above the coulee. I will let them come closer, to almost believe they can catch me.

Caballos Salvajes
Translated by Gloria Gomez Whitfield
and Aaron Leigh Whitfield

POR LA VENTANA, CABALLOS SALVAJES. Tal vez no son salvajes de verdad; son del vecino, vagando por los campos sin cercas. Para mí son salvajes. Ellos tocan algo mucho antes de monoxodil y "The Word Wide Web." El verte desnudo es ver el mundo barrido de caballos. Pero no en realidad; barrido por los caballos tal vez. La hija de mi vecino baja la ventanilla del carro y me pregunta si he visto sus caballos. Uno de ellos es blanco y negro. Algo dentro de mi quiere que me pida montar para ayudarla a acorralarlos. Montar a caballo bajando las cuestas del cañón, a la tierra salvaje donde todavía vive el centauro, montar juntos hasta que los cerros se corran. Buena suerte, le digo. Ella retrocede al lado de la calle, saluda, y sale para la casa. Caballos salvajes. Uno, pintura, con la cabeza negra en forma de violín. Puedo oler los jinetes acercándose. Los espero en el lomo arriba del barranco. Voy a permitirlos que se me acerquen, hasta que ellos casi crean que pueden atraparme.

CAROLE LOWE
Major Bear!

I HAVE TOO MANY BEAR STORIES IN MY LIFE, and they are getting progressively more frightening.

The stories started when I was a kid visiting Yellowstone with my family in the '50s. At that time the Yellowstone bears were feeding out of the open dumps. They appeared unafraid of humans. We, unafraid as well, had bear-sighting contests and played chicken—leaving tidbits for them to eat and daring each other to get close. We spotted bears at the garbage cans at the Old Faithful cabins and cried in horrified delight from inside the car as a bold one climbed up onto our hood and peered in.

We didn't see many bears in Colorado where I worked for Outward Bound during the '70s. They had long since been banished. The only bear encounter I recall was a night in the Collegiate Range while I was camping with another instructor, Nancy Smith. We heard the rustling of pots in our kitchen area during the night but weren't alarmed. Small critters often invaded camp because in those days we weren't very concerned with clean camps. I leaned over without even opening my eyes, grabbed my boot and threw it in the general direction, yelling, "Shoo! Get out of here!", then snuggled back into my bed. The noises began again. I nudged Nancy, "Your turn." She randomly tossed the other boot and we went back to sleep. Again that insistent commotion, loud snuffling, clanging of pots, … LOUD SNUFFLING! Suddenly fully awake, I sat up and grabbed my flashlight, illuminating a small black bear eating our leftover dinner.

"Nancy," I squeaked, "are you by any chance having your period?"

"Huh? … Waaa!!!"

When I moved to the Tetons, I had to become more bear aware: leaving clean camps, hanging food and never walking around blind corners in the trail without making noise. I always had my dog. I saw lots of bears during my years as a wilderness ranger in the Jedediah Smith Wilderness and had many benign encounters before I was truly humbled.

I had seriously studied grizzly bears, really wanting to be able to identify one if I should see it in the wild. My grizzled old friend, Bud Baler, a horse packer for the Forest Service and native of Teton Valley, always said, "Don't worry, Carole, you'll know one if you see one. They don't look like any bear you've seen yet."

I was on patrol in the north end of the range, walking the Bear Trail (its true name) from Badger Creek to Bitch Creek. I knew of a great huckleberry patch just on the far side of Indian Meadows and decided to make a short detour off the trail for a little snack. A few minutes later I was locking eyes with a MAJOR BEAR! Frozen with fear I quickly averted my eyes and held my breath as the bear decided my fate. She stared at me calmly, then continued stripping the huckleberries from the bushes. I slowly backed off. The forest was still. As I moved in slow motion, fear filled every pore. The adrenaline made my hair prickle and my heart race. When I was out of sight of the bear I turned and ran like hell!

Down the trail, out of energy and out of danger, I thought about what had just happened. I had come face to face with a grizzly bear in a huckleberry patch. Holy shit! Huge bear with a hump, silvery tips over a cinnamon-colored coat, big round head, little round ears and a dished nose. Now I was so excited I wanted to circle back and sneak up for a better look, but I didn't. I had already pressed my luck. Lupine, my puppy, hadn't seen the bear through the thick underbrush. She could easily have upset the bear, causing real trouble for me. This would be the first time she saved my life.

All of my memorable bear encounters have taught me a lesson and could have been avoided if I had been more careful. I became more sensitive when I made my home in bear habitat, Fox Creek Canyon. Glenn and I bought an old canyon homestead with remnants of an orchard. We worked hard to revitalize the old apple trees and were growing a pretty good crop when we discovered, one lovely autumn morning, that our trees had been ravaged. Large limbs, once heavy with the ripening apples, were lying on the ground (*sans* apples) amidst piles of bear scat! The cover to the hot tub under the trees had been caved in by something very large standing on top of it to pick apples.

I knew then that I had to "bear proof" my home in the fall, just after the first cold spell, for that's when the foraging bears would come out of the mountains to fatten up before their hibernation. The next year, as soon as I saw the first signs of bear—for which I was diligently looking—I picked the apples, every single one, in a very long day and wearily fell into bed. That night there was a bear rage on Fox Creek. In my weariness I had forgotten to put the full baskets of apples inside, but that's not all—our neighbor, Bill Boney, who was a pasta maker, had come home very late that night with a car full of pasta to sell the next day. Because the pasta needed to cool, Bill left the car windows open. Ha! The next morning, on the path through the forest between our houses we found huge steaming piles of pink bear shit. We had lots of laughs about the overstuffed bears thanking us politely for the feast and the hot tub soak!

"Have any cigars?" Hic!

Now the stories get more scary. October, 1998, on a very dark and … . I wish it had been stormy because then maybe I would have SHUT THE DOOR! But it had been a very warm day, a last opportunity to open all the doors and windows for a good airing. I mistakenly left one door open when we walked to Rob and Kate's for dinner. Coming home, laughing and stumbling through the dark, thick woods in a lovely wine haze, I noticed that Ruff and Lupine were acting very nervous, running back and forth, whining. I thought they were hungry and hurried in to feed them. There, in the kitchen, was a medium-sized black bear looking like a contented Pooh, happily ripping open cocoa packets for dessert after a satisfying meal of dog food.

I slammed the door and screamed, just like a hysterical girl, "There's a bear in the house!!!"

Glenn came running. He stood in front of the door that I had just slammed, got all puffed up and flung it open. "All bears out!" he shouted.

The bear left. We were left rolling on the ground in relieved laughter. But it was a little too close for comfort.

I hope this is the last story, because it is definitely the most scary. July, 2000. Yesterday, in fact. I had a few hours in the middle of the day and thought I would run up to Huckleberry Lake for a swim with the dogs. Huckleberry Lake is a little known place that can be reached by an obscure trail kept open only by wild game and locals who know about it. It has always been one of my "power spots"—a place where I can go to find peace and strength. I've spent many hours there. That day I was moving fast, preoccupied with my troubles. I had fallen into a deep trail trance. I did, however, notice a disgusting rotten animal smell, even said a "Whew" to the dogs, but the red flags that should have gone up had I been more "there" were still.

Suddenly, right in front of me, was a bear eating a carcass! It stood upright, looming above me. It stretched its paws into the air, looked me in the eyes and growled angrily. I bolted! For endless seconds I fled mindless, scared-out-of-my-skull, down the trail. A quick glance over my shoulder, and I saw the bear closing in on me. I stumbled over a tree, bloodying my legs. A small voice in my head said, "You can't do this. Don't run."

Then the dogs went ballistic. My brave, fuzzy buddies had gone into fight mode as I was in flight mode. They were between the bear and me in a furious standoff. At last the bear backed off.

I moved quietly down to a spring and, feeling momentarily safe, collapsed in a heap. What had just happened? I truly thought that I had been about to experience a horrible death. I felt weak and dizzy. I gave the dogs my sandwich and many grateful hugs. I gulped some water and thought back through the encounter, trying to remember every detail. To have gotten a positive identification of the bear, I would have needed eyes in the back of my head (now I know where that expression comes from). I do remember seeing a very beautiful deep, rich brown color; very big, maybe seven feet tall standing up; big, round head, very mad and—I'm almost positive I saw it—a ruffled hump behind its head! Sweet Jesus! What's your worst nightmare? BEING CHASED BY A GRIZZLY BEAR!

On the hike home I laughed out loud at the vision of myself as a cartoon character, eyes popping out of their sockets, mouth wide open with tongue flapping and little legs in a futile spin.

This morning, I woke up feeling joy, something that I hadn't felt for a long time. Seems that compared to being eaten by a grizzly bear, even a root canal—or a broken heart—is no biggie. Yesterday, on the drive home from the bear encounter, I heard a story on NPR on the proposed reintroduction of grizzly bears into the Selway/Bitterroot Wilderness in central Idaho. My immediate reaction was to yell "No way!", but this morning I'm seeing life differently. I had an elemental experience, perhaps one that my pioneer grandmother or a more ancient ancestor may have had. That unexpected link to my history has given me the strength I was looking for.

The bear was just being himself and I was just being my self and we're still alive and what joy there is in that!

LINDA MERIGLIANO
Simplicity

*" 'Tis a gift to be simple, 'tis a gift to be free,
'tis a gift to come down where we ought to be;
And when we are in the place just right,
we will be in the valley of love and delight."*

THIS SIMPLE SONG ALWAYS TAKES ME BACK TO 1986, the year of a big blizzard and the year I had the good fortune to meet Chuck Christensen. A February storm over President's Day blanketed the mountains with more than ten feet of snow. Teton Pass was closed for nearly a month. Avalanches ripped through stands of trees that had stood for hundreds of years. In March, we skied up Teton Canyon, weaving our way through forests of fallen spruce snapped into pieces by nature's power.

Three months later I returned to Teton Canyon, this time on foot. Winter had loosened its grip on the mountains, and the heavy snowpack was transformed into torrents of water. I was there as a wilderness ranger working for the Forest Service to take care of this special place that had been my summer home for the past five years. However, this year I was the sole ranger as budget cuts had gutted the field program. Fortunately, some people were willing to help out. One such person was Chuck Christensen.

All I knew about Chuck was that he was a teacher at the middle school. But the glint in his eyes and his weathered skin suggested that this was a person with lots of worthy stories. We met at the trailhead at 8 a.m. Chuck was in his late 50s at the time. His faded jeans, old felt hat, and dark red bandanna made him look part of the woods. I, on the other hand, was only 28, fresh from another year in graduate school with little experience in the woods, but eager to spend another summer learning all the mountains and its inhabitants could teach. We strapped axes and a cross-cut saw onto our packs, stuffed wedges into pockets, and headed up the trail.

It didn't take long before we ran into the first tree across the trail. We shed our packs, unsheathed the cross-cut saw, chopped limbs, and began sawing. I had only used the cross-cut saw for a short time the previous summer so had much to learn. Chuck, in contrast, had grown up using a cross-cut saw to gather firewood in the hills. As we cut, Chuck offered tips: "Don't force it, let the saw do the work. Don't bend over, move your legs with the rhythm of the saw." Tree after tree, we cut our way up the trail. With each new tree, the motion of sawing became smoother and more efficient. Rakers chiseled out wood scored by the cutting teeth and rolled the strip of wood up in the gullet, spitting out long ribbons with each stroke of the saw. Now and then, we would pause to examine the ribbons gathered at our feet. Chuck examined some, looking for whiskered edges. He found none. Responding to my quizzical look, he told me that the lack of whiskers meant that our saw was perfectly tuned for cutting well.

On up the trail, we passed through some aspens that simply demanded taking lunch, or more accurately "dinner" according to Chuck. As we munched sandwiches, fruit and cookies, Chuck said that for him there has always been something cathedral-like in a quaking aspen grove. Indeed, the sunlight filtering through the newly-formed leaves was as magnificent as light filtering through an ornate window. Chuck told me how the peace and quiet in the mountains help him feel closer to the Heavenly Father. He said that sharing trips with others is always fun, but it is the time alone that offers the real chance to learn about yourself and feel the humility that connects you to the larger world.

Back on the trail, the path was obstructed by a huge fallen spruce. Ripped from the ground by its roots, it now lay suspended across the trail. The obvious sag in the middle hinted at the tremendous tension within the tree waiting to be set free. I unsheathed the saw. Chuck studied the big tree, determining where to make the first cut. "This is going to be tricky," Chuck said. I crawled under the tree and readied myself on the other side. We began sawing. Only a few strokes into the soft wood and the cut closed. Careful wiggling fortunately freed the saw. We passed the saw underneath the tree. Again, we began cutting. A few cautious strokes resulted in a loud crack. The tree dropped several inches. Chuck instructed me to pull the saw out. "Stand away," he said. Chuck grabbed the axe and struck the tree from underneath. Two swings and the tension released. A millisecond later, the tree crashed down on the trail. I have never used a saw again without the image of how quickly a tree can snap firmly embedded in my mind.

With the tension released, the routine work of bucking the tree began. Fueled by cookies, we pulled the saw back and forth, making long, sweeping, straight strokes through the green wood. The motion became part of our bodies and the saw ran faster and faster. Two cuts through the big tree and it was ready to roll off the trail. A little nudging with a pole and the task was complete.

There is simplicity here. From the straightforward nature of the task, to the simplicity of the saw, to the beauty surrounding us, nothing seems ambiguous. Eventually, we broke out of the forest and there were no more trees to cut. We turned homeward and headed down. Each freshly cut tree spoke to our day's accomplishment. When we reached the trailhead, it was nearly dark. Neither of us had looked at a watch all day.

A few years later Chuck was diagnosed with bone marrow cancer. Instead of giving in, he headed on a 1,200-mile ride with his mules and let the mountains heal him. I saw him shortly after his return and saw how the mountains had renewed his body and spirit. He told me that horseback trips saved him. The motion of the animal made him feel just fine. "What is most precious is that you can get away from the stress and schedules and adjust your time to the sun. You can eat when you're hungry, get up with the sun, and sleep whenever you get tired. You can say that this is the place I have chosen for myself." Chuck urged me to protect wild country carefully so that when people have had enough of city and society, there is someplace they can go to get away and get re-acquainted with themselves.

It has been 14 years since I first went out in the mountains with Chuck. I have cut hundreds of trees with cross-cut saws since that day. I can still hear Chuck's voice in my head as I attempt to pass along the art of sawing to my trail crew: "Let the saw do the work, move your legs with the rhythm of the saw." The big spruce we cut in 1986 still sits along the Teton Canyon trail, testament to the simple truths of going with the flow, re-acquainting yourself with the beauty around you, and learning all you can from elders.

KELLY RUDD

Summer of Mice

Our side has taken the upper hand
since the decision was made to bait the traps
with peanut butter instead of cheese
and the campaign has turned gruesome:
crippled mice dragging traps around the linoleum
until they're corralled, taken out back,
and finished off with cinder blocks
or cord wood.

And still, when we turn on the oven
the cabin fills with the smell of mouse
     urine.
The mattress has been chewed.
The gentle Labrador Sam has had his
     tongue smashed
in mousetraps, and we continue to suffer
the predictions of hypochondriac relatives
who invoke the words "Hanta Virus"
with certainty and great doom.

I wake to a soft thumping sound and find
a mouse stuck in the wastebasket,
exhausting itself with panicked leaps.
Naked except for slippers,
I step outside and consider the options:
     getting the hose and drowning the mouse in the basket;
     waiting 'til morning and enlisting the neighbor's cat;
     crushing the mouse with something heavy …

My foot reaches out and tips the wastebasket.
The mouse with his quick shadow scurries to safety
across the moonlit driveway and into the woodpile.
I head back to bed without death
on my immediate conscience.
Off come my slippers, my head hits the pillow
and traps in the kitchen crack like artillery.

JUAN CARLOS PEREZ
My Father's Story

My dad, Dolores, came to the U.S.A. as an illegal immigrant when he was 20 years old. He came here to help his parents and to help his brothers who were really poor in Mexico.

My father was born in Tlaxcala in 1960. He is one of eight children and is second to the oldest. Like many people raised in Mexico, he was forced to begin working at a young age and end his education. The family needed the little money he could provide.

Dolores has been here for 19 years. He has a lot of stories from his experiences of coming into the U.S.A. Most of these stories are sad. One of the most interesting is this one. In the year 1979, he had an offer from one of his friends to come to Idaho and make a lot of money. He knew how hard it was to cross the border, but he was interested in this offer because he needed money to marry my mom.

This friend was an experienced "Coyote" who knew how to pass people across the border, but it was very dangerous to do it. First, my father had to pay the guy to help him make the crossing. It was expensive, 500 pesos per person. Then he went with 25 people to Agua Prieta, Sonora, south of Tuscon, Arizona.

When they got to Agua Prieta, they rested awhile. They got ready to make their dangerous trip in the darkness of the very early morning. My dad said this was the easy part. The hard and dangerous part was walking through the long desert. It took them a whole day to do it. He said he and all the people were very tired and hungry. That night was terribly cold, so cold, people died. He was lucky, because he'd brought a good, warm jacket.

Only ten people made it. Some died of the cold, and others died because they were bit by poisonous snakes. My father was relieved when the walk was over, and they were in the U.S. He was in Arizona but still far from Idaho where he was going to work.

Later they were in a hotel in Arizona, and the Coyote said they'd be leaving that night. So he showered, ate something and got ready to go on. At 1:30 in the morning, they left. Traveling in a small car, they began the long journey north to Idaho. My dad thought he'd soon be safe and ready to work and earn money.

When they reached Utah, they stopped to eat and rest for a while.

The Coyote said, "Okay guys. We've made it into America. We're safe now." But Dolores had a bad feeling. He felt someone was following them, and he was right. The border patrol had been following them from Arizona. They knew these Mexicans were illegal, so they were waiting for the right time to stop them and send them back to Mexico.

When they got to Idaho, everyone was happy and ready to go to work on the potato farm. But their dreams came down when they saw La Migra. The border patrol asked them for their visas, and when they didn't have any, took them in their vans. Everyone was so sad. Immigration took them to jail where they spent two months for being illegal immigrants. My father said it wasn't that bad because they had something to eat and the jailers took good care of them.

Two months later they were back in Mexico with no money. But my father doesn't give up, and he tried the crossing again and was lucky and made it.

When he finally reached Idaho, my father worked very hard. His boss liked and respected him. He offered to help him become a resident of the U.S. My dad said, "Are you serious?" The boss said, "Yes, I am. Do you want papers?" My father was so glad for his help.

Eventually he went back to Mexico as a resident of the U.S. and with good money to marry my mom, who was very happy. Now he is a legal immigrant and doesn't have to worry any more about being deported. But he feels bad for people who have to cross "la frontera" illegally, because he knows what it takes to survive and succeed. I feel very proud of my dad because he never gave up.

La Historia de Mi Padre
Translated by the Author

MI PAPÁ, DOLORES, VINO A LOS ESTADOS UNIDOS DE AMÉRICA como un inmigrante ilegal cuando tenía 20 años. Él quería ayudar a sus padres, porque su familia era muy pobre en México.

Mi papá nació en Tlaxcala en el año 1960. Él tiene ocho hermanos y él es el segundo mayor. Como muchas personas él fue obligado a trabajar a una temprana edad y no tener educación. Su familia necesitaba el dinero que él podía proveer.

Dolores ha estado aquí por 19 años. Él tiene muchas historias de sus propias experiencias viniendo a los Estados Unidos. Muchas de sus historias son tristes. Una de las más interesantes es ésta:

En el año 1979, tuvo una oferta de uno de sus amigos para venir a Idaho y ganar mucho dinero. Él sabía qué difícil era pasar la frontera, pero a él le interesaba esta oferta, porque necesitaba dinero para casarse con mi mamá.

Este amigo tenía experiencia como "Coyote." Él sabía cómo pasar gente al otro lado de la frontera, pero era muy peligroso hacerlo. Primero mi padre tuvo que pagar al Coyote para pasarlo al otro lado. Era costoso, 500 dólares por persona. Después se fue con veinticinco personas a Agua Prieta, Sonora, al sur de Tucson, Arizona.

Cuando llegaron a Agua Prieta descansaron un rato. Después estaban listos para la parte más peligrosa de este viaje en la oscuridad muy temprano en la mañana. Mi papá dijo que ésta era la parte más fácil. Lo más difícil y peligroso era caminar por el largo desierto de Arizona. Les tomó todo un día para hacerlo. Todos los viajeros estaban cansados y hambrientos. Esa noche era una de las más frías, era tan fría que las personas estaban muriéndose de frío. Mi papá tuvo suerte porque llevaba una buena chamarra para el frío.

Sólo diez personas pasaron. Algunos murieron del frío, y otros murieron por víboras venenosas. Mi papá sintió alivio cuando dejaron de caminar y estaban en los Estados Unidos. Él estaba en Arizona, pero estaba lejos de Idaho donde iba a trabajar.

Más tarde en un hotel en Arizona, el Coyote dijo que iban a salir esa noche. Mi papá se bañó, comió un poco y se preparó para continuar el viaje. En la madrugada salieron. Viajaron en un carro pequeño, comenzaron el largo viaje al norte, a Idaho. Mi papá pensó que ya pronto iba a estar seguro y listo para trabajar y ganar dinero.

Cuando llegaron a Utah, pararon para comer y descansar por un rato. El Coyote dijo, "Bueno, hombres. Estamos en América. Ahora estamos seguros." Pero Dolores tuvo un presentimiento malo. Sentía que alguien estaba siguiéndolos y así lo era. La Migra los siguió desde Arizona. Sabían que estos Mexicanos eran ilegales y estaban esperando el tiempo de agarrarlos.

Cuando llegaron a Idaho todos estaban felices y listos para trabajar en el rancho de papas. Pero sus sueños se estrellaron cuando vieron La Migra. Los oficiales les pidieron las visas y cuando no las tuvieron, se los llevaron en sus camionetas. Todos estaban muy tristes. La Migra se los llevó a la cárcel. Pasaron dos meses en la cárcel por el crimen de ser inmigrantes ilegales. Mi papá dijo que la cárcel no era muy mala porque tenían comida y los carceleros los cuidaban bien.

Dos meses después ellos estaban en México otra vez, sin dinero. Pero mi papá no se dio por vencido. Trató de cruzar otra vez y tuvo suerte y tuvo éxito.

Cuando Dolores vino a Idaho, él trabajaba mucho. Su patrón lo respetaba y le gustaba como buen trabajador. Le dijo que le gustaría ayudar a mi papá a ser residente de los Estados Unidos .Mi papá le preguntó, "¿En serio?" y le patrón le respondió, "Sí, le hablo en serio. ¿Quiere que le ayude a conseguir sus papeles de inmigración?" Mi papá le agradeció mucho su ayuda.

Finalmente regresó a México como un residente de los Estados Unidos y tuvo suficiente dinero para casarse con mi madre. ¡Ella estaba muy contenta! Ahora él es un inmigrante legal y no necesita preocuparse de ser deportado. Pero él esta triste por la gente que necesita cruzar la frontera ilegalmente porque sabe lo que es necesario para sobrevivir y tener éxito. Estoy muy orgulloso de mi papá por que nunca se dio por vencido.

DAN GERBER

Trying to Catch the Horses

When I give up and turn my attention
to the purr of the grass, the clatter of the aspen,
the clouds lifting off Mt. Teewinot,
I become a curious God, a tar baby,
a clump of grass they must graze.

I reach up and touch the blue with my fingers,
not just the air above my head,
but the sky itself as far as it goes.

KATE WEST

A Friday in March

THEIR FACES AND PERSONALITIES are like scraps on an unpatterned quilt. They surge and shift around me the moment my structure lets up, telling me about their Show and Tell, how Mom and step-dad got into another fight, how many books they read, and homonyms—yes, they've found so many that the "pair" tree of homonyms has run out of space. They love "butt" and "but"—that's first grade humor for you! But they love all homonyms because they understand them!

The room is big, open, carpeted, and neatly crammed with things: hundreds of books in the library corner, including their own published books; three computers; a teepee; and Legos, puzzles, string games, dollhouse, magnets, and other creative games on the table by my reading chair. The bulletin boards are crowded with their work. Three string lines running from the beams droop with art work and bump against my head. The desks are touching side by side in three rows in front of the whiteboard.

The real excitement in the room is in these small, energy-packed bodies. I hope that I'm not editing too much out of them, in my effort to teach them what they need to know.

Todd carries his shoes in and puts them on, after reminders from me. It's taken him a while to get his boots and snowpants off and stowed into his locker. Most of the others have signed in, put their mail into my mailbox (a brown dishpan), and are started on their seatwork. "Dacia, settle down and work. You are very smart. You can get caught up today." The students of the day are changing the date and counting the money in the dimes and pennies cups.

Brett shows me his new baggy pants, from his sister. Andrew tells me about his computer games. Evan hugs me, his eyes dancing with intelligence and mischief. "I brought my lunch today. I'm trying to watch my sugar, you know."

I start to read a Big Book, *Owen*, by Kevin Henkes. I say, "I have a little friend named Owen." "Me too," says John, in his soft voice. Crystal hitches nearer the easel and finally sits still, listening. The story is about a little boy who so loves his blanket, he wants to bring it to kindergarten. Their faces are thoughtful. They all relate to this.

Will has four books to be tested on for Accelerated Reader. He comes to tell me each time he passes a test. Jessie tells me in her soft voice that she has invitations to pass out for her birthday. She also practiced reading last night but forgot to bring the book back. I touch her blond hair and tell her it's all right. Rob hands me a homemade collage that says "I love you Miss Wesst." "Oh, thank you Rob, I'll put it with the other one on my refrigerator. It's beautiful!"

"Em, you need to clean out your desk," I say to this gifted, meticulous artist. "If I sneeze, everything will fall out." She smiles, her dimples showing, and nods.

Cody is such a good worker, so patient as I call on the others. He always knows the answer, and is a true gentleman. Rosa's smile shows many gaps of lost teeth. She's such a hard worker. Roberto asks in his soft voice what some of the story words mean. His English vocabulary is growing fast.

"Peter, you are so quick on your walking cast that I forget your leg is broken." His sentences of assigned vocabulary words are so carefully done! We are both proud.

"David, I can tell you are really working on reading at home."

"Teacher, did you see my new T-shirt?" he asks. "I love it, David. Did it come from your Wyoming grandma?"

Teacher Ann wheels Shyla in. "Hi, Shyla," the kids say. She raises her hand for lunch count, pushes the "Big Mac" to give us a recorded message, and listens quietly. The others fight to push her wheelchair when we leave the room.

My husband comes in to drop off my windbreaker before recess duty. "David, show him your new T-shirt. Rosa, can you read your story to him? Who can show him our wishes-on-a-star?"

It's story time—*Ramona and her Mother*. Idelia has just finished her work, but missed free play. Her English and reading are really coming along. With her shining black pony tail, wearing her new denim overalls with pink trim, she is beautiful. She kneels by the dollhouse, touching things. "Idelia, can you clean the doll house? It's all messy," I say. She nods and smiles.

Suddenly Shyla cries. The kids swarm around her to comfort her. Rob asks, "Should I get her a drink of water?" "Good idea, if you can find her cup." We dry her tears and hug her. The bell rings.

It's 3:25. Silence. The room is in order, and in the dollhouse the mama is holding the baby in her arms.

JOSH WELTMAN
Witcher, Dowser

VERL BAGLEY WAS BORN IN VICTOR IN 1916 and still lives on the family ranch there. I discovered him one fall day, went in search of him really, because I had heard he was a water witcher.

Just contacting Verl over the phone took a half dozen calls.

"Oh, Verl is out helping get the grain in," his wife Elva explained.

I finally caught up with him in front of his low-built ranch house on Cedron Road. He pulled his witching wand out of the trunk of his car and gave me a demonstration. He stepped back and held the wand above his head and took a few steps forward. Gravity appeared to take hold of that stick and it swung down in Verl's tight grip. The stick seemed to have a mind and will of its own as it dove with a staccato motion to the earth. As soon as it hit the ground the stick was lifeless again. It was pointing at the sight of his own well where he had found water in 1940.

Back in the '40s Verl was helping some well drillers and one of them, a witcher himself, showed Verl how to do it.

"It works well for me," he said. "It's kind of natural I guess, but my wife says it's just the devil in me." When the stick passes over water, "I can't hold it up."

I told Verl about my acre of land up in one of the "rugged subdivisions" in the north end of the valley. I had heard that the wells were deep there, so any leads in a spot to drill would definitely help. He said he and Elva would love to go see "the country down in the north end" some time.

A few weeks later, bringing wooden pegs to mark the spot as he had instructed, I met the couple at the old Clawson LDS Church. Verl told me he used to give sermons in the building, which now houses a furniture factory. I knew that their car wouldn't make it up the rough two-track to my land, so they climbed into my truck. Verl, at 83, crawled into the small back seat of the Toyota extended cab.

As we drove north on Highway 33 Verl commented on the old farm equipment as we passed ranches.

"There's an oldie. I've put a lot of grain through a thresher like that." Used to be, he said, horse drawn plows, mowers and rakes were used, and hay was stacked with derricks and "overshot stackers" or "beaver slides." Later, crews ran steam-powered threshers pulled by steel-wheeled tractors and still later by rubber-wheeled tractors.

We headed up Rammel Mountain Road and turned onto a tight trail into the forest.

"You really are out in the boonies," he said.

The sunlight peeked through the pines. The aspens showed the first blush of autumn. We drove through the trees and pulled into the small parking spot that is cleared at the front edge of my lot. Verl climbed out from behind the driver's seat, and Elva stayed seated.

"Mum doesn't walk so well anymore," he said.

Verl took his small chokecherry wand, walked a little way up the road and held the 'Y' shaped stick straight up, his hands grasping either end.

"I feel something already."

He took a few slow steps towards the truck. The tip of the stick began to turn down. The motion accelerated and a strained look passed over Verl's face as the sharpened tip nose-dived into the grass right by the truck. Verl looked around and asked where the boundaries of my land were.

As he fought his way through the thick underbrush, breaking sticks with his worn cowboy boots, Verl told me about some of the finer points of water witching. When the pull can be felt from far away but is not overpowering at the spot the stick touches down, the water is deeper. When the pull is faint but rapidly grows to a very strong pull, the water is shallower. At least, that was how I understood it.

"Let's try up this way. If it's an underground stream we should be able to follow it up." Verl tromped on.

As we made our way through my land, Verl walked back and forth witching his way through the trees. The stream seemed to run along the boundary on one side. It meandered slightly as he traced its path, which followed the soft contours of the land.

Verl held the stick above his head and walked slowly toward the pull. When the wand began to dip, it looked like he was trying to hold up an anvil because he staggered as he tried to balance the load. As he got closer to the source of water, the branch twisted in his fingers and pointed down to a spot on the ground. As soon as the tip touched the ground, it became a regular chokecherry switch. The one spot that he kept coming back to was right in front of my campsite.

"You got your pegs?" I held up one of the wooden stakes that I brought along to mark the well site. "Put one here," he said.

Verl was surprised at what his hands and his divining rod revealed to him that day. The spot that he first found by the truck felt like it was deeper than the spot by my tent. Through his experience underground water often follows the topography. If there is a rise in the land, the water is usually deeper at the top. Presumably the earth is thicker there. On my land at the spot by my tent Verl estimated the water to be at thirty to forty feet deep. It was slightly downhill to the spot by the truck where Verl thought the water was about sixty feet deep.

Verl told me different ways to dig a well by hand. One way is to build open-ended boxes to brace the walls of the hole. As the hole is dug, the walls fall, and new ones are stacked on top. Another method is to pound a sand-point pipe that has a sharp point and holes in the sides into the earth. If water is found, it fills up through the holes that are screened to keep out sediment. Then it is pumped up. This is the method he used when he found water for his house just 14 feet down in 1940.

The way Verl explained it, digging a well by hand seemed much simpler than paying exorbitant fees to modern well drillers. To just about anyone else, I knew, drilling a well by hand would sound absurd if modern well drillers were available.

Elva was still sitting in the truck with a contented look, reading her paperback, when we returned. Verl climbed into the back seat again, and we wound our way back toward the gravel roads. We took the scenic route toward Tetonia. Verl and Elva loved the scenery in the north part of the county. 1999 slipped away, and we entered another time frame as Elva, Verl and I drove through the dry farms and past the slaughterhouse into Tetonia and back to Clawson. As he left, Verl told me to try to find my own water. He paced out the distance on the sidewalk that he guessed would be the depth of the well. He told me, looking straight in my eyes, that digging a well would be easy up there.

That afternoon and evening I could not stop thinking about different ways to tap into my water. It would not be tough digging as the soil is deep there with no rocks. I talked to people about it and heard stories about different well drillings. In one the drill hit a rock, and upon breaking through, an open, limestone-encased channel of water was revealed at a shallower depth than expected.

In the morning Verl called. He had been thinking about my well, he said. He thought the underground stream on my land was shallow but small. It might dry up seasonally or flow slowly. If that were the case I might need a water storage tank, he said. One never can tell. On that spot in front of my campsite he thought the water could be found without the aid of a modern drilling rig.

Others had told me that the water on my land would be 400 to 600 feet deep.

I don't know yet what I will do, but think the sand-point method sounds intriguing. The old homesteaders apparently dug wells over 100 feet deep in rocky soil. On Mormon Row in Jackson a bachelor homesteader named Joe Pfeiffer dug more than a dozen successful wells in the rocky soil, usually 100 feet deep, then dug 120 feet on his own land without finding water. At least on my land the soil is not rocky.

Witching is a dying art. Often modern well drillers and homeowners pick the most convenient spot for the well and begin digging. They might be a bit pickier if they had to dig with a shovel, pulley and a bucket. Depth becomes less of an issue as machines do the digging. Some wells in this valley are 1,000 feet deep.

MARTIN VELASQUEZ

The Arrival

I WAS BORN IN MICHOACÁN, MEXICO, in 1966, the eldest of two brothers and a sister. The poverty was severe. My mother died when I was six years old. My father had to leave us children with our grandmother and go to Mexico City to seek work. Five years later he remarried, and he came back to get us, to take us to the city and send us to school.

Money was still very scarce. My brother and I started working when we were eleven and twelve years old in order to have money for school and for clothes. I finished high school with good grades, but my brother didn't like school and quit to work full time.

I tried to enlist in the army, which is a way to further one's education, gain prestige and find a good position. Academically I was qualified, but my physical exam showed curvature of the spine from doing heavy work at a young age. The army would not take me. Frustrated, I returned to Michoacán, unsure what to do next. When I was eighteen, a friend told me I should go to the U.S., but I didn't try then. I worked as a mason for the most part.

My brother got married when he was eighteen, and my sister, who kept studying until she finished college, got married when she was nineteen. My prospects were not good, and in May of 1985 I decided to try to reach the U.S.

Crossing the border was very hard. The immigration authorities caught us three times, and we had to spend time in jail every time they caught us. Those experiences were bad times for me. I remember hiding all night in the bushes by Highway 5, waiting for a break in the steady stream of headlights so that we could cross unseen. We heard that others sometimes couldn't wait and were hit by cars.

The fourth time we finally made it. We each had to pay the "Coyote" six hundred dollars to take us from Tijuana, Mexico, to Half Moon Bay, California. It took us four months to save that much money. In California the farms needed laborers, and Americans didn't want to do the work. The government finally gave us work permits if we would do farm work. We worked twenty months there and returned to Michoacán with our savings.

Life was very pleasant for a while. I met a beautiful woman with whom I wanted to marry, buy my money was spent. I told my fiancée I would go to the U.S. to work and return in six months, but I returned in three months, and we were married in 1988.

Supporting my wife was very hard in Mexico. I could not earn enough, especially after our two children were born. I had to keep returning to the U.S. to work. By that time I had a green card, so crossing the border was not a problem, but separation from my family was painful. I did that for four years.

In 1992, I was back in California and missing my family a lot. I called my wife in Mexico and told her to bring the children to Tijuana where I would meet her. We found a Coyote to bring them across the border, and we were very lucky. It was expensive, but we didn't have any problems. He hid my wife in a special place behind the refrigerator in a mobile home, and my kids crossed with other kids' green cards.

We stayed in Half Moon Bay three years. I had a good job, but we weren't too happy living there. I was under a lot of pressure all the time. I was a skilled worker, but many times an unskilled man would be preferred to me because he spoke English better. I could not get equal pay for equal work.

One day I told my wife to pack some clothes for a vacation. In four days we were driving out of California. We thought of going to Florida, where she has brothers living, but we decided to stop first to visit some friends in Idaho. I followed the roads on the map. It was my first time doing such a long drive. When we reached Idaho Falls, we called our friends to ask for directions. They were living in Driggs.

While we were visiting, our friends told us to drive around and get to know the area, including Yellowstone Park. After three days I asked my wife if she liked the place. She said yes, and we decided to stay here. I went back to California to get our stuff and came back here to start over. Getting started was hard, but we always had help from friends and other people. We didn't have money but a lot of incentives. Now I am a citizen and my family has legal status, and we are building our own house.

The longer we live here in Teton Valley, the more we like it. I haven't seen any discrimination. The Hispanic community is small, but we feel good living here, and we think we have the same opportunity as any other person living in the Valley. The people are friendly and help each other no matter what color or religion. One thing that caught my attention in the beginning was that people waved to us as we passed on the road. Sometimes my wife got mad at me because she wanted to know why people were waving to us, and I didn't have an answer. Later we learned that it is the way people are here, waving to everybody.

After living here five years, I feel like I'm living in my home town, and my wife and kids are happy here too. At first we hesitated to stay because people said the winters are cold, and storms could prevent us from leaving the house, but it is not that way. Now we see the winter differently. We are used to the snow and like it. I love being outside on those clear days when the sun brightens the snow. I even like shoveling snow if there is not too much of it.

Spring is the season I like the most. The snow starts melting, and the water starts filling the streams. The dark and white mountains gradually turn green from the feet up until they are all green with white on the peaks, and the bluebirds and sparrows that we haven't seen for six months start flying around and singing early in the mornings.

Summer is special too. The valley is beautiful, and the green and moistened ground induces people to work on their yards, fields and houses. The grass is lush, and the mowers are snipping the points with sharpened blades. The view from high in the mountains, with the symmetric lines in all directions through the fields and towns, is a temptation to take up photography. We hope that the valley will always remain as beautiful as it is today.

La Llegada

Translated by Florencia Velasquez,
Maria Teresa Mazo and Julie Martinez

YO NACÍ EN EL ESTADO DE MICHOACÁN, MÉXICO, en 1966. Somos tres hermanos y yo soy el mayor de ellos. La pobreza era muy severa. Mi madre murió cuando yo tenía 6 años de edad. Mi padre tuvo que dejarnos con nuestra Abuelita y el se fue a la Cuidad de México a buscar trabajo. Cinco años más tarde él se volvió a casar y regresó por nosotros. Nos llevó a la Cuidad de México y nos mandó a la escuela.

Aún el dinero escaseaba. Mi hermano y yo empezamos a trabajar cuando teníamos once y doce años de edad para poder seguir estudiando y pagando por nuestra ropa. Yo teminé la secundaria con grados buenos, pero a mi hermano no le gustó seguir estudiando y empezó a trabajar tiempo completo.

Yo traté de entrar al ejército. Es una forma de continuar estudiando, ganar prestigio y buscar una posición buena. Académicamente yo fui calificado, pero mi examen físico demostró que tenía un problema en la espina dorsal que fue causado por hacer trabajos pesados cuando yo era joven. El ejército no me aceptó. Frustrado, regresé a Michoacán, inseguro de qué hacer. Cuando yo tuve 18 años, un amigo me habló de ir a los Estados Unidos, pero no lo intenté. Yo trabajé el mayor tiempo en la construcción.

Mi hermano se casó cuando él tenía 18 años, y mi hermana siguió estudiando hasta terminar la preparatoria. Ella se casó cuando tenía 19 años de edad. Mis prospectivas no eran buenas y en mayo de 1985 decidí tratar de ir a los Estados Unidos.

Cruzar la frontera era muy difícil. La inmigración nos agarró tres veces, y tuvimos que pasar tiempo en la cárcel cada vez que nos agarraban. Estas experiencias eran malas para mí. Yo recuerdo cómo nos escondíamos toda la noche en las ramas al lado de la carretera #5, esperando el momento apropiado cuando no había carros para cruzar la carretera sin que nos vieran. Habíamos escuchado que a veces otras personas que no habían esperado fueron atropellados por los carros.

Finalmente la cuarta vez lo logramos. Cada uno de nosotros tuvimos que pagar $600 al Coyote por llevarnos de Tijuana, México, a Half Moon Bay, California. Nos tomó cuatro meses para juntar este dinero. En California los Rancheros necesitaban trabajadores para hacer trabajos duros, porque los americanos no querían hacerlo. Finalmente el gobierno nos dio permisos para trabajar legalmente. Nosotros trabajamos veinte meses ahí y regresamos a Michoacán con nuestros ahorros.

La vida fue placentera por un tiempo. Yo conocí a una hermosa mujer con quien me quería casar, pero el dinero se me había terminado. Le dije a mi prometida que trabajaría en los Estados Unidos por seis meses, pero regresé en tres meses y nos casamos en el año 1988.

Mantener a mi esposa en México era muy difícil. Yo no tenía lo suficiente, especialmente después de que nacieron nuestros dos hijos. Tuve que seguir regresando a los Estados Unidos para trabajar. En ese tiempo yo obtuve mi tarjeta verde, y ya cruzaba la frontera sin ningún problema, pero la separación de mi familia era muy difícil. Así lo hice durante cuatro años.

En 1992 estaba en California, extrañando mucho a mi familia. Llamé a mi esposa en México y le dije que se viniera con los niños a Tijuana donde yo me encontraría con ella. Yo encontré un Coyote que nos ayudaría a cruzar la frontera, y tuvimos mucha suerte. Estuvo caro, pero no tuvimos ningún problema. El Coyote escondió a mi esposa detrás de un refrigerador en una casa mobile, y mis hijos cruzaron la frontera con tarjetas verdes de otros niños.

Nosotros estuvimos por tres años en Half Moon Bay, California. Yo tenía buen trabajo, pero nosotros no estábamos felices viviendo ahí. Yo estuve bajo mucha presión todo el tiempo. Yo tenía habilidad en el trabajo, pero muchas veces otra persona sin habilidad tuvo preferencia porque hablaba inglés mejor. Yo no podía obtener igual dinero por el mismo trabajo.

Un día le dije mi esposa que empacara alguna ropa para irnos de viaje en carro. En cuatro días salíamos de California. Pensábamos ir a Florida donde mi esposa tenía hermanos, pero decidimos llegar primero a visitar unos amigos en Idaho. Seguimos el camino en el mapa. Esta era la primera vez manejando por largo tiempo. Cuando llegamos a Idaho Falls, llamamos a nuestros amigos por teléfono y les pedimos direcciones. Así llegamos a Driggs para visitarlos.

Por un tiempo nosotros estuvimos visitando a nuestros amigos y conocimos a los alrededores del área, incluyendo el Parque de Yellowstone. Después de tres días le pregunté a mi esposa si le gustaba el lugar. Ella dijo que sí, y decidimos quedarnos aquí. Yo fui de regreso a California a traer nuestras cosas y regresé aquí. Volver a empezar estuvo duro, pero nosotros siempre tuvimos ayuda de amigos y de otras gentes. Nosotros no teníamos dinero, pero tuvimos muchos incentivos.

Ahora yo tengo mi ciudadanía, y mi familia tiene su estadía legal y estamos construyendo nuestra casa.

Entre más tiempo vivimos aquí en Teton Valley más nos gusta. Yo nunca he visto ninguna discriminación. La comunidad Hispana es pequeña, pero nosotros nos sentimos muy bien viviendo aquí y pensamos que tenemos las mismas oportunidades que cualquier persona que vive aquí en el Valle. La gente es muy amigable; se ayuda una con otra sin que importe el color o la religión.

Al principio me llamaba la atención una cosa, porque la gente al pasar en el camino nos saludaba. Algunas veces mi esposa se enojaba conmigo porque ella quería saber por qué la gente nos saludaba, y yo no tenía respuesta. Más tarde aprendimos que así es la costumbre de la gente que vive aquí, saludar a todos.

Después de estar viviendo aquí por cinco años, me siento como si viviera en mi propio pueblo. Mi esposa y mis hijos se sienten felices aquí también. Al principio dudábamos estarnos aquí, porque la gente decía que el invierno era frío y las tormentas podrían no dejarnos salir de casa, pero eso no fue así. Ahora nosotros vemos el invierno diferentemente. Nosotros estamos acostumbrándonos a la nieve y nos gusta. Me gusta estar afuera, cuando los días están limpios y la nieve brilla con el sol. Hasta me gusta limpiar la nieve cuando no hay mucha.

La primavera es la estación del año que más me gusta. La nieve empieza a derretirse y los riachuelos empiezan a llenarse. Lo oscuro y blanco de las montañas gradualmente se hace verde, desde abajo hasta arriba, hasta que están todas verdes con la cima blanca. Los pájaros azules, y los gorriones, que no hemos visto por seis meses, empiezan volando y cantando temprano por la mañana.

El verano es especial también. El Valle es hermoso, lo verde y húmedo del suelo induce a la gente a trabajar en sus jardines, en sus campos y en sus casas. El pasto es abundante y la cortadora de pasto está lista y afilada para cortar el césped. El paisaje de lo alto de las montañas, con las líneas simétricas in todas direcciones a través de los campos de trabajo hasta los pueblos, es una tentación para sacar fotografías. Nosotros esperamos que el Valle estará siempre tan hermoso como lo es ahora.

Backcountry Skiing in Teton Valley

THREE STORIES

BEN FRANKLIN

Bonna Skis and Drying Wool

BACKCOUNTRY SKIING AND TETON VALLEY ARE SYNONYMOUS. I'm quite sure that the two were intended for each other. I've skied in other places but have never gotten the same feeling one gets from a blue-sky February day of perfect powder on Beard's Mountain with the high Teton peaks looming on the near horizon.

I showed up in the late winter of 1975 to help my NOLS buddy, Wes Krause, teach Nordic skiing at Grand Targhee resort. Another friend, Geno Forsythe, had done battle with a tree and lost. While he recovered from his injuries with the aid of several women, I took his place at the resort. There I worked with Tanna Rogers, a stylish telemark skier and a gorgeous blond who, much to my dismay, had a boyfriend. Tanna taught me the telemark turn and the fine art of Nordic track skiing.

After skiing the resort for awhile, I began to explore the area. Backcountry skiing, especially telemarking, was a fledging sport and though people had skied in the Teton backcountry for 50 years, their numbers were low. There was almost nobody on the west slope until the hippies arrived with their 210 Bonna wood skies and smelly wool clothing. I remember making four turns down Edelweiss Bowl in between the splat marks and how sore my toes were from trying to crank turns in low cut Alpha boots.

One of the first locals I met was Greg Amlong who introduced me to nearby Peaked Mountain. At the time Amlong was living in a snow cave in Dry Creek Basin behind the Targhee maintenance shed. After skiing all day, Amlong would soak in the swimming pool, spend the evening reading while drying equipment next to the fire in the lodge and retire to his straw-lined cave to rest up for another day on the slopes. Greg and I skied together for many years all over the west slope of the Tetons. His great strength and gentle nature made Greg the perfect ski companion.

I hadn't been here long when a Utah skier disappeared on Fred's Mountain in a typical Targhee storm complete with heavy snow and whiteout. His friends began to worry about him late in the day and contacted the ski patrol. By the time a rescue team was organized, it was dark.

Wes, Greg, and I rode the chair to the top of the mountain with the patrol and Michael Whitfield, who was the Forest Service snow ranger. We searched the north boundary down to Ricks Basin and had to jump behind some trees when a small avalanche came down on us. The next day we searched for Wayne Farrell on the thickly-wooded, steep slopes that lead into South Leigh Creek. It's hard to forget a name you spend 48 hours shouting into the wilderness. Unfortunately, we dug him out of avalanche debris in the bottom of South Leigh Canyon where he had been swept from the backside of Targhee to his death.

Tom and Dorothy Warren were some of my other Teton Valley first acquaintances. They came to the valley in the early 1970s and built a lodge for Paul Petzoldt. I spent my first couple winters living in that lodge, which was run by Pete Peterson, along with ski bums like Tom Fieger, Jim Buline and Dick Stokes. Pete was a crotchety old cowboy from Montana with a heart of gold who regarded us as extended family. His pancakes and coffee were legendary. If you didn't get enough pancakes, you could always chew on the coffee.

The Warrens took great care of all us wayward boys, and it was an interesting coincidence how many of us showed up at Dorothy's dinner table. I learned a tremendous amount about powder skiing and winter mountaineering from Tom. Dan Daigh, another partner in backcountry adventures, labeled our forays into the mountains "Epic Expeditions" as there was often some complication or mishap included. A winter climb of Buck Mountain with Tom became difficult when we returned to camp and were unable to melt snow for water. The stove refused to work. We spent a parched night after summiting in a storm and then rappelling with waves of spindrift washing over us on the descent.

I began a pattern of spending my summers in Alaska working as a commercial fisherman and wintering in Teton Valley. Over the next five or six years I met more skiers like Bub Talbot, Rico Young, Davey and Barb Agnew, Bev Palm, Marty Thompson, Steve Ingwersen, Dapper Dan, Kane Brightman, Bill Brandenburg, Steve King and Frank Felton. In this fine country, I spent several winters exploring places like Beard's Mountain, Oliver Peak, Mail Cabin, Taylor Mountain, Alaska Basin and

the Snake River Range.

I'm sure most if not all of the places we went had been skied before, but they were new to us, and we hardly ever saw other tracks. I also met my wife, Barbara Sprang, who was my partner on many ski adventures. One of our first trips together was into the Teton Wilderness north of Moran Junction. For five days we broke trail as the snow fell constantly. We took turns of 15 minutes, wallowing up to our waists, and fell into our sleeping bags exhausted every night. When we finally got back to the car, it was buried by the snowplows. After digging out, we headed home. Going over Teton Pass, Glory Bowl avalanched, burying the road, just as we got to the slide. As it was late in the day and the plows didn't operate at night, we had to drive around through Swan Valley to get home.

Rico Young, a lean lanky redhead from Utah, tried to teach me the way of deep powder skiing and the fine art of crack climbing. He brought finesse and a languid fluid style to both disciplines, something my bullish nature was unable to replicate. His easygoing manner made him a much sought-after companion on the ski trails. Rico may never forgive me for all the times he claims that I tried to kill him. There is that time in the Big Holes when we had a cornice break between our skis.

The 1980s bought new faces and innovations. With the arrival of Kirk

Bachman, Chi Melville and Glenn Vitucci, there were new ideas, better equipment, and a renewed vigor. Bachman and Melville partnered with Clair Yost and I to establish Teton Mountain Touring. In retrospect, we were too far ahead of our time to be a good thing. We floundered along for six years before fading into the snow, but managed to support numerous employees and ourselves.

Glenn Vitucci and Carole Lowe, who both guided for us, went on to establish Redezvous Ski Tours and have been very successful at it. Bachman moved back to Stanley where his Sawtooth Mountain Guides has prospered and grown. Clair Yost invented the Yostmark Mountain Noodle, one of the first fat skis on the market, and his Yostmark Mountain Touring ski shop in Driggs is a regional landmark.

During this time, Miles Minson became a ski partner and a good friend. An excellent all-around skier, Miles was soon kicking butt in local and regional track racing circles. Minson went on to coaching at Western State in Colorado and now works for the U.S. Ski Team.

I also renewed a friendship with Bill Danford who was one of the most gifted natural athletes I have ever seen. While his skiing prowess was exceptional, cruising with Billy was always a non-stop laughing affair even when you failed in your quest or the skiing just plain sucked. On a winter climb of Mount Owen, we reached a point just below the summit after arduous trailbreaking on a very cold day. I sat down completely worn out while Billy climbed a 50-foot chimney to the summit. When he returned to where I sat, he pulled out his camera to take my picture as the weak January sun went behind the clouds. His point and shoot camera said in this high pitched squeaky voice, "Too dark, use flash." So of course we had to play with it in the tent that night and later on the way down. We waited until the full moon rose and skied beautiful powder all the way down to Bradley Lake.

John Grassi became yet another partner during this time. John had worked on the Targhee ski patrol and now turned his sights to the backcountry. Together with Rico Young, we formed the High Tetonia Rangers, a loose affiliation of ski bums whose sole purpose was the pursuit of untracked powder. Grassi quickly became an accomplished backcountry skier and pioneer of numerous new ski descents. He was also one of the first skiers in the Valley to use dogpower, harnessing the legendary Poe who pulled him at a rapid clip while the rest of us slogged out to the car.

In 1990 we left the valley and came back to Wyoming. Though there have been many changes over the years, I still have pieces of my heart and soul in Teton Valley—probably also some tubes of wax or bits of food that fell from my pack. I know I am one with the water in the Tetons as I have fallen into nearly every creek on the west slope. At the very least, my misfortunes provided my companions with entertainment.

JOHN BORSTELMANN

Skiing at the End of the Millennium

THE SUN HAD BARELY RISEN above the Teton ridgeline to the east, yet the snow sparkled in the bright sunlight. My longtime ski partner, Lars Moller, his brother Jan Eric and I skied into the parking area at the end of the plowed road in South Leigh Creek on a cold morning right before Christmas at the end of the century. At the turnaround, several carloads of skiers loaded packs, put on skis and completed their departure rituals.

Local guide Glenn Vitucci and several of his clients were preparing to go up to Glenn's yurt on Commissary Ridge west of Beard's Mountain. Other longtime Teton backcountry skiers arrived in battered pickups and newer Subarus. But something had changed from the old days—several of the backcountry powder pigs were unloading snowmachines. "Don't you *#*@$ skiers have anywhere else to go?" hollered veteran backcountry skier John Grassi as he unloaded a snowmachine from his ancient pickup. Everyone laughed loudly.

Lars, Jan Eric and I started striding up the snow-covered road over the rolling, three-mile approach to Beard's Mountain, where we would start climbing the steep slopes. A few minutes later the snowmobiles blasted by, the last one pulling Glenn and his two clients on a tow rope.

I had skied Beard's Mountain since the early 1980s, and the long approach usually discouraged all but the hardiest skiers. I had never seen anyone except members of my own group on past trips, but this day at least six other backcountry skiers aimed for the Beard's Mountain powder. The upside was that we didn't have to break trail—a significant energy saving, and the mountain is big. And these skiers were all locals and old-timers, except the guided clients, so it felt like a powder-pig party.

John Grassi and the others had parked their snowmachines at the Wilderness boundary and skied on. Among Glenn's group gearing up for the climb, Jeff Newsom was theatrically complaining about the load of supplies he was carrying up to Vitucci's yurt to earn a night's stay. Newsom loudly wished he were skiing up with us to carve some powder turns instead of humping a load to a place with gentle slopes. "Carry on, Jeff," Lars teased. "And I do mean carry on."

We climbed the west face of Beard's, enjoying the broken trail. As we emerged from the brushy lower slopes, we climbed more easily through large, widely spaced Douglas fir. The Teton views steadily improved as we sweated our way up, telling stories as we climbed. The early birds had already left lovely turns in the west face snow, symmetrical lines carved sinuously in the snow.

Finally on top of the mountain, we met tall, soft-spoken Steve Ingwersen, another longtime local powder pig. The air remained calm, and the sun warmed us despite the cold air. We ate lunch and swapped stories, reveling in the views of Grand Targhee to the south, the main peaks of the Tetons looming to the east, the massive bulk of Mt. Moran to the northeast. North and South Leigh Creeks dropped away below us. Skiable slopes fell away in all directions, plenty of powder for all of the pinheads who could ever haul their butts up the hill.

Buttoned up for protection from flying powder snow, we swooped down the west face across the upper slopes with thin, wind-packed snow into consistent, deeper powder below. The open slopes eventually constricted into brushy areas of thick aspen, a turning challenge in the thin, early season snow. We zoomed down what had taken us hours to climb in less than ten minutes. The urge to do it again yielded to declining energy and the long ski out. As the sun dropped low in the southwestern sky, we skied steadily to the trailhead and the road home to a beer.

PATTIE LAYSER

Wyoming Journal, '97

MONDAY. GRAY DAY. Rambunctious winds. Dervishes of snowflakes whirl past my window, blowing horizontally but inching up the outside walls. I scrape soup vegetables from their death-grip on a pot bottom, but keep vigil out the window. I scribble listlessly, but crumble the notepapers into a pile of pink snowballs.

Insistent whines, like I haven't been listening, Dancing Dog hesitates before the open door. On the television, the Weather Channel is reporting

Alta, Wyoming, as "blanketed white."

Day Two. Grey day. High winds. Rollicking, frolicking, runaway snow. Our forecast is upgraded to a "dump." I spend the day writing, breaking only to walk to the window. My yard is filling with chimerical creatures of wind-whipped snow.

Day Three. Snow hurtles past the window faster than my eyes can follow. Chimney ravens noisily gulp the room's oxygen. My head aches. I don't dress. I pull on a robe with its fleece snowflakes falling down faded blue arms and dingy white polar bears gamboling around my body. For thirteen hours I cradle steaming mugs of everything liquid, sipping coffee, cider, chocolate, and tea from between locked fingers. I'm grateful for indoor plumbing.

Midnight. I flip on the porch light. One by one, outsized snowflakes sift through its narrow shaft of light. I squint until my nose hurts. Straightening up, I go to bed happy. "It's true, Dog. No two are alike." The Late Night Weather "buries" Teton Valley.

Thursday A.M. Light—diffused brightness—but certainly light, falling from the skylight. I throw the bedcovers from my sleep-warmed spot, dive across the floor to part the curtains. Fiery sundogs flank the rising sun; gilded pinks cosset the mountain's summit. Faced with the sublime, language runs dry.

Downstairs, bits of bark and leaf and anthills of dirt litter the hearth. Opening the back door a skinny 14 inches, betting Dog I can hug log to chest and beat the cold air rushing inside, I'm pulled up short. Outdoors, dry air fires ice crystals, their static glittering against brilliant cerulean sky. I fall in love with crunching back and forth across the deck. It's a carefree sound like that of eight-year-old friends raking their teeth across snowcones frozen hard. I trill my pleasure and my pain. And the neighborhood dogs answer.

Hours later, I switch off the glaring computer, pace off the perimeter of the cabin. Staring outside, roofline stalactites glisten with a film of moisture; jagged fingers of plastic snow curve inward. I think they're scratching on the window, pleading to trade places with me by the fire. "What do you think, Dog?"

He's yawning, scratching his left ear. He only does that when he's up for anything. I'm pulling on silk, fleece, Gore-Tex. "I'm in too."

Breakout! Bright sun makes me blink. I study the world while strapping on my skis. I can get away.

The wind won't hold me back. It's whimpering exhaustion. The sun's an ally. It winks through ivoried aspens.

My forward strides and darting sunlight refract the snow's glare. Now you see me clearly; now you don't.

Dog lunges ahead with syncopated leaps, the field beyond an inviting bowl of sun-popped crystals. Again and again he sinks out of sight, bursting up with an iced muzzle. Chest thrusting forward, front legs powering down, his canine breaststroke quickly outdistances me.

I ski faster. Passing the last cabin, I'm into wilderness miles. Rays of sunlight sprawl across the forest floor like kindred spirits running for freedom.

Abruptly, I change directions to track a snowshoe hare whose footprints descend rapidly to the creek. I tip off balance, with one arm dangling clumsily behind me. My half-cocked whirligig threatens to augur me into the slope.

I like the rabbit's route, but eventually we part company. His light-footed passage belies the difficulty of breaking trail through the deep powder. And he can't stay focused. He backtracks, dizzily circling. How fresh are his prints? Is he tracking me?

I rise from the creek bed gradually, leaving behind a copse of cottonwoods to ski beneath sun-heated pines and fir. Their ghostly limbs drop silent snow bombs, jetting a mist of ice-crystals between my collar and neck. The rare crystals that miss their mark bedazzle like moondust and starlight in the afternoon sun.

I ski farther, trying to figure out the figures in a tree ahead. From a distance they look like nests. Closer, I make out ruffed grouse, birds I know as loners in nature. I can't recall flushing even a pair together, so today I ski cautiously toward the lone aspen. Every branch is tipped by one pair of folded gray wings; each grouse's neck is bent gracefully as he eats his portion of aspen buds.

I turn my skis on edge to push off quietly. Winter's solitude and beauty merge with my frosty breath and sweaty exertion, creating a private epiphany. I feel bound tensions unraveling, trapped emotions sprung; pure joy released. I have grabbed this intimacy from other days of skiing, but each day's climax is a singular pleasure.

Back at home by the firelight I press fingertips to lips, blowing kisses to my restlessness of Sunday and Monday, to the yearning I felt the next two days. Spared cabin fever, I might have missed the first light piercing crystal-wrapped tree branches. I might have hurried past the sedate gathering of ruffed grouse. I might have never taken time to share life with a wild hare.

ROB MARIN
When Your Best Isn't Good Enough

THE RHYTHMIC SOUND OF THE IRRIGATION SPRINKLERS mark the painfully slow passage of time, like a noisy antique clock ticking away seconds—that seem like minutes—during a visit to some sick relative. You don't want to be there, but have you really got a choice? The potato fields around me feel vast and barren in spite of their greenness. They were especially endless a short while ago as I ran through them for miles wearing sandals and paddling shorts. They strike me as incongruous with the panorama of the Teton Range to the east: jagged peaks, still laced with the remnants of winter, the very source of the waters which helped create the present situation. As I lean against my pickup, waiting, waiting, I extract a small blue-winged moth from the corner of my front bumper. It is delicately beautiful, and very much dead.

The sun feels comfortably warm on my skin, and the rolling green furrows of the fields seem so satisfyingly, I don't know, American, against that mountain backdrop. America, the beautiful. It is a gorgeous Saturday, mostly sunny, with a mild breeze and only a hint of possible thunderhead build up, the clouds more attractive than threatening. I look down the dirt road stretching into the distance, followed by power lines from the hydro plant, trying to find the best words, the most useful words, that will aid in the task to come. No one comes for a long while, and I find myself suddenly sobbing, as I knew I would eventually. I am shot through with guilt over finding a trace of joy in this lovely day.

Finally, a cloud of dust appears in the distance, rapidly growing larger. A vehicle moving at speed, yes, a police cruiser. I dry my eyes and organize my thoughts. You can crumble later, I think. It's time to deal. Again.

FOUR-THIRTY ON A FRIDAY IN DRIGGS, IDAHO. I went on a job errand to Eagle Computer Systems, got sucked into their traditional end-of-week margarita session, and never made it back to the office. Instead, I hopped on the company bike, a total junker which we use for such trips about town, and ambled on down to Tony's Pizza to meet friends. I wore flip flops and shorts as I rode down Main, weaving casually, soaking up the afternoon sun, smiling at the casual small-town moment. As always on the company bike, that Andy Griffith whistling theme song ran through my head. I have a "real" job, I thought, but this is unreal.

It was at Tony's that I ran in to Bill Danford, a well-known local adventurer and all-around great guy, who was drinking beer outside in the sun with some buddies. Sunglasses and pitchers, smiles and tanned skin, a happy summer crowd. Billy mentioned having read an article of mine that had just come out in our magazine. We talked about it for a bit, then somehow moved on to the subject of kayaking. Did I want to run the Teton River tomorrow? Sure, but I haven't done it, what's it like? Run it lots of times, ran it last week. It's world class, in its own way, a really pretty little canyon, he said. You could tell Billy really loved the Teton. I did not know Billy well, but I thought it would be great to go boating and get to know him better. I gave him my number and said I'd like to check it out, though inwardly I was a little apprehensive at the prospect of running class V since I had done so little boating this year.

Later, while socializing at the Royal Wolf, my favorite local watering hole, I ran into Billy again, this time with his girlfriend Laurel. He talked up the Teton again, and this time I committed to meeting them in the morning at ten. It would be just the three of us. Again, I wondered if I was up for it, but I told myself I'd paddled enough that it shouldn't be a problem. Scout carefully, I thought, and if it looks ugly you can always walk the bigger drops.

On Saturday morning at five after ten I rolled up to Billy's place, eating a hurried breakfast: a cheap pastry and a container of yogurt. They were just getting motivated and had not even started gathering gear. Laurel seemed nervous and unenthusiastic. Billy was cheerful as always and was doing his best to get Laurel psyched on paddling. She made some comment about wanting to stay home and work in the garden. I felt like I should have called my regular paddling partner, Curtis, who had left a message the previous night about going boating in the morning. He probably would have wanted to head for the Falls River, a fun and easy class III run we had enjoyed a couple of weeks earlier. But, I thought, I need to do something more challenging, I need to get to know some different local runs. I had that little pit in my stomach that tells me when I'm pushing myself. I had that feeling almost every time I went out during my first year of boating, but it always gave way to a feeling of intense satisfaction and clarity by the time the paddling day was done. Higher risks, bigger rewards, I suppose. I told myself that I'd have fun, make new friends, feel more "alive."

I cranked a Pretenders CD, trying to get excited, as I followed Billy and Laurel through the spud fields north of Tetonia, a rolling agricultural region which hardly looks like a whitewater paradise. The rivers out here—the Falls, Bitch Creek, the Teton—run through basalt gorges that wind inconspicuously among the expansive fields of seed potatoes. You can't see any trace of a river until you are practically standing at the edge of a canyon wall, which comes out of nowhere as you approach.

We accessed the Teton River Canyon via a short trail through some farmer's fields. The canyon's natural beauty was something of a surprise, after miles upon miles of agricultural impact zone leading up to it. The river looked almost placid; nothing more than class I riffles, fairly wide and shallow for what I expected to be a fairly stiff whitewater run. Within half a mile, however, the riffles gave way to a class III boulder garden, the gradient increased, and things started looking busy.

Before long we came to our first scout. The rapid looked pretty easy, save a steep, narrow drop at the top. Laurel apologized for being overly cautious and walked the drop, but Billy and I ran it and came out smiling. It was fun and fast, but very forgiving.

A second major rapid definitely looked more toward the class V end of things. It required a number of moves, had some nasty pour-overs lurking in the middle, and the channel was complex. The available slots were getting extremely narrow with the dropping water levels. The river was at the two-foot level or so and had dropped a foot in the week since Billy and Laurel had run it last. The rapid definitely had a "bony" feel as I picked my way through, nearly going upside down in one narrow slot, and broaching on a small rock near the tail end of the rapid. While the water wasn't terribly pushy, it was uncomfortably shallow in places and some of the moves were almost creek-like. Bouncing off rocks was inevitable as I tried to find a clean line through.

The third scout revealed the fastest, scariest looking drop yet. It was perhaps a hundred yards long, with a short slack water section leading into another rapid. The entry was fast and turbulent, with a couple of nasties you definitely didn't want to stumble into up high in the rapid. Halfway down was a weak eddy on the left that might give you a chance to enter the crux section at the bottom with a little more finesse. I was not confident that catching that eddy would do me any good, so I decided to charge past it to set up for the bottom left slot with some momentum. That bottom slot definitely had some stuff kicking up weird fan waves in it. Billy said it would probably be a bumpy ride, but it should be doable. I took his word for it, sucked in a deep breath and headed for my boat. The previous drops had actually given me some confidence, and despite the intimidating nature of the rapid, I found myself curiously calm, almost confident. My roll is totally solid, I thought, if I go over, just make sure to hit it fast so your face doesn't get dragged across these angular basalt rocks.

I wondered at Laurel's calmness here, since this place seemed much more difficult than the short drop she had walked earlier. I decided to run last here, figuring I could use all the clues I could get from their lines. Billy peeled out, Laurel hesitated, thinking I was going until I motioned her ahead. As I turned into the current I set up for the entrance then started charging hard so as not to lose my angle in the turbulent upper section. The first couple of moves were easy. I came off the small drop near the halfway eddy and got ready to accelerate for the bumpy final left slot.

It was then I realized Laurel had pulled into the eddy and was looking down toward the slot with a look of panic. I knew from that look that I should be eddying out as well, but it was too late, I was committed. As I came into the slot I saw a nightmare in the making: Billy's boat was broached sideways, blocking virtually the entire channel, and a fan of water was pouring over his head. I desperately ferried as far to the right as I could, slamming into a rock and spinning sideways. I bumped and twisted and braced, passing perhaps four feet to the right of Billy's body, perhaps even hitting his pinned boat, I don't know. I hope not. I somehow slid off of the rock and emerged from the slot, already heading for the slack water below and looking back up at Billy, who was being pounded by the full force of the river, only his arms and the top of his helmet showing through the torrent of water. Lamely I called out his name, knowing I was looking at a man who had maybe a few minutes to live if he couldn't get his boat off the rocks or bail out of the boat.

I climbed out of my kayak, grabbed my throw bag, and started thrashing my way upstream through thigh-deep water near the bank. Laurel was already out of her boat and similarly working downstream, also with a throwbag in hand. By the time we made it out to boulders with a clear shot at Billy, his boat was already listing, his cockpit facing downstream, his face being forced completely under water. He had let go of his paddle and one arm was waving slowly over his head, reaching for help. I fired my bag just past him and the line drifted down and over his arm, sliding uselessly past his hand, past his fingers. Laurel threw her bag almost perfectly, landing directly in front of Billy's hand. He blindly missed the bag and the rope by an inch and his chances for survival began to evaporate. His arm moved drunkenly as he began losing consciousness. I pulled in my line and started making my way toward the rock where Laurel stood, which was only six or seven feet from Billy and perhaps four feet above the water level. I had to wade, then jump from one rock into a waist deep channel, then climb onto the big rock.

By the time I got there, Laurel was gone. She had desperately leapt into the channel to try and grab her drowning boyfriend. As I climbed onto the boulder above Billy I could see her swimming into the slack water below, where I had pulled my boat out. I tried hitting Billy again with my bag twice more, hoping by some miracle he would grab it and I could somehow pull him enough out of the water to keep him breathing. It was a hopeless gesture. Billy was now unconscious and his arm was only moving because of the force of the water flowing over his whole body.

His kayak was now on its side, its cockpit facing downstream and angled toward the river bottom. I tried to figure a way to get a line to one end of the boat to dislodge it, but both ends were submerged in raging water. I could see that the boat was pinned on two rocks, one on either side of his cockpit. The boat lay perpendicular to the direction of the current. It was a worst-case scenario right out of a swiftwater rescue manual. We were running out of options. I looked down at Laurel, and she was screaming at me to jump. I hesitated; it seemed hopeless, and I thought of what they always tell you in every first aid or rescue course: don't create another victim. But what was I going to do, stand there and watch him die without doing a damned thing?

I backed up and jumped, twisting in the air and opening my arms as if for a big hug. Surprisingly, I landed on his back and managed to grasp Billy around the waist. It felt like the whole cursed river was pounding on my helmet, and my face was buried into his bare back, the current having flushed his spray skirt, paddling jacket and life jacket up around his shoulders. I tried groping up toward his hips, and for a moment I felt some movement like he might break free. I was holding my breath, holding on, but nothing happened. After maybe seven or eight seconds I lost my grip and went over backwards, tumbling out of control through the rapid. I hit a couple of rocks and twisted around, feeling some tentacle-like objects swirling about my legs. I realized Laurel's throwbag was in the water, and I was swimming through 50 feet of tangled line. Just as I stroked weakly toward the left and thought I was going to make the eddy, I felt the very end of the underwater line cinching up around my ankle in a perfect hitch. It jerked taught and the current started pulling me down. I was gasping and trying to say something to Laurel as she was turning away and heading back toward Billy. My head was pulled down to surface level and I realized I was going under.

Well, shit, am I gonna drown, too?

I couldn't breathe for a moment and I started to panic when this light bulb went off in my head—you moron, you wear a knife on your vest for this very purpose—USE IT! Underwater, I reached across my vest and pulled the knife from its holster and strained against the current to reach my ankle. I swiped—nothing. Wrong side. I flipped the knife in my hands, praying I wouldn't drop it, and tried again. This time it cut the line cleanly, and I swore at that moment I'd never use my guide knife again to spread peanut butter or slice tomatoes for a river lunch.

I sputtered my way to the river bank and fell on hands and knees gasping, feeling spent but knowing that my paddling partner was dying. I felt useless, pathetic. I was ashamed at thinking of my own petty tiredness.

I tried again, wading upstream, jumping across a small channel, up on the big rock, the big jump onto Billy's back. Again, I held on for a few seconds. He didn't budge an inch, I lost my grip and swam again, banging my shins across the rocks and feeling stupid again for even noticing the discomfort.

Then once more, back up to the jumping rock, taking an eternity, knowing now that over ten minutes had probably passed since Billy lost consciousness. He was now bare from the waste up. His helmet and all his protective clothing had washed off. The boat had apparently collapsed against the rocks, pinning his thighs, preventing escape. His upper body was purple from the chest up. His heart had stopped circulating, and his blood was being forced toward his head by his position and the force of the current. I took deep breaths and leapt once more, knowing that his chances of survival at that point were basically nil. I only managed to weakly hold on for three or four seconds before the relentless water tore me off again, and as I tumbled downstream I knew for sure that I had failed. Completely. Miserably.

Tired, stunned, defeated, Laurel and I sat on rocks by the river and wondered what to do next. She began to realize that her life was changed forever. She talked of having found happiness for the first time in her life, and how suddenly, everything was different. Up to that point, I had just been reacting, dealing, and the situation seemed almost clinical. As Laurel began repeating that Billy was gone, he was gone, just like that, the scene for me became real, became tragic.

I sat there in silence by a beautiful river with a woman I barely knew, with no words of comfort, deep in a canyon in the middle of nowhere, dumbfounded, empty, overwhelmed by the question, What now?

I propped my paddle upstream of the rapid as a stop signal to other paddlers who might come along. Billy was blocking the channel and a non-scouting party might not be as fortunate as I had been. We had to make a plan. Laurel insisted she was okay, she could stay with Billy as I went for help. Help was a body recovery at that point. I ferried across the river, pulled off my jacket and put on sandals. I grabbed a water bottle and started the 600-foot scramble out of the gorge though a break in the cliffs.

At the rim of the canyon I entered that other world: the fields, the irrigation wheel lines, the panorama of the Tetons. I ran. The car was maybe three miles away, across the interminable fields. The entire mission was to get Search and Rescue to come and recover Billy's body and to give comfort to Laurel. Unbeknownst to me, within minutes of my departure Billy's boat somehow washed off and carried downstream. Once again, I was destined to fail.

The day went on forever after that. I finally reached the truck, ran into a family with a cell phone on the way to the town of Felt, and help eventually arrived. Hours passed, a search began. But as Laurel pointed out as we sat on the canyon rim, none of the details mattered. After the first six or eight minutes down at that rapid, nothing really mattered. Later, as I hauled Laurel's kayak on my back, then mine, up the loose scree to the canyon rim, I thought of Jesus bearing his cross, and Sisyphus rolling his stone forever in Hades. Somehow recovering equipment seemed shallow and insensitive, and the struggling effort felt like penance for some sin. Perhaps the sin was that I could not help but dwell on the beauty of the place, or that I felt so "alive." My senses felt sharpened, yet my spirit felt absolutely dead.

It's Monday night, now, and the search for Billy has been suspended due to bad weather. They spotted him in a log jam on Saturday, almost nine hours after the accident. The Search and Rescue team managed to cut him loose, but his body sank and disappeared again, and he hasn't been seen since. The sheriff says the search will resume toward the end of the week when the water drops further, and grimly, "changes in Billy's body chemistry" should bring him to the surface.

I will descend Teton Canyon once more to look for my lost friend. The best we can hope for is an extremely hollow victory. I will continue to kayak, I'm sure, but I doubt I'll ever run the Teton again.

The whole valley knows. They look at me like a ghost. They stop me and want to know details. They comfort me, they say don't blame yourself, you did all you could, you did your best. But the fact remains, it wasn't enough.

They go on and on with the cliches about how he died doing what he loved the most. I wonder if Billy, slowly losing consciousness as his beloved Teton River took him away, would whole-heartedly agree.

We Are Not Extreme

At Billy Danford's wake, Andy Breffeilh said, "We recoil at the description of our passions as extreme sports, as much as we would recoil at our descriptions as either heroes on the one hand or daredevils on the other. Our outdoor enthusiasms are not extreme. They are simply us."

Early adventurers George Dewey and sons during an early ascent of the Grand Teton from the West side.

DAN GERBER

Smoke

I MUST HAVE LAIN HERE A LONG TIME, in the sun, in the dry grass. I must have fallen asleep, although I don't remember waking. My dog lies curled by my thigh, and the last yellow leaves of the cottonwood tremble. Near Victor a pillar of white smoke rises from the grass and fans out against the sky. All summer the great fires in Utah and eastern Oregon softened the mountains and zeroed the sun down to a resolute ball. Our eyes watered and our noses cracked but we saw flames only on the evening news, 200,000 acres they said, in 7,400 separate fires. Before dawn I saw lights from the football field at Driggs. The potato harvest is on and the Redskins practice early to get the crop in while the weather holds. Snow already in the timberline. A ladybug inching up a long brown stalk makes a leap of faith to my knee, and a few flies buzz in the drowsy thistle heads. A pickup sweeps by down on Hatch's road, from here about the size of the ladybug it seems. Elk season, and a shot rings down from the mountain. How old is this spidery thistle branch? How many day's walk is the sea?

SUSAN AUSTIN

Quatrains for a Backhoe

Dragon's black diesel breath
Yellow rumbling syncopate
Mechanical bucket mind
Not one chokecherry left for the waxwings

Tractor treads portion out even shares
Make a road to make a road
Sheep fescue 〜〜 moose bed 〜〜 harrier nest
Blue grouse fireworks in sage

Level your blade
This road is not a road home
Those yellow fingers thumping my chest
Smell of aspen sap

White trunks burled and scarred black
Moose rump bear scratch porcupine wind

K.H. and M.H.
1906

Shallow brotherhood of roots
Pushed over they pop like femurs
Stillborn moose calf tangled in wild rose
Bedrock for a parking place

Coyote sits patient
While mice scatter
Across a juniper avenue
The sage grouse pedaling circles

You, old sagey breath!
Who sings such a tidy mess
          Trot off
A banquet in your jaws

AFTER OUR BONES ARE ASHES

PETER ANDERSON

Home

INDIVIDUALS IN THE MACHINE-LIKE TEETH of powerful systems and institutions usually emerge the worse for wear. A bit of that happens every day in Teton Basin. The machinery is elsewhere, outside the valley, all around us, giant, grinding machinery far beyond the control of this community, or any community. There's no wizard behind the curtain. The machinery is driven by national population growth, dispersal of wealth and a popular culture which continuously for the last century and more has steered people deep into the Intermountain west.

A hundred and forty years ago, the government offered free land to entice settlers west. But in the last four years more new households were established in the Rocky Mountain states than during forty years of the original Homestead Act.

Growth indeed resembles a clanking, gear-driven system, a predictable function of economics and demographics. It's an amoral phenomenon, and the results here in Teton Basin will, ultimately, be neither good nor bad. Farms convert to subdivisions. Small businesses cave in to larger, stronger competition. Families alter patterns from self-sustenance to middle-class employment-dependence. It's a story old as the hills, and will mean little more than graphs in history books, when all's said and done.

But viewed at the daily, personal level, the events unfolding locally sometimes seem to string together into a long chain of little tragedies. Almost every day each resident of Teton Basin hears about an old friend who's sold out and moved away, a new out-sized building proposal, an expansion plan, a growth objective, another familiar thing diminished or lost.

It's all about growth. Teton Basin's battles are fought on growth's terms, principally arguments concerning land-use. The toll, in vague, messy, un-systematic human values, mounts silently in the background. Greater Yellowstone Coalition Director Mike Clark, quoted in Robert Kaplan's visionary book *An Empire Wilderness*, says, "If everyone gets 20 acres, then we all might as well be dead."

A dour comment, that one, and yet it gets right to the heart of the matter. Can everyone who wants to live here cut out a little space for themselves and still leave a reason for us all to be here?

But I don't think the enquiry ends there. More pointedly, I'd ask what, if everyone carves out a little piece of the west, is signified about our desires, our wishes, our tolerances, and the future of our micro-culture.

Because the carving up is already at hand. It's somewhat too late to wonder whether people are coming west. They are.

The physical future of Teton Basin — what we do with the landscape of the valley floor—is the system about which we hear most of the shouting. It's the only system most people can imagine as eligible for us to affect.

The social future of Teton Basin — what we feel about our communities, how we nourish the lives of individuals — seems, to many residents, beyond the purview of manipulation or even comprehension.

I'd suggest the two futures are so closely linked and intertwined they're practically indistinguishable. And the future needn't be frightening.

IF YOU DON'T KNOW WHERE YOU ARE, writer Wendell Berry observes, you don't know who you are. True, I think, but I would add that if you don't know who you are, then where you are doesn't matter much.

To get at who we are in Teton Basin requires some knowledge of its history.

Grousing café chatter aside, the present epoch is certainly not the worst moment in the Teton Basin's human annals. Recorded history of the area kicked off smashingly with a lethal gunfight between hungover fur trappers and irritable Indians in 1834. A century later, in 1935, martial law was imposed and the state militia sent to Teton Basin to clamp down on striking Mexican farmworkers and bitter disputes over water rights. Terrible winters, with prayer vigils held to plead for improved weather, have come and gone. There were horrible accidents, friends and family killed on farms, the girls killed in the Wind Cave in 1951. Individuals have done evils; murders, rapes, vicious abuses, thefts and fights have torn folks apart here.

In short, despite illusions, this has always been a typical, real human community.

Once, this was a busy, crowded valley. Before World War II, the population here far exceeded what it is now. A big family on every hundred and sixty acres. Twenty-three schools. Six grocery stores. Daily train service. Following that came the long sleep. Now, noisily, the valley is resurgent.

One needn't throw tea leaves, dice or animal bones to glimpse the future; the runes of statistical forecasts foreshadow our fate. When America's population hits 300 million (in roughly twenty years), 20,000 people might live in Teton Basin. Likely, one fifth of them (one-third higher than the estimated current percentage) will be Mexican. Maybe a third will still be Mormon. Political distribution will roughly balance between liberal and conservative. The average age of valley residents will have risen. So will the median education and inflation-adjusted income levels.

It's clearer what Teton Basin won't be. It won't comprise an easily identifiable culture. And it won't be identical to any of its neighboring regions. I happen to think that's great.

Sociologists called upon to describe why people are opting to move to the Intermountain region use the phrase "amenity-based in-migration." Imagined pleasures, perhaps mirage-like, lure people here.

But why do they stay? Family obligations. Business enterprises. Proximity to Jackson Hole. Farming operations. Fond remembrances of Vacationland. No better options at the moment. A low-stress place to retire. A loved one likes it here. Mountain sports. River sports. Natural surroundings. Small town life. Imbedded personal roots.

Motivations are as diverse here as in an urban area. This complexity isn't duplicated in neighboring communities. Jackson Hole, for instance, is filled mostly with move-ins, and one moves to Jackson Hole (and places like it) to forget. Jackson Hole is the Land of Forgetting.

On the other extreme, the traditional, intractable, mono-ideological farm communities around us—Ashton and Aberdeen; Teton and Terreton; Ririe and Rigby—seem oddly doomed to remember themselves forever.

This broad disparity of motivation for moving to or staying in Teton Basin is actually fertile ground for a new culture. It may bring weeds at first, but something new, distinct and lush could spring up here. That's hopeful.

I'm here because this is where I've chosen to settle. It's as close to a permanent home as I've had, or likely will ever have.

Like many, I find it's not necessarily easy to be here. In living here, I sacrifice daily exposure to arts — symphonies, avant-garde theaters, ballets, jazz clubs, experimental galleries, buskers, touring plays, operas, museum exhibitions, blues bars, lectures, street performers, all the things I love that people do.

But automobile traffic is sparse.

Here, I don't get ringside seats to the great dramas of national and international importance. I learn about things after they've happened, after tempers have cooled, dignitaries have gone home, posters have come down, fads have suburbanized. I learn current events from news magazines and PBS and NPR and the internet — in other words, third-hand knowledge, at best. I'm always a step or two behind. I don't scent history afoot, hound-like, in the streets.

But here people know me, and say hello in the bank, and order books from me when I'm buying groceries or collecting my mail.

Here, sometimes, I feel very alone.

But I know most all the valley's elected and appointed officials personally.

I sit in my store sometimes for hours hoping, aching, for a customer to come in.

But there's very little shoplifting.

No offense to my friends who own restaurants, but living here I miss the depth and richness of a vibrant restaurant scene. Likewise, I miss the pure, joyful stimulation offered by an immense variety of shops, markets and bazaars, from sublime to ridiculous.

On the other hand, who has money to buy things?

Here, even though I'm constantly crushingly busy just trying to make ends meet, I often seethe with the anger engendered of boredom and ennui.

But I can hike Table Mountain early in the morning and be back in time to open my store.

Nothing remarkable about all this — it's just mountain-town life.

But am I satisfied with the trade-offs? Is this enough for me? Is my family proud of me? Will I be proud of myself? Will I leave any sort of mark on the world, or by choosing this place, am I ensuring that I'll glance off of time and my species leaving no imprint?

These are the quandaries and fears with which many who live here, and most of those arriving, will grapple indefinitely.

WHICH CONNECTS DIRECTLY to the oft-heard assertion that people who live here don't expect much of life other than their instantaneous pleasures and the luxury of being left alone. Nonsense. Life here isn't that simple, and the people aren't, either.

Poverty in Teton Basin is self-imposed, I've heard. But that's commonly said of everywhere, usually by well-off people.

Life here moves at a slower pace, I've heard. But that doesn't account for the seventy mile-per-hour commuter traffic over the Pass and back each day.

People here don't work very hard, I've heard; they're content to settle for less. Then how to explain the aggressively growing regional land trust, the active Humane Society chapter, the exemplary hospital, the recycling program, the Teton Valley Museum project?

People here don't want change, I've heard. I'll agree that each person hopes some things remain the same indefinitely, but has there ever existed a time or place where everyone wanted everything to remain unchanged forever?

Paraphrasing Hegel, the only thing on earth worthy of fear is the petrified situation, the era which fails to produce movement. None advise change for the sake of change; but intelligent change works courage, maybe even sanity, back into its own soil.

CHANGE IMPLIES TRANSIENCE. Teton Basin culture feels transient now, and probably will indefinitely. Unlike other locales, almost everyone living here claims they may move on. They're keeping their options open. It's not the general ambition to grow old and die here. The lines one hears most often: "If I get tired of Teton Basin, I'll find somewhere more interesting," or "If Teton Basin changes too much, I'll head for greener pastures."

That's another reason it's hard now to live here, and becoming increasingly difficult. Other places lend the illusion, at least, of permanence in culture, friendships, social structure and status quo, landmarks in the fog against which to take one's bearings and navigate. Here, the fog is very thick.

Transience isn't all bad, perhaps. It accelerates cultural evolution, something we could use more of around here. But transience in a community, another aspect of social adolescence, destabilizes and makes cohesive effort nigh impossible.

CAST AN EYE OVER THE HILL TO JACKSON HOLE. Our neighboring valley, as button-bursting tourist destinations tend to do, has inadvertently appropriated its outlying areas as support and spillover regions. Jackson Hole has four such: Buffalo Valley, Bondurant, Alpine and Teton Basin. Of the four, our community is the closest and most-affected.

In Jackson Hole, Teton Basin is the butt of jokes. Jackson Hole (generalization noted) looks down on Teton Basin as less attractive, interesting, progressive and worldly.

Why should Teton Basinites care? Only because, pardon the image, we're in bed together. Since settlement days, this has always been true to a certain extent. It's true now more than ever, and increasingly.

At the same time that Jackson Hole's culture castigates Teton Basin as a sub-alter-ego, the territories out below, downriver, are growing increasingly chagrined at Teton Basin's emancipating political climate and state of mind. Staid, conservative (and down-at-the-heels) Wyoming views Jackson Hole as an alluring but maddening foreign kingdom to whom they're cruelly betrothed. Before long, mainstream Idaho seems likewise likely to view Teton Basin. The two Teton Counties, dubious siblings astride their namesake range, will come to be paradoxically dependent on each other and annoyed by each other, simultaneously.

More tangibly, as the stakes in Teton Basin grow, Jackson Hole (and Boise's power structure) can and will likely deliberately exert increasing influence on the valley's local politics, economics and social affairs. It will be in their interests to do so. It will be in Teton Basin's interest to grow more autonomous, to head outside interests off at the pass.

In some respects, the future looks like a battlefield. Seen differently, regional politics emerges as another opportunity for this community to develop its own distinct personality and voice.

The little bricks-and-mortar public amenities that appear in the valley over the coming couple of decades will greatly influence the quality of the social community to be found here. Will there be wetlands parks and education areas? A network of bike paths? Public transportation? Pedestrian-oriented town cores? A substantive library and conference center? A rec center? Public restrooms? Public art?

Yuppified and urban though these ideas sound to many residents, the truth is that civic projects like these can serve as salve to heal a community rent asunder along demographic fault lines by growth and change. If many of this sort of project come to fruition, the social quality of the community will be greatly strengthened. The benefits of such projects, in other words, aren't just the projects themselves.

The same is true of less-tangible social services. Efforts like assistance for the elderly, recycling, alternative schools, community education programs and crisis outreach services, when instituted, create a sum much greater than the parts.

Teton Basin's adolescence reveals its fundamental schizophrenia, too.

Most peaceful places conceal a social schism of some sort. That may be natural, or even healthy, to a limited degree. Here, the taxonomical division lies between the Mormon half of the community and the incoming non-Mormon settlers.

There's no jihad imminent. Rather, a frosty delimitation, all too familiar to locals, fences in many so-called public enterprises. They have their events and we have ours, say the intimidated ones. The local subcultures don't readily mix, invited or not.

It's true that the old-time community is far harder on its own members than on outsiders, a fact lost on most newcomers to the region. Conversely, the in-migrants are usually most publically resistant to other newcomers, not the old Mormon farm families.

Growth is less than comfortable for those under its wheels. Old-time residents know the feelings: The dispiriting experience of walking into the grocery store or lumber yard and recognizing no one; the bewildering experience of learning about the activities of local organizations and businesses you didn't even know existed; the humiliating experience of having to introduce yourself and explain your background, even describe where your long-standing family property is located, to county employees, store staffs, local politicians, all of whom used to know these things automatically, as if you'd moved here yesterday, as if you were just one of an anonymous crowd. A lifetime sense of belonging is erased in a snap.

But recent arrivals aren't the only people carrying a burden of due cultural sensitivity. Many of the valley's long-time residents insist that being born and raised here confers particular status. But history teaches that nostalgia and systems of seniority are hallmarks of fools and doomed civilizations, respectively.

And anyway, the in-migrant ski-bum history of the valley is now more than 30 years old. That's almost a third of the valley's white-people tenancy, and represents a huge contribution to local history. So Teton Basin's story doesn't belong solely to the pioneer families any more.

Sharing territory, especially between divergent cultures, is always humankind's toughest assignment.

WALLACE STEGNER FAMOUSLY DESCRIBED the western landscape as the geography of hope. He meant many things by that, most of which, I believe, are still true of Teton Basin.

Our best hope lies in the consilience between our physical and social futures. What we accomplish in the way of designing a beautiful valley-floor landscape will depend on the social climate that evolves here in the coming few years, and vice versa.

If we deteriorate into a place where people simply convene to play, bringing little regard or concern about the ethics of community life, then we may not graduate from that adolescent period I've described. At its worst, this valley could become a clot of monomaniacal outdoor adventurers and people untroubled with thoughts about why they do anything.

If, conversely, we manage to grow more cohesive, effective and powerful—a civilization to match the scenery—then we could make great strides in helping the valley avoid becoming just like all the worst once-were-lovely places in the West.

THE SOCIAL FUTURE MUST LEAD THE PHYSICAL FUTURE, not vice versa, because good leadership and community resilience are best-suited to bring intelligent, consensual management of growth. Intelligent management doesn't form after the fact, alchemy-style, out of construction debris, the detritus of foregone conclusions.

EVEN THE SOCIALLY-RESPONSIBLE AMONG US must strive to be multi-faceted, to recall that our obsessions du jour must take into account the whole community, including its past and present.

How can residents fight wilderness issues while dismissing how Mexicans are treated?

How can residents wrestle resort development and ignore the local school district's funding crises?

How can residents advocate hunting culture or skiing culture, but fail to address the widening social schism in the community?

How can residents argue over roads and sewer systems but skip local arts events?

How can residents promote the business community knowing nothing of valley history?

In point of fact, they can't. All seemingly-unrelated human matters eventually interact, especially in a small town. And the parallel is also true: A human community's natural environment is irretrievably attached in millions of subtle ways to its social matrix. The loop is complete.

I'd suggest that when the clock ticks down, how many ski runs you got in or how many elk you shot or how many quilts you sewed or how many children you bore won't mean much. Meaning will lie in the skill with which you drew the best from human history and knowledge and used it to till good soil for the future.

ONE SUNNY SPRING AFTERNOON, feeling unusually resistant to my overswollen ledger of uncompleted tasks, I set out in my rusty old car on a slow tour round the perimeter of Teton Basin. As I drove, it occurred to me — some laconic springtime intuition — to stop at the Cedron Cemetery. I did so, and walked awhile among the graves, recognizing many pioneer surnames, as would any alert person who has lived here even a short time.

I had the lonely hillside to myself. A line of distant cottonwoods hung blurry between land and sky like in a Russell Chatham painting. A snow-chilled breeze stirred the new leaves on the solemn little grove of aspens adjacent. Far off, tractors worked the fields at the Buxton's and the Drake's, and Augie Busch's jet descended silently toward the Driggs airport.

I knelt in the muddy gravel to wipe the dirt from an old carved marker or two. You earth-passengers gone ahead, glancing back, perhaps, over your shoulders at followers such as I: I salute you for nothing in particular, just that you were each here, and now you've gone. A simple truth; those are the finest.

I didn't know the people buried here. I don't carry the freights of their histories. But soulfully I find I've stepped into line behind them. They've broken trail.

I like cemeteries, in a certain mood. I've visited them worldwide. It's not a macabre habit. On the contrary, strength for living lies in the equilibrium between one's forward and rearward perspectives.

Death knocked for me a few years ago (a brain-stem stroke, from which I'll never fully recover). What bit of beauty will I leave behind? Shouldn't a person live in each home, I'm constantly reminded, as if it were the last?

Indifference, then, is the truest enemy. Art, I believe, is the confession that simply existing is not enough. An artist friend once described art's fundamental function as the liberation of people from indifference. Human beings are only truly alive as long as they're not indifferent — to history and culture, the natural world, their lovers, themselves. Curiosity, eagerness, sensitivity, passion — these are the antitheses to indifference. These define the boundary between existence and life. These form our art.

I drove on north and circled back, stopping awhile at each of the Basin's little cemeteries: Bates, Haden, Cache, Darby, stories notched letter by letter into the parsimonious farmland. They're the burial grounds of the old community. Few of the newer generations of residents have gotten around to dying here yet.

Eventually I came to the Victor Cemetery. It's larger than most of the others, Victor being once the beating heart of the valley. Here the wind blew stridently from the canyon, but over it I could hear cars distantly on the highway, rushing home from Jackson Hole, their tires singing like children.

There I stood, among a cluster of gravestones, some tended and others weed-riven and aslant in the thinning sunshine, bereft of flowers wild or cultivated. A grave lay fresh-dug and dark, awaiting an occupant not yet arrived, and I, though not having heard who had died, whispered a few silly words beside the mound of displaced earth (better soil here for planting things, they say, in the alluvium from the canyon), beside the tidy, straight-edged hole in the planet, hoping my respects would not be unwelcome, had anyone known. There I stood in the rough grass surrounded by inadequate evidence of others gone before.

I think when many of us have carved out our little pieces, reason will indeed remain for us all to be here. The reason will lie partly, as it does today, with the mountains and rivers, lonely roads and windswept spaces, and partly, as it always has, with our need for each other.

I do recommend it. Everyone should wait alone for a spell, just once in a while, quietly among the shards of unknown souls. It's hard to leave.

It's hard to decide that you've found a home.

But I do recommend it.

DEBRA PATLA

In Time for Frogs

AN EVENING IN EARLY MAY, last week's snowstorm seems an old memory as you pause along a quiet road in Teton Valley. You could keep pedaling vigorously until dark as planned, but soft breezes and wispy clouds gently steal away your ambitions. Late sunlight winks from puddles and pools. Snowmelt and rain have filled every low place, and water seems to have won a short respite from its endless rush between sky and land. Warmth and moisture are weaving magic spells, creating life from land that so recently felt still and hard but now pulses with sparrow song, insect buzz, and leaf rustle.

"Preeep?" says a startlingly loud voice from the pool of water near your feet, a sound rather like fingertips drawn over the teeth of a comb but rising in inflection. "Pree-ep.", comes an immediate response, slightly different in pitch. "Preeep?" the first voice trills back. From farther away, another similar alternating duet begins, and another, and soon the area around you reverberates with calls, too many voices to count, every acoustic space filled.

You walk toward the nearest voice, straining your eyes, wetting your feet. You see nothing in the water, except perhaps a quick ripple, and suddenly there is a hole in the chorus where the voice was. You wait, motionless. At last, two tiny eyes above a brown head and snout appear just above the water surface. Under the snout, a silvery bubble the size of a jawbreaker juts out, "Preeep?", and suddenly deflates. The loud sound seems impossibly out of proportion with the size of the creature, but again and again it repeats the performance.

The captivating caller is the Boreal Chorus Frog, tiny enough to perch comfortably on your smallest finger. Sometime between March and early May, these frogs emerged from under wood or leaf litter or tangles of willow roots. They spent the winter in a deathlike sleep, with body fluids frozen, limbs stiff, and hearts stopped. Somehow, in ways yet vague to scientists, the tiny glimmer of life preserved in the frozen bodies rekindled, and wetlands of Teton Valley resound with the spring chorus of resurrected frogs.

The calls are purposeful, finely honed by the variable survival and reproduction of frogs stretching back over countless generations and millions of years. Male Boreal Chorus Frogs call to attract females to the ponds and pools used as breeding sites, and also to announce and stake out their individual breeding territories among the other males. Female chorus frogs, who lack the throat sacs used to produce calls, silently arrive at the scene and select among the males based on their distinctive voices and locations. To accomplish mating, the male frog embraces the female from behind, with his forelimbs encircling her chest just behind her forelimbs. Thus paired, the male will cling to the female even as she swims and dives until she excretes eggs, which he then fertilizes with a cloud of sperm expelled into the water. The shell-less eggs, attached to vegetation just under the water surface, hatch into tadpoles within a week or two.

By mid or late summer, barring the disaster of their pool drying up, the tadpoles sprout legs, absorb tails, and develop wide gapes to replace their small round mouths. Converting from a vegetarian diet to exclusively carnivorous (insects and worms), the new generation of frogs emerges from the breeding pool and disperses to live in moist meadows or woodlands. Less than one and a half inches long when fully grown, these green or tan, black-striped frogs are so inconspicuous that seeing one anywhere except right around the breeding pool is a rare event.

While the calling of chorus frogs in Teton Valley can fill the human heart with wonder and the joy of spring, such thoughts are chilled by knowledge that amphibians are not faring well. Silence in lieu of frog voices signals a troubled world, and the silence of the frogs has become apparent worldwide. Not all amphibians in all places, but declines are common enough so that it is distressingly easy to find people able to recount stories about "disappeared" frogs, toads, and salamanders in places where they once thrived. Some biologists conservatively estimate that one third of all amphibian species in the U.S. are experiencing population declines, others think it justifiable to state that nearly all species are in decline in portions of their ranges.

Modern threats to amphibians form a long list. Most prevalent is the loss of amphibian habitat due to development and massive human-caused changes to aquatic and wetland systems. Habitat fragmentation, caused by roads and developments, make it increasingly difficult for amphibians to safely reach critical breeding and wintering sites. Pesticides, herbicides, fertilizers, and a vast array of chemicals pollute water and air, deadly poison to amphibians which breathe and drink through permeable skins. Livestock overgrazing removes vegetation, tramples amphibians, and pollutes ponds. Logging takes away the woody debris and turns moist shady places into land too dry and exposed for amphibians to inhabit. Introduced predators, such as trout stocked for sport fishing, gobble up amphibians. Ozone thinning increases the amount of ultraviolet radiation reaching the earth, killing amphibian embryos in their transparent eggs. Climate changes bring increased temperatures and drought, drying up the breeding pools too soon. Outbreaks of strange deformities occur, producing horrors such as five-legged or eyeless frogs. Previously unknown diseases result in mass die-offs of amphibian populations.

In Teton Valley and surrounding areas, the status of amphibian populations is uncertain and the existing information troubling. Long-time valley residents, such as Elma Wood, can recount how toads were once common in gardens and ditches but now seem to have almost vanished. Others can tell about catching "green leapers" (leopard frogs) at Mud Lake, which appear to have recently vanished, or about silence where chorus frogs used to be almost deafening in Teton Valley in spring. Recent surveys and observation reports show that Columbia Spotted Frogs currently thrive in some areas in the Tetons and occur along some of the mountain streams that extend into the valley, but Boreal Toads are now rare and appear to have declined in both valley and mountains. Tiger Salamanders and Boreal Chorus Frogs are the most widely distributed and common amphibians. But since no federal, state, or local agency has the funding or mandate to monitor amphibian populations in Teton Valley and its environs, no one knows if the area's rare species are imperilled, if common species are declining, or how severe declines from past abundance may be.

Development that eats away at Teton Valley's remaining natural areas and contributes chemicals to soil and water is no doubt steadily taking its toll on amphibian populations. Draining and fragmentation of wetlands inexorably diminishes the number of places where amphibians can breed and survive. Frogs crushed under automobile wheels have nothing in their 200-million-year past to help their species cope with this hazard. Pesticide applications, such as the spraying for mosquitos that often follows in the wake of development near wetlands, will further decimate amphibian numbers.

Although fortunately surrounded by public lands and clean headwater streams, Teton Valley itself is likely to become no-frog's land if development continues at current rates. Islands of remaining habitat in the valley may not be sufficient. Frogs and toads who colonized the valley after the last ice age will be banished to ever smaller pockets of habitat, their isolated populations eventually winking out one by one as natural and human-caused disasters strike.

No development project is ever likely to be stopped to protect amphibians in Teton Valley. No elected official is likely ever to say out loud or listen with a straight face to a plea that a frog population is more important than a developer's need to spawn another Second-Home City and Super-Wonderful Golf Course. No newspaper headlines will announce the demise of frogs and rally citizens to action. Inevitably, collectively, our decisions will culminate in a loss that is mourned quietly and privately only in the hearts of those that remember, and perhaps angrily by generations that follow.

And yet, humans (with the great big brains of which we are so proud) could chart another course for the future of Teton Valley, a future where the natural world is cherished and preserved, where our homes and businesses and ways of movement integrate with rather than dominate the living landscape. A future where frogs wake from their death-like winter sleep to find a world that yet welcomes them. Can this come about, in time enough?

ARTHUR FRAKT

The Future: Problems and Perspectives

I AM NOT FROM HERE. I spent my early years in Newark, New Jersey, where my exposure to nature was limited to the occasional snowfall in Weequahic Park, a one-time owl in a tree opposite my fourth-grade classroom, and of course, the exotic fantasies that a little bookworm derived from Jack London, John Steinbeck and Marjorie Kinnan Rawlings.

Mountains always played a major role in my imaginings. One teacher had erroneously informed us that the beginning of the Piedmont Plateau, which led to the Appalachian mountains, was at a hill on Chancellor Avenue about a half-mile from where I lived. I would tread up that little slope with the same kind of excitement that most kids reserved for their backyard diggings to China.

I would read the high-altitude directions on the side of the Bisquik box, with a distinct mental snapshot of a cabin perched precariously on a steep slope, with biscuits on the stove and smoke pouring from the chimney. And when, in my 27th year, I first saw the Rockies arising from the high plains west of Denver, I knew that I had come home.

LIVING HERE IN THE FOOTHILLS OF THE TETONS after a lifetime of coast-to-coast migrations is the fulfilment of those youthful dreams. And in every season, there are times when the view from our windows reveals a landscape that comes close to being an earthly paradise. But as with all idealized visions, reality presents a picture that has flaws and faults, and which requires careful maintenance lest it deteriorate and fade into something ordinary and unattractive.

Of course, in terms of the human horizon, the mountains will always be with us, and, despite the threat of global warming, it is unlikely that our climate will change radically within the next 100 years or so. The vast areas of national park and forest which surround our valley will continue to provide a buffer and barrier to prevent excessive development and radical change in the landscape beyond the Teton Basin. While controversies and arguments may rage over land swaps, competing recreational uses and timber and grazing practices in the forests, there is no chance that much of these federal lands will be privatized in the foreseeable future.

We who live in and care for this valley must be primarily concerned with the intertwined land uses and social issues whose development and resolution will shape the human environment, not just for the next few years, but for generations to come.

Throughout the West, as demonstrated time and again, a failure of imagination, political will and understanding occurs at a time when our region is at that evanescent point between its rural past and problematic urbanized future. Such a failure may ultimately result in a community whose problems are insurmountable and whose diminished quality of life satisfies no one.

We live in a time when the art of compromise and cooperation seems to have been largely lost. The propensity for people to stake out extreme or immovable positions is almost a universal phenomenon in our society. Whatever the root causes of this development, the emphasis on the virtues of one's own interests and disdain for those seen as competing and threatening make any kind of coherent planning difficult.

We see this in Teton Valley as the seemingly endless search for villains and demons. Consider this list: the Forest Service, with its difficult balancing act among its multiple, congressionally-ordained responsibilities; proponents of various forms of recreational activities, including skiing, snowmobiling, hiking, horseback riding, mountain biking, hunting and fishing; and a wide spectrum that includes ski area operators, subdivision developers, environmental activists, and federal and local officials. Further intensifying the polarization is the propensity of the region's federal and state elected officials to cynically play upon and exaggerate these conflicts in pursuit of their own political ambitions.

The over-riding reality is that significant residential development is inevitable, and while changing economic conditions may slow or speed it up at different times, the future human geography of Teton Valley will be much different from that of the past. Under current land-use and zoning laws, literally thousands of residential lots may result from perfectly allowable subdivision.

About 190 homes currently exist in that relative small part of Teton Valley that's part of Wyoming. Regional planning authorities expect more than 1,200 homes (not including the allowable "guest houses") if all the rural land is developed like the rest of Teton County, Wyoming — and that number is not the legal maximum. While the county's comprehensive plan does require a substantial amount of open space in each subdivision, the most likely pattern will see individual houses built on lots of two to five acres sprawling across Alta and Leigh Canyon.

Land use and zoning in Teton County, Idaho, is far less stringent than in Wyoming, so the potential building lots on the relatively flat land in the valley and up in the foothills of the Big Holes number in the thousands.

If the currently proposed and highly controversial land swap between the Forest Service and Grand Targhee Ski Resort is implemented, population increase and development will advance more rapidly. Emotions aside, the continuing decline of agricultural land value and family farming, and the inevitable increase in the value of undeveloped land for residential purposes, will increase population growth in the valley of both full- and part-time residents for the next 20 to 30 years.

Historic boom and bust patterns cause some to believe that massive growth is not inevitable, but technological developments dictate otherwise. The era of electronic communications and business relations is here. Growing numbers of professionals will seek congenial rural settings like Teton Valley, knowing they can conduct business by computer, fax and cell phone; they may leave the valley only for a few days a month to report to a home office or for business purposes.

Those in the top one-half of one percent in earnings may continue to purchase property and build primary or secondary homes in places like Jackson Hole, Aspen and Sun Valley. Those whose income does not allow the purchase of building lots and homes in the million-dollar and higher range may still have earnings and yearnings that result in the desire to emulate the super-rich, and these folks are drawn to areas like Teton Valley. Their in-migration will lead to increasing demands for the proliferation of services they have become accustomed to.

If we used a crystal ball to look 30 to 50 years into the future, what are the worst—and best—scenarios for Valley development?

The former is easiest to envision, because it has already occurred in so many other places: a pattern of contiguous but essentially unconnected, suburban-type subdivisions occupying more-desirable locations, including elevated areas bordering on or near Forest Service land, waterways (Teton River and the various creeks) and those with scenic views. Most homes will be on lots large enough for pride of ownership but too small for any practical value. People working in service industries or the remaining agricultural and livestock operations will largely be confined to modest housing units (including a substantial number of trailers and manufactured homes) within Driggs or in the mixed-use sprawl along the highway from Victor to Driggs and around Tetonia.

We will not likely see the classic European mountain development with clustered housing, surrounded by large amounts of open space for recreation or agriculture.

With no planned road and pathway development, Little Avenue and Ski Hill Road will be subject to substantial traffic jams and tremendous hazards for anyone wishing to ride a bike, or—perish the thought!—walk.

Similarly, the Route 33 corridor could become a traffic nightmare, particularly during commuting hours to Jackson and during bad weather. Because services will be spread out along the highway, shopping will involve a series of short auto trips and very little opportunity to walk from store to store.

Problems of trash disposal, water-table and air pollution, and a general lack of connectedness between the developments and those who live within them are likely. With many childless people moving in, provision of educational, recreational and cultural services for children and teenagers will become a critical issue as young people may feel alienated and/or ignored. Efforts to provide better services could be resisted by adults who do not believe they will benefit from them and thus will oppose tax increases and bond issues.

This scenario is not inevitable.

In the best case, a thoughtful re-evaluation of land-use planning will take place. Government agencies, working with organizations like the Teton Regional Land Trust, could make every effort to preserve the most critical view corridors, river frontage and land of high-passive or low-impact recreational value as open space and for agricultural purposes.

Contiguous trails and pathways for biking, hiking, horseback-riding and where appropriate, snowmobiling, should be an integral part of the planning-and-development approval process. The creation of the Teton Trails and Pathways organization is a positive step in that direction.

Subdivisions could also be required to devote part of their land, or pay substantial assessments, to allow needed services to keep pace with growth.

Cluster zoning and town-home developments could be encouraged with density bonuses in appropriate areas. Such projects, unfortunately, bear a poor reputation in much of the country because they have often involved shoddy construction, too-little preserved green space and minimal recreational opportunities—but these disadvantages can be improved upon. Developments such as Woodbridge in Irvine, California, demonstrate how desirable clustered developments may be when they result from intelligent planning.

Appropriate housing plans must be available for working-class people and the younger, less-affluent individuals and families critical to a healthy economic and social mix. This has not been the case in other vacation-land areas. Currently in Jackson Hole, the income of those moving into the county is five times that of those moving out, resulting in an unbalanced community where much necessary work is either not getting done or being provided by people who live in unacceptably-poor conditions.

While creative zoning and land-use plans are often greeted with skepticism if not outright hostility in the mountain West, such schemes should be considered. The use of dedicated conservation easements to preserve open space (and reduce taxes for landowners) is a preferred means of encouraging voluntary donations to land-trust organizations. The transfer of development rights, from a parcel appropriate for conservation to another where development makes sense, can provide a reasonable profit to a seller while achieving the same conservation goal. Unfortunately, tax relief alone may not be a sufficient incentive for struggling farmers as the value of their land for development purposes rises to many thousands of dollars per acre.

Beyond the preservation of open space, zoning and planning should encourage the kind of business and commercial opportunities that will reduce sprawl, minimize the counter-productive use of cars, and promote the kind of positive social interchange that a well-planned urban zone helps provide.

OTHER SPECIFIC ISSUES, if not unique to Teton Valley, are not universal and do not fall within the parameters of traditional land-use planning.

Our Hispanic population is growing. Many of these individuals and families, who came here originally to engage in agricultural work, are now settled here permanently and are branching out into the building trades and other professions. It is critical to the social fabric of the community that those of Hispanic heritage are welcomed and encouraged to integrate into the larger community. Prejudices and stereotypes must be avoided. Law enforcement officers, teachers, service providers and businesses must seek to learn the needs and appreciate the values of this population. The richness of cultural diversity that non-Anglo residents bring to life must not be reduced to an acknowledgment of an expanded ethnic foods section in the grocery.

Isolated mountain communities with long winters and limited cultural outlets and social services also have an unfortunate propensity for domestic violence. All too often in the past, both law enforcement and religious leaders discounted this problem's significance. An encouraging note—Family Safety Network has recognized the realities, and cooperation is increasing between traditional providers of aid and activist young women to ensure that shelters and services are available to both help prevent abuse and protect its victims. With growing numbers of economically stressed couples and young families in Teton Valley, and with the concomitant likelihood of increasing levels of drug and alcohol use, this problem must continue to be addressed.

For the most part, the LDS community has shown good will and a positive spirit toward the increased number of non-Mormon residents and their institutions, cultural preferences and social structures. Recent immigrants generally appreciate the values and sensitivities of those who pioneered Teton Valley. Still, it is important for the Valley's future health that contributions and continuing vitality of Mormon society are honored.

At the same time, those whose families have lived here for generations must recognize that one of the enduring virtues of the U.S. Constitution is the requirement that every resident is automatically a citizen of the community and state in which he or she lives. Recent residents have all the rights and privileges of local citizenship. Efforts should be resisted to exclude them from the political process; it's counter-productive for resentment to build against them for their desire to express a significant say in the life of the community, educational programs and other aspects of local society.

In sum, volunteer organizations, public officials, agencies, private individuals and enterprises all have a responsibility to help develop Teton Valley in a manner that not only meets current needs but also provides a positive environment for a high quality of life in the future.

Human talents and resources abound here. I believe prospects are promising for a rich and rewarding life for the generations who live in Teton Valley during the next 100 years — but only if narrow, parochial and self-centered attitudes may be overcome in recognition of larger needs and values others hold dear.

Certainly, we who live here now have a unique opportunity to create an infrastructure that will ensure that the quality of life will complement the physical magnificence with which we've been blessed.

JEANNE ANDERSON   FICTION

Letter to Sarah

Feb. 26, 2026

To: Sarah Divine Pinti
         Edmonds, Washington

Dear Sarah,

Yesterday was my 70th birthday. A landmark, and I'm celebrating by writing you to catch up on all our valley's news.

First, to fill you in on the personal stuff. Peter's doing well; the Institute celebrates its 20th anniversary of think-tank programs this summer. Various foundations sustain the financial end of things, and the rigorous meeting schedule keeps his staff on its toes. Linking it to the new community college has turned out more positively than we ever expected.

We celebrate our 45th wedding anniversary in May—and hope you and Bill can be here for our party. It would be great to see you and compare wrinkles.

As for me, I never thought "retirement" could be so busy. Between serving on the bookstore's co-op board, helping with Institute fundraisers and doing other volunteer work, I'm always heading here and there.

We still love to travel, of course. We haven't yet heard if the Peace Corps will take our old bones, but we asked for two special places (Slovakia or Mexico) about as far apart as possible geographically.

The valley! Where do I start? It's kind of amazing, actually. So much has changed since we moved here, and I have so much to tell you about since you last visited.

When the population reached 25,000 last year, I thought we were maxed out, but with the neighborhood communities again redeveloping—very similar to the old LDS-ward system that was prevalent in the early settlement days—it doesn't seem as crowded as we thought it would. The old five-acre "ranchettes" that were built before the clustering laws in 2010 seem pretty out-of-place now; a surprising number of them are being moved into pre-planned sites within the residential villages, especially Packsaddle, Trailway (what grew out of the old Pass Road controversy) and Willow. (Remember Gary Johnson whom we knew in Seattle? This last project was the old Willow Creek subdivision; he moved here to build that the same summer we arrived here, our very first "it's a small world" in Teton Valley experience.)

Of course, census numbers don't include the additional one-third or so second-home owners (a fairly stable percentage, actually) who've contributed so much in tax revenues and seasonal commerce over the years. The good news is that they've become such an integral part of the basin that some of the old psychological divisions about them don't count much. (I suppose it's also helped by the fact that so many full-time residents of Teton Valley now have their *own* second homes elsewhere—Cabo, Belize, St. George.)

The county's clustering decision also limited further expansion of core development between Driggs and Victor, pushing a lot of services to locations east and west. It was about time! But the writing was already on the wall when the "fingers" were added in either direction to join the light-rail that runs from Felt to Teton Springs. That speedy system was developed as an alternative to cars when gas finally hit $7 a gallon, and it's much more efficient than electromobiles. It has made it possible for people from all over the basin to access all the areas we need to, without the pollution and traffic of motor vehicles.

Light-rail has truly served us well. Sometimes I can't believe we thought it was normal for every single person to drive themselves up and down the old Highway in a gas-guzzling car. (But then I thought that in Seattle in the early '80s!) It seems amazing that such a small population can support mass transit, but we do. As far as riding the light-rail goes, I never tire of the view out those big windows! And it makes the connection to the Jackson Pass Tunnel so much easier.

Most folks coming over "the hill" ride the bullet train through the Tunnel to the Springs. Real estate is again on the fast-growth track over in Jackson after a series of "busts," but a surprising number of people commute to provide service workers so high in demand on this side. It's easier on people now that the trip is fast and safe, and the two counties are working together so well to solve mutual problems. Never thought it would happen, but Jackson's decline taught us all many lessons.

As you know, the return to "authenticism" has been a boon for our economy but the downfall of our sister-city. Despite its problems, however, it's still kind of fun to go and see the restored relics of cowboy "kitsch" and drive through the old "trophy homes." Many have been turned into workers' housing or short-stay lodging for wilderness guests, which really helps the Parks. It's been a great option, particularly since the feds limited overnight accommodations and now completely prohibit single-vehicle excursions in Yellowstone and Grand Teton.

Must say, however, the turnaround in the environmental damage caused by old-style visitors has been phenomenal. Old Faithful's erupting again, on somewhat of a regular cycle (once every hour and a half, where it used to be about once every 70 minutes.) The no-lodging decision also means that the new Jed Smith Wilderness National Park won't ever have the same traffic congestion as the older parks.

Tolls on the Teton Pass Scenic Road, however, remain higher than most of us would like (that's what primarily funds the joint Teton projects). It makes a simple trip of wildlife viewing and/or reaching Glory Bowl Ski Area on the pricey side. Luckily, our senior citizen status makes it possible for us to purchase a lower-cost sticker for our electromobile. Glad it's annual or we'd go broke in the summer taking guests up there.

Some things don't change — Teton Valley's two seasons remain "winter" and "company." You, Sarah, haven't contributed to that problem, however. Remember the welcome mat is always out!

We don't have much to complain about. Grand Targhee's skier days are reaching capacity, due largely to the perception of the place as the "last best place" to ski with your family. The 25 private homes at the base are in great demand for rental—a compromise reached when the extensive land exchange proposal was dropped after 12 years of legal battles.

Everyone loves the free Italian-style funiculare that runs up the hill from Alta Town; what a speedy and scenic way to arrive safely! The former cat-skiing area is fully laced with runs, and they expect skier days to hit an all-time high next year as the popularity of the resort rises.

The corporation of owners, which now includes a lot of us basin residents, is fairly pleased with the sustainable-partnership arrangement created in the courts; now *that* was a piece of revolutionarily cooperative decision-making! "Ski Hill Road" retains some of its charm because the upper section is only accessible to those with computer-keys to the village homes. Alta Town will likely become Alta City, soon.

Over on the Big Hole side, the Kaufman/Hibbert/Robson snowmobile center attracts an ever-increasing number of those addicted to the thrill of the quiet speed of high-tech snowmachines. Every once in a while, an old-fashioned (noisy) job goes by, but pretty much, the world of this sport has changed. The feds were also wise to create huge open areas where fast-riding snowmobiles could still hit the backcountry without endangering slower riders or cross-country skiers. Again, all it took was some alternatives becoming more attractive for people to begin to see doling out the space and protecting the environment in a new way.

Everybody's on the green bandwagon now—and we really have no choice. Remember sorting our trash in Seattle way back when we shared the house in Montlake when Peter was at school? Another urban trend that definitely sifted to this more rural area. You'll be proud to know our recycling center, expanded many times from that old hanger built around the turn of the century, now collects more per household for its size service area than any other in the country.

And another plus: the Land Trust's conservation efforts now protect more than 200,000 acres of open-space. This land has been preserved through the good efforts of property-owners of all stripes, and the Teton River remains closed to further development. Your grand-kids will always have a place to fish! Of course, it took a lot of vision to get that going. It's Mike Whitfield's legacy and a damn fine one.

You'll appreciate that intellectually we're thriving too. The public now enjoys the tremendous collections of books and computer resources available at the libraries in Victor in the south and at Dry Ridge up north. The new Paul Allen library outglosses the original Valley of the Tetons, but both have their charm. It looks like a Driggs facility will finally be opening within the next couple of years. We've already decided to leave our extensive private collection for public use here. (Who knows, the entire Anderson compound may evolve into what we originally hoped it would be—a writer's camp.)

The Packsaddle Physics Project, started by Leon Lederman and others from the Fermi Lab, gathers a wide array of scientists who love this place as a retreat and a relief from urban congestion. They are all so willing to stop by the Institute and lend a fresh perspective to Peter; it never would have gotten off the ground without an initial boost from them. I understand that the Project folks are developing new theorems on the time-warp ratio and other naturally-occurring phenomenon.

The Eastern Idaho Heritage Center is now fully developed near the fairgrounds. When that effort started, we all wondered if it would happen, but wow, it's something to see—a hands-on fully-experiential multi-media museum. (It may even remind you of the original Pacific Northwest Museum in Victoria.) The displays that cover geology and natural history are especially engaging, along with the walk-in sense-and-sound dioramas of Native Americans, mountain men, outlaws, Mormon pioneers, snowpea and seed-potato pickers as well as extreme skiers and early mountain-climbers. "Petzoldt's Panorama," a huge 3-D holograph of the view from the Grand, is really something, and the giant chart of population growth remains a popular feature.

The companion theme park, Ag-land, is also near completion. We're especially pleased the petting zoo will be so large; so many kids today never see a pony or a calf alongside the road. Plus the Buxton tractor—an enormous climb-aboard sculpture crafted by the prizewinner in an Arts Council contest—is sure to be a draw.

We also think the greenbelt running through the center of the old towns of Driggs, Victor and Tetonia is pretty special. The public art includes all types—sculpture, mosaic and a huge clock near the original county courthouse on the plaza. Each of those areas is so pretty now!

Speaking of art, Ralph Mossman and Mary Mullaney are being inducted into the Glassblower's National Hall of Fame at Corning next week. Their careers have been fun to follow.

Mary and I continue to do a little African drumming at Abdoul's summer sessions each year at the RhythmFest. (You know she wrote the original grant to the Idaho Commission on the Arts to bring him here in 2000, back when I was TAC chair.) It was great to have you participate with us—and Emma might be here with her kids this year, yes? We hope to host 50 drummers and teachers from all around the world—another record for the books. (And hopefully, schedules will allow them to arrive in time for the Balloon Extravaganza, as the Chamber expects some 150 hot-air craft over the Fourth.)

Both of these events have really put Teton Valley on the map for those seeking a fun summer scene. RhythmFest, especially appeals to looky-loo urbanites, I guess because it takes place in Driggs itself. There are plenty of places to sit and enjoy the sunshine and daily concerts, especially by Courthouse Plaza. I like it *way* more than Westlake Center! Widening the sidewalks on Main was a key part of it. Then building the retractable cover for winter keeps the visitors happy, even in the coldest winters. (And it doesn't hurt for little ol' ladies like me and you, either!)

As far as government goes, the county is firmly ensconced in its new complex on Fourth Street across from the Old Driggs City Park. With so much commercial in town, we're thankful that jurisdictional business has a new home where it's still easy to park and access the Main Street pedestrian mall.

Little Avenue is now commercial all the way to Fifth Street, with Yostmark's "watch how Noodle-skis are made" factory center one of the prime attractions. The hospital's grown to 50 beds, and the senior care-facility rivals many urban-area offerings. We're all going to need it eventually, some of us sooner rather than later!

You asked about our "towns." Felt's probably the most changed community of all. It's thriving, and the Saturday Mexican-style market is a great tribute to some of the people who have lived up there for decades. It remains most economical to live in the north part of Teton Basin, but there is plenty of affordable housing spread-out among the open spaces, with the main clusters provided in Tetonia, at North Bates and near Bennion.

Well, this letter's rambling on and on, so better go for now. I do look forward to hearing about your grand-kids and Bill's continued progress on the Pinti estate.

I think that brings you up to date on the many, many changes here in Teton Valley. Can't wait to see you again and show you all these things in person. I'll charge up the electromobile and await your arrival.

Love always from this special corner of the sky,

—Jeanne

STEPHANIE O'BRIEN McKELLAR

Speaking of the Tetons

If our mountains had a voice,
What would they say?
Would they tell of the time
when the great Creator spoke
and, as if chiseled by a master's hand,
they were formed?
Would they speak of the Valley's grass,
of roaming herds, or gracious-winged birds?

Or perhaps they'd tell of the many men they've known.
Of bloody battles between warrior tribes,
or the first white men, dressed in furs and bearing pelts,
traipsing over the crusty-white snow.
Perhaps they'd speak of the sheep-herders,
the homesteaders, the cheese-makers, and the crop-growers.
How many times they've seen seeds planted,
harvested, and planted again.

These mountains have seen many years go.
They've seen the work of the families, laboring in the fields,
many trips to church,
many family prayers.
Many births,
And many deaths.

But, one day,
They will again hear the voice of the Creator,
and as He spoke and they came to be,
so He'll speak again,
and the mountains will see the graves open,
and whole, perfect bodies come forth.
Then not only will the mountains speak,
But sing.

MERLIN HARE

Main Street Metamorphosis

1840

1920

2000

2080

Acknowledgements

THIS *SPINDRIFT* ANTHOLOGY, part of the Spirit of the Northwest Project, was funded by the National Endowment for the Arts and administered by the Idaho Commission on the Arts. Special thanks go to past ICA interim-director Julie Numbers Smith who initiated the original Spirit Project. Appreciation also goes to the outreach directors from Idaho, Washington and Oregon, Kathleen Keyes, Bitsy Bidwell and Bill Flood, for their advice and creative input.

The project is the result of partnering between the Teton Arts Council (TAC), the Teton Regional Land Trust and the Teton County Historical Society. As TAC wrestled with choosing an appropriate project on which to use the Spirit funds, it was members from these groups, especially Mary Maj, Dale Breckenridge and Mike Whitfield who kept feeding us ideas and support.

Special thanks go to Elizabeth Kelly whose response to the ICA's original query was the reason our community was chosen to participate in the Spirit Project. Thanks also to Kelley Coburn who helped in the capacity of editor as the first entries were submitted.

Abrazos to Alan McKnight for his generous sharing of time and talents; Alan proofread drafts, designed the book template and illustrated the cover. Thanks as well to his wife, Kate West, who helped in many different capacities.

Appreciation goes to Mary Lou Hansen who formatted the entire book and has had patience for our changes.

At the beginning of the project, two creative writing workshops were held, facilitated by Laurie Kutchins and Amil Quayle. Thanks to them for their planning and inspiration.

Three ladies helped in translating the stories of immigrants from south border way; they are Florencia Velazquez, Maria Teresa Mazo and Julie Martinez. Aaron Leigh Whitfield and Gloria Gomez Whitfield translated the pieces by Mary Maj and Dan Gerber. We are indebted to them for the time put into the difficult task of accurately conveying meaning in another language.

We have had help from Deb Barracato and Karen Russell; from TAC members Arthur Frakt, Shauna Crandall, Josh Weltman, Gretchen Notzold and John Bozek. Appreciation goes as well to Francie Froidevaux, Cheryl Letchworth, Allen Stewart, Jacki Cooke, Kate Yaskot, Mary Mullaney, Michael Beaumont, Eva Dahlgren, Reina Collins, Chi Melville,

Carla Sherman, Dan Sitarz and Rick Ardinger. Indeed, so many have assisted on this project that it's difficult to remember everyone; please forgive us if you have been inadvertently omitted.

We appreciate Christina Adam who helped to embed a literary tradition in Teton Basin when she started the Pilot Knobs Writers' Group. This anthology is a natural evolution of the work she began.

The greatest effort has been put forth by the anthology team consisting of the editors and project whip who have met every Wednesday for the last five months. Gratitude goes to Jeanne Anderson upon whom much of the responsibility for the anthology fell this last winter; to Mike Whitfield who held us to a high standard; to Marilyn Meyer who provided renewed energy, insights and humor when she agreed to fill Kelley's spot; and to Bonnie Krafchuk who wrote the original proposal and budget and has encouraged us to completion before the millennium.

Finally the book would not have been possible without all the folks who submitted work; thanks to everyone who sent us prose, poetry and artwork. The anthology reflects the work of nearly 60 contributors.

And more finally, thanks to family members and spouses Peter Anderson, Bob Meyer, Liz Davy and Rico Young for not only tolerating all the time we've had to spend on this effort, but for understanding and ideas offered when needed most.

Contents Notes

WALKING THE LAND

"Walking the Land," title of the first section, was used in a poem by Kate West, submitted but not chosen for inclusion in the anthology.

"Still Life with Hawks and Storms" (page 17) and "Poems to the Quaking Aspen" (page 28), by Laurie Kutchins, originally appeared in *Between Towns*, published by Texas Tech University Press (1993).

Drawings by Julia Hibbert (pages 6, 11 and 139) are copyright Wolf Track Studio, Tetonia.

"Cranes Signal Spring" (page 8), by Mary Maj, originally appeared in the *Teton Valley Independent*, April 19, 1995.

HARD ROAD TO TRAVEL

"Hard Road to Travel," title of the second section, was used in a song lyric written by Ben Winship, submitted but not chosen for inclusion in the anthology.

In "Proving Up" (page 45) the quote from William Hubbard's letter appeared in *Hubbard Heritage, An American Story* by Eloyce Hubbard Kockler, published by Family History Publishers (1992) and provided courtesy of Dale Breckenridge.

Several pieces in "Hard Road to Travel" used as sources *Driggs Idaho Stake Diamond Jubilee, 1901-1981*, printed by Ricks College Press in 1982, and *History of Teton Valley* by B. W. Driggs, Harold Stanford Forbush and Louis J. Clements, printed by Arnold Agency, Rexburg (1970), a revision of *History of Teton Valley* by B. W. Driggs, originally published by Caxton Printers, Caldwell (1926).

"Our Mountain Home So Dear" (page 58), by Don Coburn, was written with information provided by Grant Wilson, Lorin Kearsley, Michael Holmes, Leigh Fullmer and Ruby Schiess.

"Harry Had a Pontiac" (page 64), by Ben Winship, was originally recorded by Ben Winship on *Early Times* with Loose Ties, and published by Fried Acres Music (ASCAP).

"A Christmas Story" (page 71), by Helen Nelson Richins Kunz and Ella Nelson Griggs, as told to Jon Richins, was published (in a somewhat different form) in a booklet called *The Cowboy Actor*, printed by Little Buckaroo Enterprises, Tucson, Arizona.

In "Hearty Hymns Were Sung" (page 77), by Lori McCune, help was provided by Harold Forbush, editor of *History of Teton Valley*. Forbush also authored the recently published *Tales of the Big Hole Mountains*.

"The Grand Old Man" (page 89), by Michael B. Whitfield, was originally published as "Trap Lines in the Mist" in *Teton Valley Top To Bottom*, Summer 1999 issue.

"Roosevelt's Tree Army" (page 89), by Barbara Bohm-Becker, was originally published (in a somewhat different form) in the *Teton Valley News*, September 22, 1983.

"An Essential Life" (page 93), by Marilyn Elliott Meyer, was originally published (in a somewhat different form) in *Living Idaho Magazine*, Sept-Oct. 1981 issue, under the title: "Chet Miller: Fishing for the Challenge."

"Little Spare Time" (page 98), the oral history of Kerry Gee, was written by Adam Edwards for an English class taught by Carol Call at Sugar-Salem High School in November 1998.

Photos by Florence McCall (pages 107 and 119) were part of *Portraits of Teton Valley*, a project funded by an Idaho Commission on the Arts grant.

COMING HOME
"Life in the Basin Selectively Recalled" (page 112), by Jean Liebenthal, was originally published in *The Christian Science Monitor*, May 1, 1997, under the title "Life in the Country, Selectively Recalled."

"Going 'Out Below?' "(page 116), by Russell Jones, was first printed in the *Teton Valley News* on February 15, 1979, and reprinted April 27, 2000.

"Back in the Saddle Again" (page 124), by Michael McCoy, was originally published (in a somewhat different form) in *Mountain Living*, Spring 1997, under the title "Desperately Seeking Aunt Bea."

"Wild Horses" (page 130), "Trying to Catch the Horses" (page 143), and "Smoke" (page 171), by Dan Gerber, originally appeared in *Trying to Catch the Horses*, published by Michigan State University Press (1999).

In "A Friday in March" (page 144), by Kate West, names have been changed to protect privacy.

AFTER OUR BONES ARE ASHES
"After Our Bones Are Ashes," title of the last section, was used in a poem by Jeanne Anderson, submitted but not chosen for inclusion in the anthology.

About the Contributors

CHRISTINA ADAM divides her time between Teton Valley and southern New Mexico. She was awarded an Idaho Commission on the Arts Fellowship in Literature, and her stories have appeared in *The Atlantic Monthly* and *Cosmopolitan* as well as in anthologies and literary journals. Chris founded the Pilot Knobs Writers Group, which for several years brought writers such as William Kittredge, Kim Barnes, Mary Clearman Blew and Robert Wrigley to Teton Valley for readings and workshops.

BARBARA AGNEW was born in Minnesota. As a child, she loved sports, and also spent a lot of time in the library. She received a BS in psychology and sociology, and obtained her teaching certification at

ISU, where she currently studies library science. She teaches fourth grade at Tetonia Elementary and spends as much time as possible biking, hiking, and skiing. "I was raised on the prairies, and when I came here, it was such an open valley, it felt like where the prairie came together with the mountains," she says.

JEANNE UPHOFF ANDERSON was born in Cheyenne, Wyoming, and spent her first 17 years there. She eventually graduated from the University of Wyoming after three years as a cast and staff member in Up With People. Her free-lance writing and editing career now centers on newsletters and magazines after a three-year stint as editor of the *Teton Valley News*. Jeanne currently chairs Teton Arts Council. When not at the bookstore or working under some deadline, she and Peter can usually be found reading or working on the place they built on the flats north of Driggs. They share a passion for traveling as well.

PETER ANDERSON, his parents and three brothers migrated West from Ohio in the late 1960s, and he graduated from Jackson Hole High in 1976. Peter and his wife, Jeanne, returned to this area from Seattle in 1994 to again live near family. Now a free-lance writer and editor with regular columns in the Idaho Falls *Post Register* and *Teton Valley Top to Bottom*, he is also a traveling scholar and facilitator for literature and legal-ethics courses for the Wyoming Council for the Humanities. He holds degrees in psychology, English and American literature. The Andersons own Dark Horse Books in Driggs.

SUSAN AUSTIN lived with her husband, Greg Amlong, on the Hollingshead homestead for twelve years. Her life and her writing continue to be informed by Karl and Miles Hollingshead and their thoughtful way of life.

BARBARA BOHM-BECKER was born in 1949 in Greenwich Village of Austrian Jewish refugees. She was raised in New York City and its suburbs. Lured by big sky and public land, she left home as soon as possible, heading steadily West. She earned a BA in English from Hiram College in Hiram, Ohio, and a BFA in ceramics from Utah State University. While raising her two children here in Teton Valley with her husband, Lew, she maintained her sanity with art work and part-time writing for the *Teton Valley News*. For the last 10 years she's worked as a bicycle mechanic in Bend, Oregon, and recently became a licensed U.S. Cycling Team mechanic.

JOHN BORSTELMANN grew up loving snow but feeling an acute lack thereof in North Carolina. After earning a history degree at Stanford and spending a year of law school at Duke, JB fled to the mountains, ultimately landing in Teton Valley in 1981. He has worked as a carpenter, nordic ski instructor and coach, climbing guide and real estate agent. Struggling to start a career as a freelance writer, JB's day job is serving the needs of the outdoor-playing public at Yostmark Mountain Equipment. He received a masters in journalism at the University of Colorado in Boulder. So far his writing has surfaced in the *Boulder Planet* (a defunct weekly) and will soon appear in *Couloir, Wild Earth* and the soon-to-be-reborn *Mountain Gazette.*

ANN-TOY BROUGHTON moved to Teton Valley from Connecticut, where Yankee mailboxes meet their demise at the hands of overactive teenagers with baseball bats. She and her husband enjoy playing outdoors in the mountains so much, now that their children are grown, that her writing aspirations rarely succeed in getting her onto a chair's seat. If they ever do, she will probably write about people and connection and the complexity of the human spirit, with a lot of genuine admiration and a lot of sincere irreverence.

MIKE CLELLAND is a former New York City yuppie turned ski bum. Mike divides his time between illustrating for climbing instructionals and teaching mountaineering and skiing for National Outdoor Leadership School. He's one-half of the partnership that has produced *Allan and Mike's Really Cool Telemark Tips, Allan and Mike's Really Cool Guide to Backcountry Skiing* and another really cool guide yet to be released by Falcon Press.

DON COBURN, born in Driggs in 1924, received his BS degree in pharmacy from Idaho State University, and he owned and operated the Coburn Drug Store in Driggs for many years. Donald and Clarice Mae were married in the Idaho Falls LDS Temple in 1946. He has been actively involved in his church, serving in many different positions. Writing has been a lifelong hobby and source of much personal enjoyment. His only story previously submitted for publication, "Eight Pounds of Love," was published by the *Improvement Era* in 1963. Reading this Christmas story about the faith and courage of Alta Green, one of our early pioneer ladies in Alta, Wyo., has become a holiday tradition in many homes.

GWEN DALLEY CRANDALL is a Teton Valley native, the daughter of Iris Neilsen Dalley (of Cache) and Milo Hulet Dalley (of Alta). She and husband Robert W. Crandall made their home in northern California for about 35 years. They returned here after Bob retired as an executive from the Port of Oakland. "I told my husband I was coming back, and he could come if he wanted to," she says. She designed their house in Alta, and they started building in the summer of 1991. They have 12 grandchildren; their sons live in San Jose, Portland and Heidelberg, Germany, and their one daughter, Shauna, lives here. Although she likes gardening and the arts, Gwen's real passion is crocheting fine lace.

ADAM MICHAEL EDWARDS was born in Ogden in 1982, the son of Shane and Louise Ricks. He has lived in Sugar City for most of his life and graduated from Sugar-Salem High School in May 2000. He worked for Kerry Gee the last four summers, where he'd look out at the Tetons whenever he could take a break from moving pipe, swathing and baling hay, feeding cattle, fixing equipment and doing other farm chores. An all-seasons outdoors guy, he loves to fish and go snowmachining. A hard worker in whatever he tackles, Adam is now employed by a bricklayer in Rexburg.

ARTHUR FRAKT was born at midnight on a stormy Halloween, 1939, in Jersey City, just after Hitler's invasion of Poland. His schooling consisted mostly of disciplinary detention and suspensions. He was educated largely by random reading including *The Yearling, The Red Pony* and *David Copperfield*. After serving as a deputy attorney general for civil rights in New Jersey, he became a law professor and dean at some of America's largest law schools. Desperately trying to atone for foisting thousands of lawyers on an innocent public, he moved with his long-suffering spouse, Janna Rankin, to the Tetons where he teaches some tennis to kids and unsuccessfully tries to stay out of trouble.

BEN FRANKLIN was born in New Jersey and is somewhere close to 50 years old. He came to Wyoming in 1969 with NOLS and never looked back. He spent 15 years living in Driggs, which along with commercial fishing in Alaska, NOLS, eight years of educating in Pocatello and a 21-year relationship with Barbara Sprang, has been a major influence in his life. "I feel very fortunate to have a plethora of friends and family scattered from hell to breakfast, so I'll always have someone pleasant to dine with and a companion to scream with when I get roasted and tortured," he says.

DAN GERBER received *Foreward* Magazine's 1999 Gold Medal Book of the Year award in poetry for *Trying to Catch the Horses*, his most recent book of poetry, which included the three poems reprinted in this anthology. He has published five earlier collections of poems, three novels, a collection of short stories and a book on the Indianapolis 500. Recent poems have appeared in *Poetry, Witness, New Letters, The Ohio Review* and in *The Best American Poetry 1999*, published by Scribners and edited by Robert Bly. A volume of selected essays, *A Second Life*, will be published next year. He and his wife, Debbie, divide the year between Teton Valley and Santa Ynez, California.

BERTHA CHAMBERS GILLETTE was born to James and Berla Stevens Chambers on land now known as the Wildlife Refuge in Jackson, Wyoming. It was a very poor community. Bertha and her neighbors existed mainly on elk, pork, fish and garden produce. She attended a one-room log school until the eighth grade, then graduated from Jackson High School. She married Wendell Gillette and had two children, Glen and LaVon. In 1936 the family moved to Victor where they bought a garage and sold Fords, Plymouths and Chryslers. Bertha and Wendell celebrated their 50th wedding anniversary in 1984; he passed away just before their 60th. Bertha's book, *Homesteading with the Elk*, describing the hardships of her childhood, is in its seventh printing. She owns the Quilt House in Victor.

NEIL GLEICHMAN moved to Teton Valley in 1994. He teaches and coaches cross country at Teton High School. Other passions include climbing, bicycling and trail running. He is currently building his first home in Victor.

MARY LOU HANSEN grew up in Denver, Colorado, earned an English degree at Brigham Young University, then moved to the Tetons. She met her husband Paul while working in Grand Teton National Park and they settled in Teton Basin in 1980. Mary Lou serves on the Driggs City Council, works as a bookkeeper and runs a desktop publishing business. Founder, editor and publisher of the *Teton Valley Independent*, she writes for *Teton Valley Top to Bottom* and other clients, including the Teton Soil Conservation District. She and Paul have two daughters, Martha and Robin.

MERLIN HARE has lived outside of Victor for the past 15 years, working as a wildlife research pilot and computer graphic specialist. He constructs and flies experimental aircraft and enjoys wilderness backpacking. He spent most of his school years in Paris, France, with summers in the Absaroka Mountains of Wyoming.

JULIA HIBBERT was raised on a farm near Heise Hot Springs. As a young girl she began painting and drawing, using the farm and landscape around her as subjects. Living and traveling near several national parks as a young woman, she continued to paint the natural world around her, seeking out artists and teachers wherever she went. For 15 years she drew Arabian Horses for specialty publications; 23 years ago she moved to Teton Valley. Julia was one of the founders of the Teton

Arts Council in 1992 and remains very involved today. She, her husband Dee, and their son David live in Tetonia.

RUSSELL JONES is the son of Jerry and the late Fern Jones of Victor; he grew up in Victor, attended Teton Valley schools and graduated from Teton High in 1970. He graduated from Idaho State University in Pocatello with a degree in journalism. From 1979 to 1982 he was editor of the *Teton Valley News*; later he served as news editor for the *Morning News* in Blackfoot, writer and editor for Harris Publishing in Idaho Falls, publisher of *Snowmobile West* and *Potato Grower of Idaho* magazines. Russ and his wife Barbara have resided in Boise since 1988 where Russ works as a corporate communications specialist for IDACORP and Idaho Power.

JESSICA KERR is the 10-year-old daughter of Dr. Darin and Myra Kerr of Driggs. A fifth-grader at Driggs Elementary School, she's lived in Teton Valley for nine years. She plays the fiddle and the piano and is the middle sister of Megan and Caitlin. She has three pets—a dog named Licorice, a mouse named Stuart, and a bird named Chip. Jessica plans to follow her father into the dental profession and become a hygienist.

BONNIE KRAFCHUK is a second-generation Ukranian-American who is grateful not to be living in eastern Europe. Born in New York City, she's had the good fortune to live in Teton Basin half of her fifty years. She currently works with immigrant Mexican teenagers at Jackson Hole High School. She believes the influx of Mexicans to the region brings challenges and enriches the cultural fabric.

LAURIE KUTCHINS grew up in Casper, Wyoming. Her family purchased property in Teton Valley in 1979, and since 1986 she has spent her summers in the valley. She is the author of two books of poetry: *Between Towns* (Texas Tech University Press) and *The Night Path* (BOA Editions). She teaches creative writing at James Madison University in Virginia.

EARLE F. LAYSER is a forester and biologist who retired from the USDA Forest Service in 1990. He returned to the Greater Yellowstone area, where he had worked in the 1970s and 80s, to do natural resources consulting and writing. A resident of Teton Valley since 1992, he has written and published numerous technical and scientific articles and studies, including research papers on grizzly bear, mountain caribou, plant ecology and a book on the flora of northeast Washington and north Idaho. He has recently had popular stories and photographs published in a wide variety of local, regional and national publications. He and his wife, Pattie, also a writer, reside in Alta, Wyoming. Both enjoy the outdoor activities, scenery, and people of Teton Valley.

When PATTIE LAYSER married, her playing fields became both her home and her work place. She sold her art gallery in Montana, moved to Alta, Wyoming, and began writing freelance. Now widely published in both regional and national magazines, when Pattie writes about fly-fishing, cycling, skiing, or hiking the Valley with her husand Earle, it's all in a day's work.

JEAN LIEBENTHAL was born in eastern Idaho and grew up near St. Anthony. The first thing she wrote was a Sunday school talk. Unlike the other children, Jean thought it was great fun to write this, and she's been writing ever since. She has published articles, short stories, and poetry in *Redbook, Poetry Magazine, The Christian Science Monitor* and other publications. Four short novels have also been published. She enjoys all genres of writing, but poetry is her favorite.

CAROLE LOWE was born in Ogden, Utah, and lived for a few years in Colorado before moving to Teton Valley in 1977. Love of the back-country and the peaceful lifestyle brought her here, and she has listed as her career, "doing whatever it takes to stay here." Consequently, she has had many jobs, but since 1988 she has been a co-owner and operator of Rendezvous Ski Tours and Chalet.

CAROLE LUSSER is a wife, mother of two daughters and new grandma this year of a beautiful girl born in January and a handsome boy in August. When at home in Driggs, she and husband René enjoy gardening and hiking in summer. Winter finds the family skiing or boarding at the resort or surrounding mountains. Spring and fall, Carole and René travel to the family farm in central Illinois to crop share with René's 97-year-old maternal grandmother. Carole, a registered nurse, works at Teton Valley Hospital.

SUSAN TRAYLOR LYKES grew up in Colorado and received degrees from the Universities of Vermont and Montana. After living in most of the Rocky Mountain states at various times following college, she settled in the shadow of the Tetons in 1995 with her husband, Mayo, and their dog, Pearl. A left-brainer dabbling in the right-brain realm, Susan has been drawing—albeit somewhat sporadically—for most of her life. These days, travel is a significant part of the Lykes' existence, and it provides a catalyst for much of Susan's artistic expression.

MARY MAJ served as stewardship director of Teton Regional Land Trust until December 1999, when she moved to Missoula, Montana. Educated as a wildlife biologist, her master's thesis research was a study of trumpeter swan nesting ecology in Idaho and Wyoming. Mary returned to the Forest Service as a wildlife biologist, a position she formerly held in Clark, Fremont and Teton counties in Idaho. She has taught courses throughout the Northern Rockies and in far east Russia. The most prevalent attribute of Mary's person, she says, is her "gypsy-like tendencies."

ROB MARIN quit a perfectly decent desk job as a cartographer on the Colorado Front Range and promptly took off to kayak in Africa. After a year of travel he somehow washed up in Teton Valley. With a graduate degree in geography and years of experience as a whitewater guide, his nomadic instincts are apparently stronger than a need for mainstream employment. A contributing writer for the Driggs-based magazines *Teton Valley Top to Bottom* and *Teton Home*, he plans on river running until he's too old to pick up a paddle.

FLORENCE McCALL has been a photographer for almost eight years, starting off in San Francisco as a newspaper/portrait photographer. After two and a half years, Flo moved to Driggs, shooting skiing, sports and editorial photographs. She initiated a black-and-white photo documentary of the residents of Teton Valley through the Idaho Commission on the Arts. That project got her name known and put her on the road to doing serious portrait work. After four years, Flo moved to Jackson, opened a studio and now does weddings and portraits year-round, as well as ski photography in the winter. She shoots in both black and white and color. For more examples of her work, see http://www.FloMcCall.com.

MICHAEL McCOY was born in Wheatland, Wyoming, and raised in Boone, Iowa. After earning a BA in anthropology at the University of Wyoming in 1973, he performed archaeological field work in Mexico and throughout the Rocky Mountain West. More recently, McCoy conceived and researched Adventure Cycling's Great Divide Mountain Bike Route. He has authored eight cycling and travel books, including *Journey to the Northern Rockies*. Besides his freelance writing, Mac currently serves as managing editor of *Jackson Hole* magazine. Of the first time he laid eyes on Teton Valley's mix of mountains and farmlands in the early '70s, he says, "I felt like I'd come home."

LORI L. (CHERLAND) McCUNE, along with her husband and two teen-age children, has been a Teton Valley resident for five years. The family came here for a job and stayed for the life. She is very active in helping the Hispanic community and enjoys serving in various capacities in Teton Valley Community Church. She taught English as a

Second Language, Spanish, French and various primary grades before landing in the Basin, and the family enjoyed a 13-year stint in Peru and Bolivia as Christian missionaries. Presently she runs her own business, McCune's Bilingual Services, providing legal workers for businesses around the Intermountain West and beyond.

STEPHANIE O'BRIEN McKELLAR's ancestors came to the Valley for a variety of reasons— to make cheese, herd sheep, teach school, to stake claims and farm land. They came with the common faith of the LDS church. Children grew up and married others from the Valley, and so did their children. Stephanie, born and raised here, loved hearing their stories; her favorite reading is a simple life history, a journal, diary, or letter from the past. She is the daughter of Dee and Chris O'Brien. People are most important to her family, as shown in her parents' occupations as school teacher and nurse. Stephanie and her husband, Tyler McKellar, also of Driggs, reside in Bountiful, Utah, with their two daughters, Kate and Lauren.

ALAN McKNIGHT was born in Boston and grew up in the northeast. He has an MA degree in English, but prefers pictures to words, and returned to school to study art in the 1980s. Since his wife, Kate West, introduced him to the West, he prefers the mountains and canyons to the coast, though he still studies seashells as well as wildflowers and the stars.

CHI MELVILLE moved to Teton Valley in 1980 to work as a backcountry ski guide and partner of Teton Mountain Touring. TMT ran a retail ski shop in Driggs and built a backcountry skiing hut system in the Big Holes. Chi is one of the founding members of Teton Valley Trails & Pathways. For the past five years, he has worked as a graphic artist, website designer and computer-networking consultant. He enjoys photography, fly-fishing, hiking, bicycling and cross-country ski racing. Chi and his wife René live in Alta.

LINDA MERIGLIANO came to Teton Valley in 1979, drawn by snowy mountains and the chance to care for wild country. Over the years, the land and people have created bonds that keep her and husband Mike rooted here. Linda currently works for the Bridger-Teton National Forest, serves on the board of the Teton Regional Land Trust and on the grants committee of the Community Foundation of Jackson Hole. She and Mike spend as much time as they can hiking or skiing, sharing experiences together and with friends. Her other loves include tennis, music, reading, and being entertained by Dale the cat.

MARILYN ELLIOTT MEYER grew up in southern Idaho. She earned

a BS in journalism from Northwestern University, put in a few years on daily newspapers in her home state, then quit to wander aimlessly through Mexico, Central America and the West. In 1978 she built a house on Fox Creek. During the next 20 years she married, raised two sons, worked for local newspapers and ran a retail business in the valley with her husband. Now retired from those activities, she is relearning spontaneity and hopes to head south often.

JACKIE O'CONNOR was born in Michigan and has lived in Teton Valley for 25 years. She taught third grade for 10 years, and for the last 10, has taught physical education at Victor Elementary School. She, her husband Patrick, and their two sons, Will and Ryan, live in the Chapin area.

DEB PATLA is a biologist conducting amphibian surveys and monitoring in the greater Yellowstone-Teton area. Since moving to Teton Valley in 1986, she has devoted most of her free time to conservation activism, particularly the local effort to prevent the privatization of national forest lands around Grand Targhee.

JUAN CARLOS PEREZ was born in Mexico City in 1985. He spent 11 years in Mexico, then moved with his family to the United States. He is currently a high school student in 10th grade and enjoys soccer and most sports.

JON RICHINS is a Driggs native whose family has farmed and ranched in Teton Valley since the early 1900s. Now living in Tucson, Arizona, he is a cowboy poet who regularly works with young authors at schools and has participated at many poetry gatherings and events throughout the West. A singer and self-taught musician, he plays guitar and banjo using finger-picking, clawhammer and frailing styles. Jon has published and co-edited several books of poetry, along with musical collections. He has been a featured performer at the Western Music Association Festival in Tucson. Much of his material comes from stories passed through his family.

KELLY RUDD was born and raised in Spokane, Washington, then moved to Salem, Oregon, to attend Willamette University where he was nearly expelled due to a series of misunderstandings that were subsequently resolved. Kelly came to Teton Basin in 1997 to work as a fly-fishing guide. He lives in Victor, with Courtney Kelley and two dogs, Huckle and Sam J.

KEN SMITH was born and raised in Driggs. His poem, "Spring in Alaska Basin," originally appeared as a letter to the editor in the *Teton Valley News*. At that time, he was living in Parker, Colorado. The poem was suggested for inclusion in the anthology by Julia Hibbert.

STANFORD SORENSEN was born in Tetonia, the third of Douglas P. and Lette Hulet Sorenson's seven children. Soon after his birth they moved. He grew up in Darby and Alta, graduated from Teton High School, served in the army and fulfilled an LDS mission to Brazil. He earned degrees from BYU and the University of California at Berkeley.

J. M. (JULI) SPENCER was born in southern California just after World War II. She completed a Bachelor's degree in Fine Arts at the University of British Columbia in 1976. For the next 21 years she lived in the Rocky Mountain region of North America, from northern British Columbia to Colorado. She is currently working on several short stories and poems.

MARY CAROL STAIGER has lived in Alta, Wyoming, with her husband, Dick, for 12 years. His hunting camp stories provided the humorous material for the "Donkey Joe" story and many more.

SUE TYLER, an Idaho native, has lived in Teton Valley for 15 years. Her work reflects a celebration of nature, animals, people and cultures. Sue has been an active member of Teton Arts Council since the organization was founded. She currently teaches drawing, painting, ceramics and photography at Sugar-Salem High School.

MARTIN VELAZQUEZ was born on a small ranch in the state of Michoacán, Mexico. Searching for adventure and a better life, he ended up in Teton Basin, Idaho. He says he didn't listen to his father when he told him, "If you go to school, you will have a better life." Now he finds himself telling his kids the same thing. He hopes they will be smarter, keep learning and have satisfying lives.

JOSH WELTMAN, originally from the suburbs of St. Louis, settled in Teton Valley in the fall of 1994. Seasonal forest service trail-crew jobs had acquainted him with the area and helped develop an interest in local history. While on field study at Hampshire College, he spent a semester researching the history of Mormon Row in Jackson Hole. He often researches local history when he's not woodworking, writing or making telemark ski bindings. He encourages anyone with local knowledge who is interested in recording or discussing their history to contact him.

KATE WEST was born north of the Adirondack Mountains in New York state. She loved adventuring in the outdoors and was a voracious reader. She received her BS and MS in elementary education and also was certified to teach reading K-12. After many years of teaching, she has retired to spend more time fiddling, reading, writing, and outdoor adventuring.

MICHAEL B. WHITFIELD is a native son with a four-generation heritage of love for the people and natural resources of Teton Valley. He is a conservation biologist by training and has published research results on bighorn sheep, bald eagles, and other birds of prey. He has taught natural history in the Northern Rockies and far east Russia for several universities. He was founding Board President and is current Executive Director of the Teton Regional Land Trust.

BEN WINSHIP grew up in New England and settled in Teton Valley in 1986. After studying and practicing forestry for several years, Winship's passion for the mandolin overcame him, and he chose the life of a troubadour. After actively touring for 13 years, he now stays closer to home, dividing his time between performing, recording, writing and working as a studio engineer/producer. He lives in Victor with his wife, Caroline, and sons Owen and Sam. (For more info visit www.benwinship.com)

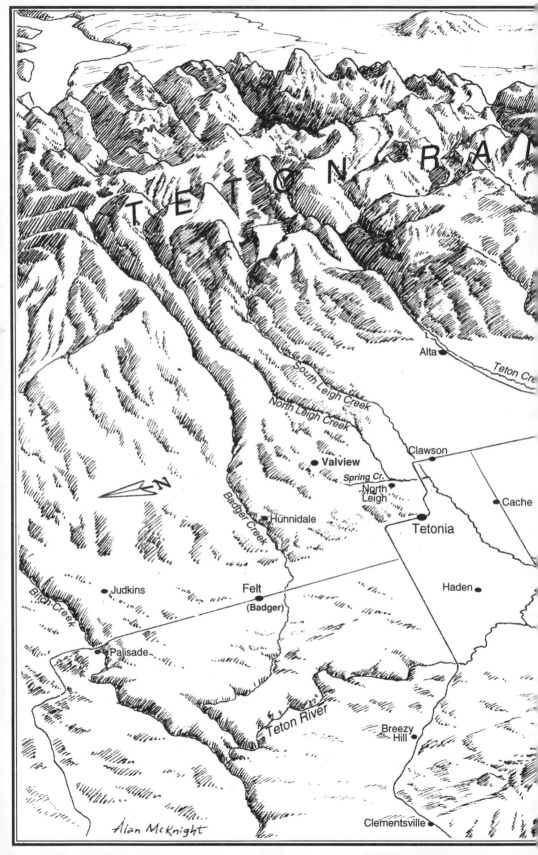